Great Artists
from Giotto to Turner

Great Artists
from Giotto to Turner

Tim Marlow with Phil Grabsky and Philip Rance

faber and faber

Tim Marlow
with Phil Grabsky and Philip Rance

First published in 2001
by Faber and Faber Limited
3 Queen Square London WC1N 3AU

Design by Stephen Coates at August
with Marit Münzberg
Printed in Italy

A CIP record for this book
is available from the British Library

ISBN 0–571–20908–4

2 4 6 8 10 9 7 5 3 1

Contents

Introduction

This book is written for the numerous visitors to museums and galleries all over the world; to those who are enthralled by art but who are not professionally involved in its creation or distribution. It is intended as both an enlightening, sometimes entertaining read and as a reference book. It spans over five hundred years of art history and cannot hope to cover anything but a tiny fraction of human creativity during this period. It can however, offer an insight into some of the major moments and the most profound achievements in Western art.

Over the past century art history has undergone almost as many changes in approach and style as art itself. Without wishing to immerse the lay reader in a quagmire of academic wrangling, the subject has undergone a radical transformation partly as a result of various ideological battles between certain art historical camps: formalism against iconography, Marxism going head to head with connoisseurship, and so on. In the seventies and early eighties, a quiet revolution took place in art history which led to the emergence of what is still, rather blandly, called the New Art History. At its best, this approach was expansive and open-minded. It applied new intellectual ideas to the art of the past ranging from feminism and film-studies to psychoanalysis and post-structuralism. In broad terms it explored painting and sculpture in terms of the political, social and economic conditions in which they were made and wrested art history away from a patrician establishment who still believed that art somehow encapsulated universal truths which applied across time, place and culture. This has led to an inclusive view of art history. One which seeks to look beyond the mainstream, to ask questions about why women have failed to be recognised as major figures largely until the twentieth century; to challenge the traditional view of who and what were considered to be significant. The New Art History has also, however, at its most dogmatic, challenged the idea of studying art history monographically, of looking at the life and work of individual artists, particularly those who have been accorded the status of great or, worse still, 'genius'. The idea that all aspects of art history must be questioned is a healthy one, as is the notion that little or nothing should be taken for granted.

Certainly, the idea that art history is dominated by a handful of individuals endowed with a superhuman talent which somehow removes them from their immediate world is a fallacy, and the term 'genius' is largely one which came into play during the Romantic movement in the early nineteenth century, which virtually invented the cliché of the isolated figure in his (rarely her) garret, wrestling with how to express radical ideas to a largely uncomprehending world. But using the artist's life as a starting point in a quest to explore how art was made, what it intended to convey, how it was perceived and subsequently how it has been viewed seems entirely valid. Indeed it seems to offer the simplest and most rigorous structure from which to apply many of the approaches of the New Art History. Over the ensuing chapters I hope you feel that numerous different ways of seeing are being applied but without ever being dogmatic or closed in their meaning or intention.

The notion of 'Great Artists', however, is a little trickier. Twenty years ago, it would have been difficult to publish any such book, but now, I think, the climate has changed. In a culture which refuses to take anything at face value and which has learned to question whatever it is confronted with, traditional approaches can still be relatively sophisticated ones. In a culture obsessed with celebrity and now reading more biographies of the great, the good and the bad, looking afresh at celebrated artists has a strong contemporary resonance. Finally, in a world which embraces the visual arts more broadly than ever before in human history, that is more visually literate than any previous one, the idea of selecting a dozen or so artists whose work has, by broad consensus, had the greatest impact, which is seen most profoundly to evoke the world in which it was made and which has continued to strike a chord over the centuries, seems both playful and productive as a means of exploring some of the spine-tingling, eye-opening, heart-stopping, gut-wrenching, mind-blowing art of the past. Celebratory? Certainly. Critical? Absolutely. Comprehensible and entertaining? I hope so.

There is, however, another factor in this project which has helped to shape it strongly, that most powerful of all twentieth-century visual media and one whose stranglehold looks unlikely to diminish into the twenty-first century – television. Over the past decade the dominant mode for what little arts television there has been was broadly thematic and often nation-based: a history of British art; American history viewed through the lens of the visual arts; the Renaissance revisited; and various idiosyncratic explorations of the art of the twentieth century. So when Michael Attwell, the commissioning editor responsible for arts at Channel Five, asked me, Phil Grabsky and Philip Rance to come up with a large, ambitious but accessible idea for a series of thirteen half-hour programmes we thought laterally, quirkily and even ludicrously for a few days but kept on returning to the idea of the 'Great Artists'. After all, the most enduring book on art written by the man often hailed as the father of art history – Giorgio Vasari – was called *The Lives of the Most Eminent Painters, Sculptors and Architects*. In addition, the bestselling book on art, Ernst Gombrich's *The Story of Art*, began with the memorable lines: 'There really is no such thing as Art. There are only artists.' Naturally, we wouldn't claim to be writing such grand narratives but we could view the legacy of those art historians through both the post-modern frame of television and the intellectual framework of the New Art History. And that, essentially, has been our approach.

Selecting thirteen artists from any period of history is difficult, but over the time period we proposed it became a game of cultural bartering. Artists have been (and indeed still are) mainly urban animals and we wanted to explore the social, economic and creative nature of various European cities at certain times in their history, as well as looking at the evolution of particular artistic styles and attitudes. An artist like Caravaggio, probably the most glaring omission, was left out because there was a danger that the selection was becoming too Italianate and that Rome loomed a little too large. It was, however, never our intention to come up with a definitive list – it would be impossible and odious to try such a thing – but just to make it clear the definite article was banned. This, therefore, is a book surveying the life and work of various great artists rather than THE great artists. And there can always be a sequel.

The Renaissance was the obvious starting point, not least because the idea of the artist as we now understand it was nurtured in fourteenth- and fifteenth-century Italy. It was here that painters and sculptors began the slow shift from artesan or craftsman – serving an apprenticeship, learning a trade and belonging to a guild – to socially and intellectually lauded individuals. Reverence for the artist and freedom from the guilds occurred largely in the sixteenth century, notably with Raphael and Michelangelo in Rome and then Titian in Venice being fêted by popes and princes and treated as men of learning and imagination as well as skill.

There are always exceptions to broad historical generalizations but it is largely the case that the idea of artistic fame, of greatness, came from the ancient classical worlds of Greece and, to a lesser extent, Rome. No work by the celebrated Greek painters Apelles and Zeuxis survives, but their reputations do, notably in the writings of the Roman encyclopedist Pliny the Elder. In Latin initially but in Italian after 1473, scholars and – more crucially – artists could read not just of the perfect likenesses that

Apelles was able to render with brush and pigment but how he was revered and honoured by Alexander the Great to the extent, so the story goes, that when he was commissioned by the Emperor to paint the royal mistress Campapse in all her naked glory, Apelles fell in love with her and was duly 'given' the woman as a token of Alexander's admiration. Notwithstanding sexual politics or the hoary old chestnut about the relationship between artists and their models, this kind of story authenticated the professional aspirations of numerous artists in Italy and then beyond. In addition to being celebrated for his talent, Apelles and other ancient-world artists were portrayed as men of learning and of elevated social status – gentlemen artists of the kind that Michelangelo and Raphael, and later Rubens and Velázquez, sought to become.

The rebirth of classical art and learning slowly but significantly challenged the domination of Christianity in European art and culture. Aside from the emergence of broader subject matter in painting and sculpture inspired by ancient history and mythology, the excavation of the pre-Christian world – literally and intellectually – helped to place man closer to the centre of his known world. The intellectual movement known as 'humanism' which was largely responsible for the revival of classical scholarship in Florence at the beginning of the fifteenth century encouraged a new focus on the achievements of individuals who had made their historical mark. Commissions to commemorate the lives of famous men flourished, a new form of patronage which glorified individuals (or dynastic families such as the Medici of Florence or the Gonzagas of Mantua right up to the Egremonts of Petworth, who patronized Turner) and which proclaimed their taste, wealth and power but also promoted the creative power of the artists themselves. In turn, when the Catholic Church began to harness the increasingly celebrated talents of numerous painters and sculptors in a bid to spread the Christian word and to fight back against the Protestant Reformation, they empowered artists and bolstered reputations still further. The growing number of visitors to the Sistine Chapel or to Antwerp Cathedral were making artistic as much as religious pilgrimages; paying homage to Michelangelo or Rubens as well as to their God. In the twentieth century, for many people, art galleries became the new cathedrals of the modern world.

Fame – as our own era shows perhaps more powerfully than any other thanks to the expansion of mass media – is addictive and often self-perpetuating. What began as a desire to emulate the achievements and status of the ancients snowballed into a quest to surpass that of one's immediate predecessors and one's peers. Michelangelo and Leonardo went head to head in a much mythologized competition in Florence in

1503–4; Velázquez 'beat' his artistic rivals at the Spanish Court in 1627 in a competition arranged by King Philip IV; Turner and Constable vied for the greatest impact on the walls of the Royal Academy in London in the early nineteenth century by touching up their canvases in situ right up to opening day; the Dutch Protestant Rembrandt reworked numerous subjects painted by his Catholic Flemish rival Rubens, who had previously copied and reworked paintings by Titian in an almost endless cycle of emulation and reaction, of paying homage and of pushing out in a new direction, of healthy rivalry and sometimes of self-obsession. And it was all fuelled by the increasing mobility of the population and the wider dissemination of ideas. People began to travel further afield and more frequently. Art became an international currency during the sixteenth century with Italian artists as the gold standard. With more people being exposed to a greater amount of art than ever before and almost every major artist across Europe (and certainly all the ones explored in this book) visiting Italy at various times in their careers, Spain, Germany, the Netherlands, France and finally even Britain produced art to rival that of the south.

The other major shift in emphasis, aside from but inextricably linked to the changing status of the artist over the five centuries covered in this book, was art's growing obsession with itself, its methods and its visual language. The idea of art for art's sake was only fully expressed towards the end of the nineteenth century, but the seeds were sown from the time that individuals became prominent internationally at the beginning of the sixteenth century. The idea of a mainstream European tradition in art developed as artists established a new form of training institution to rival the essentially medieval workshop – the academy. Initially created as informal clubs, they became the dominant means through which artists were educated. The first official academy was formed in 1563 in Florence with Michelangelo and Duke Cosimo I de Medici as honorary presidents; within thirty years Perugia, Bologna and Rome had followed suit. Over the next two centuries the concept of the academy swept through Europe, dominating the production and exhibition of art but exerting an increasing stranglehold. This caused various young artists to challenge its authority in the middle of the nineteenth century, first in England with the Pre-Raphaelite Brotherhood and then, more momentously, in France with Edouard Manet and the Impressionists. Within the space of ten years, beginning in 1863 when Manet and others established the Salon des Refusés in protest against their exclusion from the academy's official Salon, they had provoked moral and critical outrage in equal measure and established the pre-eminent role model for artists over the next century – the avant-garde.

Art history is far more dominated by lines of continuity than by radical breaks with the past, but it is still fair to say that the onset of Modernism nearly a hundred and fifty years ago, was a dramatic moment of change. Fuelled by the development of photography, it forced numerous artists to rethink what they did and how they did it. Turner was both a precursor of the Impressionists and a lifelong academician, perhaps the last great academic artist. That is why he is the final figure in this book.

These then are some of the broader sweeps of history running through the lives and times of the thirteen great artists selected for both book and television series. The project, however, begins and ends with the smaller sweeps of a painter's brush. All of our enquiries into meaning and significance emanate from a confrontation or communion with the work of art itself. One of the pleasures of writing this book has been to see, in the flesh so to speak, almost all of the work discussed. With the onset of mass media, many feared that the endless reproduction of art would reduce the power of seeing painting and sculpture at first hand. They need not have worried. Coming face to face with art is, I think, among the richest and most intensely rewarding of all human experiences and I hope this book fuels your own desire to look, see and understand.

Tim Marlow, London 2001

1.

Giotto
1267–1337

Detail of Hell from The Last Judgment, c.1303–06, Arena Chapel, Padua

There is no doubting Giotto's status as one of the towering figures in Western art. His life spanned a period of profound change, when strong political, economic and social forces challenged the values and unity of medieval Christendom. Correspondingly, his work embodies the beginnings of that transition from the medieval to the modern world.

Although Giotto devoted his life to traditional religious subjects, he introduced a new realism and emotional intensity, which, together with his ability to narrate complex stories in seemingly simple but immensely powerful and subtle images, was broadly believed to have revolutionized European painting, eventually leading to the Renaissance, the bedrock of Western culture for centuries. Near the beginning of his famous *Lives of the Artists*, the sixteenth-century writer and painter Giorgio Vasari makes the following assessment of Giotto's achievement:

> he alone, although born among inept artists, revived through God's grace what had fallen into an evil state and brought back to such a form that it could be called good. And it was truly an extraordinary miracle that such an ignorant and incompetent age could have inspired Giotto to work so skilfully that drawing, of which men during those times had little or no knowledge, came fully back to life through his efforts.

It's a potent combination: Vasari, the man frequently described as the father of art history, championing the work of the artist he established as the father of Western painting. It underpins much of what we know about Giotto and how we view him centuries later. Vasari was a myth-maker, a cultural spin-doctor with an agenda to put his native Tuscany at the heart of Western civilization. Much of what he says is true and full of insight; some is disputable; a little is wrong. To see the clearest picture of Giotto requires us to read between Vasari's lines.

Giotto di Bondone was born around 1267 in the Tuscan hamlet of Colle di Vespignano, about fourteen miles from Florence. His father, Bondone, was a local farmer and, as soon as he was old enough, the young Giotto joined his father tending the family's sheep. How the shepherd-boy Giotto became one of the most celebrated artists in history has always been something of a mystery. According to the most popular story, first recorded by the great Florentine sculptor Lorenzo Ghiberti in 1452, it was Cimabue (c.1240–c.1302), the most successful Florentine painter of the day, who discovered Giotto by chance, when he came across the young boy sketching one of his father's sheep on a flat stone. Cimabue was apparently so impressed with Giotto's skill that he persuaded the boy's father to let him become a pupil in his workshop in Florence. Another story has Giotto originally apprenticed to a wool merchant in Florence, but spending so much time hanging around Cimabue's studio that eventually the master offered to teach the boy. Whatever their veracity, the abiding theme of these stories is to stress the importance of the older master, Cimabue, in teaching Giotto; recognizing his early talent and establishing the idea of an artistic succession from master to pupil.

What a shock it must have been for the young farmer's son to find himself beginning his apprenticeship in the hubbub of Florence. With a population of nearly 100,000, thirteenth-century Florence was not only the greatest city in Italy, but also one of the largest cities in Europe, roughly four times the size of contemporary London. Throughout the twelfth and early thirteenth centuries, the cities of Tuscany – Florence, Siena, Pisa, Lucca – witnessed tremendous economic growth. Giotto's earlier life as a shepherd points to the origins of Florence's success. At that time, finished cloth was Europe's single most important product. Florence grew rich as the manufacturing centre of the finest cloths and woollens in Europe. Building on this commercial and manufacturing success, important banking houses later developed, and Florence's gold coinage, the florin, became the standard currency throughout Western Europe for over two centuries.

The Italian peninsula in which Giotto was born, however, was torn by wars and factional disputes. For generations, popes and Holy Roman Emperors had battled on Italian soil over their conflicting claims of secular and religious supremacy. Consequently, these super-powers were overburdened almost to the point of exhaustion, which meant that the Italian city-states became more independent and self-sufficient, but the price was bitter disputes both between and within cities. Italian cities formed and changed alliances with kaleidoscopic variety, and Florence was often at war with her neighbours Siena, Lucca and Arezzo. Every city and town in the peninsula had its Guelph (papal) and Ghibelline (imperial) parties. Throughout the thirteenth century, government in Florence was extremely volatile, though the Guelphs were usually in ascendance. These divisions were echoed at a local level, with every city riven by power struggles between the older aristocratic clans and the newly wealthy commercial bourgeoisie, which in turn sought to suppress the aspirations of the artisan class. In Florence, successive constitutions failed to establish political stability, and continued factional disputes led to the exile of some of the city's most famous sons, including the poet Dante Alighieri (1265–1321).

Giotto's world was still essentially medieval, a world in which Christendom was the only unifying concept in Western Europe, but one which was now subject to profound change. The crusade against the Muslim infidel was still regularly preached, but in reality the last Christian strongholds in the Holy Land fell in 1291. In Giotto's youth, the papacy gained victory in its long conflict with the Holy Roman Emperors, but the struggle had severely weakened it when faced with other challenges to its authority. New mendicant orders such as the Franciscans and Dominicans, placing emphasis on a more spiritual life based on absolute poverty, contrasted starkly with the wealth and worldliness of the regular Church. Heretical holy men issued apocalyptic predictions of the 'Third Age' of the world. But perhaps the greatest threat to the papacy's universal claims and to the unity of medieval Christendom came from the rise of England and France as powerful embryonic 'nation states'. This was the changing world in which Giotto would live and work. During his lifetime he would see a pope die as the result of a bungled French kidnap attempt (1303), followed by the election of a French pope who established the papal court at Avignon, where it would remain for over seventy years (1305–76). Giotto's art can be seen, at least partly, as a quest to affirm Christian stability and strength.

Cimabue's workshop, where Giotto learned to paint, was one of the busiest in Florence. Artists at this time worked in the manner of craftsmen in large workshops run by one or two 'master painters', aided by several assistants and apprentices, training for anything up to thirteen years according to a handbook for craftsmen written around 1400. Direct information on Giotto's life during this period is purely anecdotal. There is a story that the young artist once painted a fly on the nose of one of his master's figures, an image so lifelike that Cimabue repeatedly tried to shoo it away. Such tales fall into a collection of anecdotes that portray Giotto throughout his life as something of a prankster. In reality, apprentices were found a variety of tasks – initially Giotto may have had to grind pigments for paints; he may also have learned carpentry in order to construct altarpieces and to prepare panels. Gradually, he would have learned how to draw an apostle, a Virgin or a Christ according to a strict set of rules dictated by the Byzantine tradition, diligently copying from pattern books. When he had mastered these artistic conventions, he would probably have assisted on the unimportant aspects of his master's commissions: the background, for instance, as well as the application of areas of unmodulated colour on robes. Individual creativity, innovation and originality were not required of an artist, let alone an apprentice. Far from the lone creative genius familiar to the modern world, the late medieval painter was more a craftsman than an artist, his work a trade rather than a gift.

The overwhelming influence on Western painting in the thirteenth century was the artistic tradition of the Byzantine Empire. This was in part due to direct contact between Western Europe and the eastern Mediterranean during the Crusades, though Italian cities were more broadly subject to these cultural influences on account of their proximity and trading connections. Byzantine art supplied a model for sacred painting of the highest majesty and power. This painting did not seek to portray subjects in anything approaching a naturalistic manner. Instead, the painter's task was to arrange a set of conventional and familiar religious images in order to convey most effectively a story or scene from the Bible. Figures are stylized, symmetrical and seemingly immovable. They gaze as if into another world, mask-like and without any discernible emotion. In Byzantine art, symbolism and strict iconography prevail over realism, naturalism and the depiction of human feeling.

Giotto's teacher, Cimabue, is widely regarded as one of the most outstanding painters in Italy during the later thirteenth century, not least for tentatively beginning the process of trying to break free from the stylized forms of medieval art. However, though much of what remains of his work is breathtakingly beautiful in its otherworldliness, it

THE BYZANTINE EMPIRE

After the break-up of the Roman Empire in the fifth century, the centre of political and cultural activity shifted firmly to the east. Its capital was Constantinople, named by the Emperor Constantine, who had made the city his capital in 330. The city had previously been known as Byzantium, which led future scholars to refer to the 'Byzantine Empire',

but in effect it was a continuation of the Roman Empire until its demise in 1453. By the Middle Ages, the city had a population of around 1 million and was the largest and wealthiest city in Christendom. It is now known as Istanbul.

The emperors of this eastern empire looked back to Rome for their tradition, symbols and institutions, but were also very heavily influenced by the great

Asian empires such as that of Persia. The empire was enormously prosperous in its early days, with emperors trying to regain the majesty, power and intellectual qualities of the western empire. The centuries brought varying degrees of success, but, by and large, the city and empire were home to intellectual development – ancient manuscripts were recopied;

nevertheless remains rooted in the Byzantine tradition. Cimabue's *Santa Trinita Madonna*, painted around 1290, is a brilliantly crafted work, but the Virgin appears rigid, static and posed. She stares out from flat eyes, her spiritual aura somewhat undermined by the clumsy way she holds an oversized infant Jesus.

Medieval artists, on the whole, were not interested in attaining greater naturalism and made no attempt to create the illusion of realistic space. Yet a movement towards naturalism can gradually be perceived in Europe at this time. The achievements in contemporary sculpture are particularly notable. The primary influence here came from north of the Alps. From the early thirteenth century, the cathedral sculptors of southern Germany and France created more realistic portrayals of the human form, with naturalistic posture and drapery and even hints at emotional expression. These developments in Italy benefited from a greater awareness of the classical heritage, surviving in scattered remnants of ancient Roman statuary. Certain Italian sculptors strove tentatively to recapture that lost naturalism of Roman sculpture. In particular, Nicola Pisano (*c*.1220–84), and to a lesser extent his son Giovanni, (*c*.1245–1314), working for the most part for Florence's rival, Pisa, produced sculpted reliefs which, though still medieval in composition and arrangement, were deliberate attempts to imitate the naturalistic qualities of classical art.

These artistic developments were mirrored in contemporary religion and literature. Franciscan and Dominican friars, leading lives devoted to poverty, chastity and obedience, sought a more direct and emotional experience of God. They also retold the Scriptures to the illiterate in plain Italian rather than in Latin. Similarly, writers like the great poet Dante Alighieri and, later, Francesco Petrarch (1304–74) and Giovanni Boccaccio (1313–75) applied vernacular Italian to all forms of literature; indeed, Dante, in championing the vernacular,

---

encyclopedias were compiled; mathematics, astronomy and literature were considered vital. On the whole, Byzantine intellectual and academic activity tended to produce unoriginal, encyclopedic collections, essentially preserving classical texts and knowledge rather than making new contributions and developments, but the preservation of ancient Greek manuscripts meant that this intellectual history did not die. Sometimes overlooked, Byzantine art is often monumental in conception, deeply moving and stylistically distinctive. It deeply affected much of the art of Europe, in particular, through its religious icons and mosaics.

Although Byzantium received financial and political assistance from Western Europe and the First Crusade (1096–9), it was eroded by failing political and military power and by other nations taking advantage of its weak position, not least by the Crusaders themselves, who allied themselves with Venice and plundered Constantinople in 1204. The Ottoman Turks demolished what was left of the empire during the 1300s, finally taking Constantinople in 1453.

for many the father of modern European literature.

These were the cultural and artistic influences that surrounded the young Giotto; indeed, Vasari calls Dante Giotto's 'contemporary and greatest friend'. Giotto, however, brought to them his own particular genius, a genius that was perceived to have enabled him to break from conventional artistic forms. When only in his twenties, Giotto's skill was already deemed to have surpassed Cimabue's, as he began to apply the naturalistic achievements of sculpture to painting.

Dante wrote:

> Cimabue thought he held the field
> In painting, but now the hue and cry is for
> Giotto, and the other's fame is dulled.

(Purgatorio, XI, 94–6)

Vasari elaborated more fully:

> in a brief time, helped by his natural talent and Cimabue's teaching, not only did the young boy equal the style of his master, but he became such an excellent imitator of nature that he completely banished that crude Greek style and revived the modern and excellent art of painting, introducing good drawing from live natural models, something which had not been done for more than two hundred years.

There are significant problems in narrating the life and achievements of a late medieval artist. Signatures were scarce and supporting documentation scarcer still. There's the odd contemporary chronicler like Riccobaldo of Ferrara, who details certain commissions undertaken by Giotto, as well as eulogizing accounts by later artists like Lorenzo Ghiberti, who were subsequently influenced by Giotto. Most of

---

THE FRANCISCANS

The Franciscan Order is one of the most significant to have developed in the medieval period. Its founder was Francis Bernardone (later St Francis), who was born around 1181, the son of a rich merchant of Assisi. In his early twenties, while on a pilgrimage to Rome, he exchanged clothes with a beggar and spent the day begging. He then renounced all possessions and determined to live a life of poverty. His wealthy father disowned him but, undeterred, Francis persevered. He claimed to have experienced a vision in which Christ told him to rebuild his churches – and Francis strove to do so.

He started to gain a following and when the number of his followers reached twelve, he drew up a simple rule, the *Regula Primitiva* (now lost), which eventually gained the approval of the Pope. Francis based the Order in Assisi in a small chapel obtained from the Benedictine abbey. Here they built a small community – in voluntary poverty – preaching and trying to imitate the impoverished circumstances in which Christ himself was thought to have lived.

In the medieval world of the twelfth century, Italy was undergoing a significant transformation. Trade, banking and, in particular, textile industries fuelled a rebirth of cities which, in turn,

what we know about his work, however, comes from the *Life* compiled by Giorgio Vasari published well over two centuries after the artist's death. Vasari attributes to Giotto a huge number of works commissioned by different patrons in locations as diverse as Rimini, Rome and Naples. But it is very probable that this catalogue exaggerates the number of finished paintings, both accidentally and deliberately. Vasari may have been mistaken in some of the works he attributed to Giotto. Various surviving paintings that bear a signature are almost certainly by his pupils, the signature being merely a 'trademark' denoting a product of Giotto's workshop. Furthermore, the facts that Giotto was famous and his work prestigious even in his own lifetime created a great incentive to attribute works to the master. Vasari refers to one Florentine gentleman who collected and greatly venerated the works of Giotto, 'who completed so many works that it would be unbelievable to hear them all described'. Vasari also notes a painted crucifix by Giotto, from which a later artist 'took the design for making many copies throughout Italy, since he was greatly practised in Giotto's style'. Vasari appears even to have changed his mind about the extent of Giotto's achievements. He produced two editions of his *Lives of the Artists*; in the second edition (1568), he attributes many works to Giotto that he had assigned to other artists in his first edition (1550). Fact, fiction, myth, legend and cultural propaganda are inextricably bound together in Vasari's account. Like Giotto himself, Vasari was a Florentine, and it suited his account of the great artists of the Renaissance that fellow Florentines should figure so prominently.

The first signs that Giotto was discovering his own artistic voice began to surface in the late 1290s in the Basilica of San Francesco at Assisi in Umbria. This building was consecrated in 1253, three decades after the death of St Francis, who lies buried in the crypt. Cimabue and

---

encouraged a stream of immigrants from the countryside. Conditions for these new city-dwellers were often grim – and it was specifically at this new urban poor that Francis targeted his sermons. It was for them that Franciscan churches, capable of holding hundreds of people, were built, frequently on the edge of towns. It was for them that the internal decoration was kept simple, with a particular emphasis on illustrating the

pain and piety of Christ's life. Like Francis himself – who used theatricality to enthrall his audience – wall paintings were intended to affect the viewer, to make the stories of the Bible alive and significant.

Francis is credited with the first reconstruction of the nativity scene. At Christmas 1223, he decided to construct a three-dimensional representation complete with models of Mary, Joseph and the Child in a crib. Animals

stood alongside in straw. Eight centuries later, the tradition continues.

Francis died in 1226, was canonized in 1228 and the first stone of a new double church (a Lower and an Upper, one on top of the other) on the hill of Assisi was laid in the same year. An earthquake struck the church in 1999, but the frescoes which adorn the walls have been restored.

his workshop had been involved in the decoration of the church from around 1277 and it is likely that Giotto had been part of the team in Assisi from the late 1280s onwards. The recently built Upper Basilica, rising out of the great Franciscan monastery like a fortress, in the hilltop town had become a magnet for any young artist worth his salt and there seems little doubt that the atmosphere was highly competitive. In addition to Cimabue's Florentine workshop, there were others engaged in the vast project, including various workshops from Rome. So, when Cimabue left in the mid-1290s to fulfil work commitments elsewhere, a power struggle seems to have ensued, and certain art historians deem Giotto to have emerged as the leading artist. Consequently, he was asked by Fra Giovanni di Muro della Marca, Minister-General of the Franciscan Order, to paint a series depicting the life and deeds of St Francis. This, at least, is the traditional view, stemming in the main from Vasari. But it's a contentious issue, with a number of art historians now of the opinion that an unknown Roman, the so-called 'St Francis Master', was the main creator of the frescoes. Recently a painter named Cavallini was hailed as the potential creator, but this suggestion has been dismissed by most of the major scholars of the period. Broadly speaking, though, the Italian art world opts for Giotto and in spite of a growing scepticism, consensus still favours the Tuscan artist

The frescoes depicting *The Legend of St Francis* at Assisi were created as an early and almost definitive visual account of the life of the saint. St Francis had died only in 1226, barely out of living memory. Written accounts of his life blossomed after his death, ranging from St Bonaventure's biography, commissioned by the general chapter of the Franciscan Order, to the *Legend of the Three Companions* compiled by three of Francis's disciples. Armed with this material, the young Giotto was given a blank canvas, or rather a white wall coated with wet plaster, on which to bring the saint vividly to life and to establish a model for almost all future representations of St Francis.

The story of the forty-four-year life of the rich merchant's son Francis Bernadone unfolds in twenty-eight scenes running like a cerebral cartoon strip around the north and south walls of the church below the tight niches created by the elaborate arches and windows of the Gothic building, which were also decorated. The cycle begins with a scene clearly recognizable as contemporary Assisi, with the wealthy young Francis tersely acknowledging a man who kneels reverently before him, having spread his cloak on the ground. In the next image Francis gives away his own cloak to a poor man and so begins his abandonment of worldly possessions in a quest to mirror the poverty of Christ. God, for Giotto, was present in the detail as well as in Francis himself. Architectural settings carefully create illusionistic spaces that amplify the drama as it unfolds. Likewise, the landscape around Assisi is lovingly recreated as a backdrop to the various miracles that Francis performs, from the spring which bubbles forth to quench the thirst of a parched farmer to the extraordinary vision of Christ wrapped in an angel's wings giving Francis the stigmata, or wounds from the Crucifixion. This scene, marking Francis as an imitator of Christ, is remote and unworldly in many ways and yet the landscape seems real enough, certainly by the standards of the day. Indeed, Giotto is credited with introducing a naturalism hitherto unseen in religious art.

Above all, the figures seem to suggest strong, if subtly drawn, human emotions, from the extreme joy of Francis's growing band of followers to the deeply felt pain of his death. Rather than appearing as symbolic characters in a religious narrative, the people Giotto creates would have seemed more real to a thirteenth-century eye. Just as St Francis appealed to the poor and dispossessed who identified with his ascetic life of poverty and struggle, so Giotto produced simple but powerful images which were recognizably human, conveying events which had only recently taken place. Likewise, the revolutionary aspect of St Francis's life, his establishment of a religious order based on poverty, chastity, obedience and the spreading of the Christian word through preaching to all and sundry, which so threatened the wealthy rulers of the Church, was subtly conveyed by an artist who was himself developing an approach to painting which became revolutionary.

By the turn of the fourteenth century, Giotto was accomplished enough to have set up a successful workshop in Florence and to have realized a commission, universally accepted as the work of the Tuscan artist, to paint a monumental crucifix for the Dominican Church of Santa Maria Novella on the edge of the city. Here, unlike his teacher Cimabue, Giotto emphasizes the physicality of Christ's death in an image where the body seems drained of life. Light and shadow amplify the naturalism of the work and hint at what was to come in Giotto's art. Meanwhile, his reputation was spreading beyond the boundaries of his native province. Vasari tells the story of how Pope Boniface VIII (r.1294–1303) sent a courtier around the cities of Tuscany in search of artists suitable for papal commissions. He was to interview likely candidates and to collect samples of their work. The courtier visited Giotto's workshop and requested samples so that his work might be evaluated. Giotto dipped his brush in red paint and with one continuous stroke drew a perfect circle. 'After he had completed the circle, he said with an impudent grin to the courtier, "Here's your drawing."' Giotto then assured the dissatisfied and protesting courtier that the worth of this sample would be recognized. When the Pope and his court heard the account and saw the image, they 'instantly realized just how far Giotto surpassed all the other painters of his time in skill'. In Tuscany, 'Giotto's O' became proverbial for perfect circularity.

Some time around 1300, Pope Boniface summoned Giotto to Rome where he was commissioned to produce numerous works within St Peter's, few of which survive. The most famous of these is the *Navicella*, a mosaic over the entrance of the portico, which depicts Christ walking on water. This piece, which has been restored and reworked to the point where Giotto's hand is no longer discernible, was perceived by some to be a miracle of sorts itself. It also serves to remind us that the so-called break with Byzantine art was nowhere near as emphatic as Vasari and others would have us believe. Mosaics were at the heart of Byzantine creativity and it seems more accurate now to view Giotto as having built on the achievements of various Byzantine masters rather than dismissing their work out of hand. Giotto was also employed to decorate the loggia of the Lateran Palace, commemorating Pope Boniface's proclamation of the first Holy Year in 1300. These commissions had important implications for Giotto's career; association with such a prestigious patron not only made him extremely wealthy, but advertised his talents to a wider audience. An artist who had worked for the Pope himself was an impressive commodity. As Vasari notes: 'Giotto therefore richly deserved the reward of six hundred golden ducats that the Pope, who considered himself well served, gave him, besides doing him many other favours, so that it became the talk of all Italy'. Giotto subsequently received commissions

The Lamentation, or Mary Weeping over the Body of Christ
c.1303–06, Arena Chapel, Padua

Giotto's vision of the *Pietà*, or Mary's lamentation over the body of her dead son, is a pioneering image in the depiction of tangible human grief. The remote, dispassionate tone of Byzantine art is superseded by an image with which the viewer can immediately identify.

All the eyes in the picture focus on the lifeless form of Christ, but none are more searingly griefstricken than those of his mother, who seems weighed down by her son's body and by her own emotion. It is an image full of gravity, both in mood and in the heaviness of the figures who are rendered with the monumentality of sculpture, partly inspired by the recent carved stone reliefs of Nicola and Giovanni Pisano in Pisa.

St John ('the disciple whom Jesus loved') throws his hands out in a gesture of dramatic despair. Behind him, Nicodemus and Joseph of Arimathea look on in stunned silence. The statuesque figures who crouch with their backs to us lead the viewer into the scene and push at the boundaries of the picture frame, creating an illusion of depth. In the background, nature is stripped bare, with a single, skeletal tree as a distant reminder of the cross on which Christ has just been crucified. The otherworldliness of the angels who flutter melodramatically above is partly brought to earth by their contorted, griefstricken faces. They, too, hint at the resurrection and ascension to come.

Like all the panels painted by Giotto in Padua, *The Lamentation* is both a self-contained image and an integral part of an ongoing saga. It is the spiritual low point, but, for many, the artistic high point in the painted life stories of Christ and Mary, full of nuance, expressiveness and, above all, an identifiable human experience of emotional and physical suffering.

in numerous other Italian cities, from as far afield as Ravenna and Naples, but, like so many of his works, few of these have survived.

Giotto's most celebrated surviving work came when he was in his mid-thirties. In 1302 he received an unusual private commission from a wealthy Paduan called Enrico Scrovegni. Giotto's fresco series in Padua has been universally recognized as one of the most important works in the history of European painting. Here the artist not only established his voice but proclaimed it from the rooftops. It is incontrovertibly by Giotto, an extraordinarily ambitious cycle of twenty-eight frescoes in the Scrovegni, or Arena, Chapel, so-called because it occupied the site of a Roman arena in Padua.

It is likely that Giotto was originally summoned to Padua by the Franciscan friars to paint frescoes in the church dedicated to St Francis there, which have since been lost. One of Padua's richest and most influential citizens, Enrico Scrovegni, then commissioned Giotto to paint his family chapel. Enrico's father, Reginaldo, had amassed a great fortune as a moneylender, a practice that the Church condemned as sinful. Indeed, he had achieved such a notoriously bad reputation that in the *Divine Comedy* Dante consigns him to the Inferno. Enrico was probably a usurer himself – wealthy and powerful, some contemporaries called him a hypocrite. The chapel was a conspicuous display of his wealth and influence, but also an act of atonement for the sins of his family.

Work began in 1303 and Giotto's frescoes are usually dated around 1305–06. The frescoes run around the entire interior. The main wall areas have three registers of frescoes portraying scenes from the life of the Virgin and her parents, St Anne and St Joachim, as well as scenes from Christ's Passion. Below are figures personifying Virtues and Vices, which are painted to simulate statues and sculpted reliefs. These three-dimensional optical illusions on a flat surface are called *grisailles*, and this is their first appearance in Western art since classical antiquity. Giotto's remarkable grasp of space and his ability to create the illusion of depth on a flat surface were two of his greatest innovations. This is also demonstrated in the false transepts that he drew in the corners of the chapel and above all in *The Last Judgment*, which adorns the west wall of the chapel. Here, in a scene of hellfire and damnation unprecedented in its power, Christ emerges triumphant amid the thronged multitudes of heaven, flanked by two figures peeling back the firmament to reveal a sparkling new Jerusalem. Likewise, below, a cleric's robe is painted by Giotto as if hanging out of the picture and on to the frame of the door from the chapel. In both instances, one epic, the other mundane, Giotto draws attention to the process of painting as an illusion but suggests, through these visual sleights of hand, that it might be real. This must surely have staggered fourteenth-century observers. It certainly continues to amaze visitors today, one of whom recently likened the chapel to a vast multiplex, a world where Giotto's imagination was projected over and over again on almost every available square inch.

It is clear that Giotto drew on the sacred theatre of the day, mystery plays and passion plays performed by travelling actors recreating biblical stories culminating in the life, death and resurrection of Christ. The architectural spaces that were created in Assisi are elaborated here and in certain instances – notably the birth of the Virgin Mary, her Annunciation and the birth of Christ – it is as if Giotto has created stage sets in which characters play out their sacred stories. He is also influenced by contemporary sermons, those impassioned performances from mendicant monks inspired by St Francis who incited pockets of religious fervour all over the Italian peninsula. In some ways, Giotto emerges as a kind of Franciscan preacher himself, but one who uses images rather than words and whose sense of drama is there on the wall for all to see. Finally, the impact of contemporary sculpture on him is striking. The growing naturalism in the work of Giovanni Pisano and his son, which almost seemed to bring stone to life, is invigorated still further by Giotto. His figures have solidity and weight, both physical and moral; they seem weighed down by gravity, even, paradoxically, when

The Last Judgment
c.1303–06, Arena Chapel, Padua
This work, which fills the west wall of the Arena Chapel, is the climax of Giotto's work in Padua. It shows Christ triumphant, the judge supreme and king of heaven. He is framed by a rainbow-coloured mandala and is depicted against a backdrop of rich gold, all of which amplifies his stature and gives the impression that he is powerfully real, almost as if he has been projected from one world into another.

The picture is multi-layered in its composition and its meaning. On either side of Christ sit the twelve apostles, themselves topped by choirs of angels who, in one of numerous illusionistic devices used by Giotto, disappear behind the actual windows of the chapel. Below are those who are to be judged.

The dividing line is the central symbol of Christianity – the wooden cross, to the left of which lies redemption. Kings and queens, saints and priests, the devout from down the ages – even, by tradition, Giotto himself (front row, fourth from the left, wearing a white hat) – are saved. So is the repentant son of a usurer, Enrico Scrovegni himself, seen handing a model of the very building the viewer is inside to the Virgin Mary, St John the Evangelist and St Catherine. It's almost as if time itself is conflated, whereby past, present and, by implication, future merge into an eternal moment.

To the right of the cross are the damned, spiralling downwards into the pit of hell amid twisted tongues of fire. It's a violent, seething and chaotic mass of apparently depraved humanity. Little or no detail is spared. Figures hang by their hair and genitals; one unfortunate individual is turned on a spit which runs through his mouth and out of his anus while the giant figure of Satan devours and then excretes a multitude of hapless sinners.

Giotto's vision of the Last Judgement is surpassed perhaps only by that of his fellow Florentine, Michelangelo, two hundred years later. It's a sophisticated, highly charged pictorial drama with a stark moral message about repentance and damnation whose impact was made all the more powerful to the late medieval faithful who came to worship at the chapel because it was the last image etched on to their imaginations as they left the building.

they are suspended in the heavenly skies. Above all, they have a real physical presence, amplified by what could be described as Giotto's rich palette of human emotions.

It was very unusual for a private individual to commission a work of this type and when it was completed it was criticized as too ornate a display of personal wealth. Scrovegni himself was depicted in *The Last Judgment* on one knee, presenting the building to the Virgin. The family chapel incited the anger of the monks of the neighbouring Eremitani monastery, who complained that this lavish display took God's name in vain. Nevertheless, many people flocked to the chapel because of a papal bull granting dispensation from penance to those who visited the chapel on specific holy days, and to see for themselves whether the rumours of blasphemy and extraordinary creativity were true and whether the frescoes actually warranted the growing attention they were receiving in and around Padua.

In the fractious world of fourteenth-century Italy, other city-states wanted some of the reflected artistic glory and Giotto was increasingly in demand. His native city lured him back soon after the Arena Chapel was finished and he was commissioned to paint a *Maestà* for the Ognissanti church (the church of All Saints). The *Maestà* is a devotional image of the Madonna surrounded by saints and angels, literally 'in majesty'. Giotto's commission was for the altar of the Ognissanti church in the western quarter of Florence, where the Benedictine Order of the Umiliati specialized in weaving woollen cloth that in turn paid for the work. The

Ognissanti Madonna
c.1309, Uffizi, Florence
This painting was commissioned as an altarpiece for the Ognissanti church in Florence. It is a devotional picture which shows the Virgin Mary and her infant son surrounded by a host of the saints to whom the church was dedicated. The supporting cast turn their enraptured gaze towards Madonna and Child led by the two angels in the foreground who form the base of an arc of figures which mirrors the architectural throne at the centre of the picture. This frames the two main figures and once again shows Giotto's mastery of the art of spatial illusion. The richly mottled marble step draws us into the picture and creates a more natural and emphatic sense of elevation for the enthroned figures than the dislocated compositions of most medieval painting. Of course, the Gothic throne is symbolic in its emphasis on ascension, on making us all look up (whether we're inside or outside the picture) but it also enhances the weight and solidity of the figures. Here, then, are gravity and grace deftly combined. Colour is delicately controlled, with haloed heads emerging from a sheet of shimmering gold and complementary reds and greens creating a lustrous web intricately woven around the throne. The vases of flowers held by the angels are filled with lilies and red and white roses, symbols of the Virgin's purity and future grief and painted as *trompe l'oeil* garlands, as if lifted from the real altar below which the picture was hung. The solemn drama of the scene is nowhere more powerful than in the depiction of the Virgin's veils, a rich contrast of translucent silk and traditional dark blue velvet pulled aside to reveal the contours of a real mother, the outline of breast and nipple subtly visible as if to emphasize the Madonna made flesh and blood. On her lap sits the Christchild, plump and well nourished by his fecund mother, gazing into the distance and making a gesture of benediction; the focal point of the painting, a blessing for the devout viewers who came to worship at the Ognissanti.

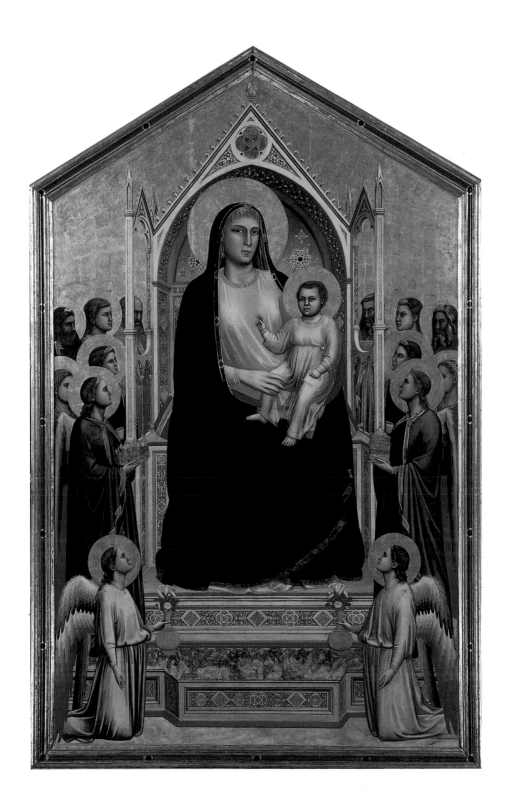

Ognissanti Madonna now hangs in Uffizi Gallery in Florence next to the S. Trinita Madonna by Giotto's teacher, Cimabue. They provide an object lesson in how codes of representation had shifted in two decades. Mary actually looks like a young mother, holding her child in a way that is caring and believable; she is situated in a spatial construction that enhances her corporeal presence as well as that of the saints around her.

By his mid-forties, Giotto's fame had already spread far beyond his workshop. During the next twenty years of his life, he continued to travel far and wide. He worked for popes, prelates, kings and noblemen. Biographical references place Giotto in locations as far apart as Pisa, Ravenna, Naples, Milan, Verona and even Avignon. Around 1313, a Roman cardinal, Jacopo Stefaneschi, commissioned Giotto to make a large altarpiece for St Peter's in Rome. By this time, however, the papal court was in exile in Avignon. As if to affirm its commitment to return to the Eternal City as quickly as possible, the Pope concerned himself with the ongoing decoration of his primary church.

The *Stefaneschi Altarpiece* was created as a triptych: three wooden panels painted on both sides, with Christ enthroned in heavenly splendour on one and St Peter, the first pope, enthroned on the other. Just as Giotto had painted Enrico Scrovegni presenting his building, so he illustrated Stefaneschi handing over a model of the altarpiece itself to St Peter. Here, for the first time in Western art, is an image of a picture within a picture. Indeed, if you look closely, it's possible to see the picture repeated once again in the model. One of the central characteristics of modern art is its self-referential obsession, where the artwork often refers to itself in a way we describe as self-knowing. Giotto, however, explored the territory well before the nineteenth- and twentieth-century avant-garde. Likewise, his sense of visual illusion was unrivalled at this stage in art history. As if to emphasize this, having effectively turned the work inside out through the device of a picture within a picture, moving around from one side of the altarpiece to the other, Giotto flips Peter through a hundred and eighty degrees from a throne to his crucifixion, upside-down in order to distinguish himself from his Lord and Saviour. The effect is dynamic: a few subtle twists and the world depicted seems alive, in flux even, with Christ the calm, reassuring centre of everything.

Giotto's late work was mainly back in Florence, where two wealthy banking families built chapels to honour both their God and their family name – just as another family of bankers called Medici would do a century or so later. Both the Peruzzi and Bardi families commissioned Giotto to paint devotional chapels in the Franciscan church of Santa Croce. First, a fresco cycle celebrated the lives of the two Johns – Evangelist and Baptist – for the Peruzzis. Space once again is paramount, and to enhance the idea of looking at a real scene viewed through an architectural opening, Giotto began to truncate some of the buildings and even on occasion the figures. He was also experimenting technically with the process of fresco painting. Instead of applying pigment to a wet plastered surface, Giotto tried working with dry plaster. This gave him more time and control. Unfortunately, in the eighteenth century the fading images were whitewashed before being restored (effectively excavated) a century later. Tragically, they have lost a good deal of detail and lustre mainly because the paint wasn't as deeply saturated into the surface as it would have been had Giotto used the established technique. As if to acknowledge that the process hadn't worked, Giotto returned to working with fresh plaster in the 1320s with the decoration of the Bardi Chapel. Here, as if to reiterate his prime position as *the* visual chronicler of St Francis, he worked through the life of the saint once again, although on a much smaller scale than in the frescoes in Assisi.

The Bardi family may well have been instrumental in Giotto's elevation to the role of court artist to the King of Naples in 1330. The Florentine family operated a branch of their bank in Naples and may well have introduced the artist to Robert of Anjou who ruled the Neapolitan kingdom. Giotto was granted the title of '*familiaris*' (or member of the household), for which he received a large salary, assistants, apprentices and materials. Little or nothing survives from the five years he spent in Naples, although it seems clear that his work was often that of an overseer for the decoration of rooms and chapels in the palace as well as the odd church. His rise from shepherd boy to courtier was complete and Vasari wallows in the reported accounts of Giotto's familiarity with the King. On one occasion, 'the king said to him, "Giotto, now that it is so hot, I would put aside my painting for a while if I were you." And Giotto answered, "I certainly would too, if I were you."'. Another anecdote, which Vasari quotes from Franco Sacchetti, relates that a rather pompous but minor knight brought his shield to Giotto's workshop in Florence and demanded, 'Paint my arms.' Rather than depict the knight's coat of arms, the artist covered the shield in illustrations of weapons and armour. The resulting uproar culminated in a court case, in which the knight was forced to pay Giotto his fee.

Giotto himself also became a wealthy landowner. As well as being a hugely successful artist, he was a shrewd business entrepreneur who knew how to profit from his creative talent and how to circumvent the laws of the time. One of the few surviving documents from Giotto's life shows that he was in the habit of hiring out his loom at a very high price, a clever and popular subterfuge for making money at the

Baroncelli Polyptych

c.1334–37, Santa Croce Church, Florence

Although the work is signed by Giotto, it was almost certainly painted by his protégé Taddeo Gaddi and Giotto's workshop, with the master overseeing the project. It serves, however, as an example of the expansive vision and practice that Giotto adopted in his later years. It is an elaborate small-scale work, a gilded fanfare to the Virgin Mary painted some time between 1334 and the artist's death in 1337. The five-panel altarpiece was commissioned by the Baroncelli family for their chapel in Giotto's favoured Florentine church of Santa Croce. In the central panel, Christ crowns his mother, rendered as a tender, sombre gesture of love. On either side, and painted as if floating off into the distance, are the heavenly horst. From a distance, the faces look uniform, golden symbols of Christian virtue. Look closer, though, and Giotto continues his pursuit of truth to emotion and human individualism with each celestial spectator presented as a unique, sentient human being. Perspective, however, is thrown out of the delicately arched window as a blanket of gold threatens to overwhelm the picture thus condensing the space.

In this respect, it is unlike almost everything else that Giotto produced, with the two oversized figures of Christ and Mary dislocated at the heart of a celestial vision. This emphasizes their importance but also signals a late shift in Giotto's workshop in which he permitted his assistants to embrace part of the burgeoning style of late Gothic. It is a radiant vision, a cacophony of vibrant colour and imaginary sound from the angelic orchestra in the foreground. From the elegant drapery of the saintly robes to the softer, less weighty handling of the figures themselves, Giotto, Gaddi and their assistants seem to be responding to the growing success of his Sienese rival, Simone Martini.

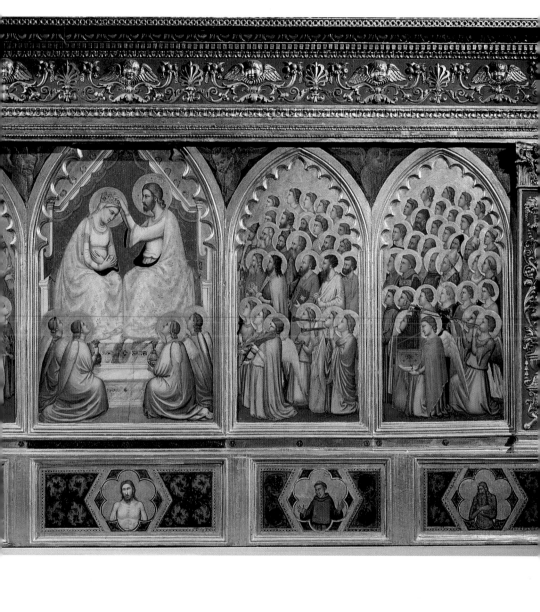

time without being guilty of the sin of money-lending.

Giotto's very last works are both the culmination of a lifetime's learning and a form of response to the increasing fame of his rivals, notably the contemporary Sienese painter Simone Martini (c.1283–1344), who had imitated and refined Giotto's style and technique under the influence of the French Gothic style. Martini himself was acquiring an international reputation to rival Giotto's. Giotto therefore modified his own style, introducing greater ornamentation, delicacy of colour and pictorial softness, notably in his final work at the church of Santa Croce. The *Baroncelli Polyptych*, as its name suggests, is a multi-panelled altarpiece commissioned by yet another wealthy Florentine family (the Baroncellis). The chapel itself was decorated between 1328 and 1335 by one of Giotto's more illustrious pupils, Taddeo Gaddi, with the master becoming more involved, after 1334, in the completion of the project. Giotto's workshop produced five panels, at the centre of which Christ crowns his mother, surrounded by a vast array of saints and angels. Each image is framed by an ornate Gothic arch, but the composition suggests one continuous space. There is a much more ethereal feel to this work than anything else Giotto produced, which was perhaps the result of his more supervisory role in his late work. Figures still seem weighty in the foreground but they begin to float off in a sea of rich gold as the eye travels up each image. There is a suggestion of heaven as an infinite space, the like of which we cannot quite comprehend. Vasari omits any reference to the work, even though it is inscribed at the foot of the central panel 'OPUS MAGISTRI JOCTI FLORENTIA' – 'Work of Master Giotto of Florence'. This is partly because the work is chiefly by Taddeo Gaddi and the workshop, but it also shows how Giotto himself was prepared to permit a shift away from the naturalism of a classically inspired tradition and to allow his workshop to embrace the more mystical style of the late Gothic. His practice is that of a mature artist trying to maintain his position in the face of new artistic trends and reserving the right, as all great artists do, to reinvent himself or at least reassess what he does and how he does it.

In 1334, the city of Florence honoured Giotto with the title of *Magnus Magister* – Great Master – and appointed him Master of Municipal Construction Works and Master of the Cathedral Masons' Guild, with the substantial annual salary of one hundred gold florins. In the same year, the foundation stone was laid for the famous campanile (bell tower) of the cathedral of Santa Maria del Fiore in Florence, over which Giotto presided as the dominant creative individual in the city. A sketch attributed to Giotto and now owned by a museum in the rival city of Siena details designs for the immense campanile which was built over the next twenty-five years under the supervision of two of Giotto's successors. Although the campanile looks rather different from the drawing, ask any Florentine or consult any guidebook and they will tell you that the original architect was Giotto.

With the campanile barely off the ground, Giotto died on 8 January 1337, at the age of seventy, and was buried a few feet away, just inside the entrance to the cathedral of Florence.

To the modern eye, the paintings of Giotto are very much products of the medieval world. They certainly lack the technical knowledge of perspective and anatomy possessed by painters of the Renaissance. Yet Giotto's achievement lies in his breaking away from an art of rigid appearance and formulaic craft and his creation of scenes which were charged with the physical presence of real human beings existing in something akin to naturalistic space. Above all, he could imbue a scene with rare and subtle emotional intensity, capturing a moment of crisis, stress or revelation and showing something of what it was to be a living, breathing, feeling human being. Giotto was the most 'human' and direct artist of his day. His immediate influence was stifled in subsequent Florentine painting by the popularity of late Gothic, but he inspired later generations of artists, notably Masaccio and Michelangelo. His long-term contribution to the Western tradition of painting is incalculable and this significance was recognized by many of his contemporaries.

The celebrated scholar and poet Giovanni Boccaccio, writing a generation after Giotto's death, offers the following assessment of his life and career:

> Now, since it was he who revived that art of painting which had been buried for so many centuries under the errors of various artists who painted more to delight the eyes of the ignorant than to please the intellect of the wise, he may rightly be considered one of the lights of Florentine glory.

2.

Leonardo da Vinci
1452–1519

Few artists have been as lionized as Leonardo da Vinci. In a life lasting sixty-seven years, he barely completed twenty paintings but this was enough to ensure his status as the outstanding figure of the Italian Renaissance. The *Mona Lisa* and *The Last Supper* are perhaps the two most celebrated paintings in Western art history: venerated, copied, parodied and stolen – once literally so in the case of the *Mona Lisa* in 1911, and metaphorically pilfered by advertisers and manufacturers the world over in products ranging from keyrings to condoms. Though Leonardo aimed to elevate the status of painting from a manual craft to an intellectual pursuit, he was at all times so much more than just a painter. He investigated, among countless other things, anatomy, botany, aviation, hydraulics and architecture. He devised schemes to divert rivers and even designed clothes. He had an intellectual curiosity more diverse than that of any other figure of his, and some would say any, time; and yet in his own terms Leonardo's career was a tragic if noble failure. 'Tell me if anything was ever done' was written across his voluminous notebooks, a frustrated refrain from a man who saw more of his world than anybody else but who, correspondingly, realized how little he knew and could achieve in his lifetime. This, perhaps, is the true, undeluded nature of genius.

Leonardo was born on 15 April 1452 in the tiny village of Anchiano near the small town of Vinci in the hills which lie to the west of Florence. The circumstances surrounding his birth are obscure and were later embroidered with legend. He was the illegitimate son of a local notary, Ser Piero da Vinci, the result of a liaison with a peasant girl, Caterina. She married a lime-burner in 1457, but Leonardo remained in his father's family. Leonardo thus grew up in Ser Piero da Vinci's large and prosperous household; a life with his mother would have been very different. Stories about Leonardo's childhood maintain that he quickly developed a profound love of nature in all its forms. Apparently a vegetarian, he is reputed to have purchased birds in the marketplace in order to free them. This unusual, even eccentric, aspect of Leonardo's character was to be manifest, and later exaggerated, throughout his life. In youth, the stigma of illegitimacy may have alienated him from his peers. In later life, his superior intellect, and perhaps his homosexuality, led him to live an often reclusive life.

Although the immediate environment in which Leonardo was raised was relatively traditional, the wider world around him was changing rapidly. It was an age of discovery in the broadest sense. Overseas exploration opened up new continents. Technological innovations like the printing press, the compass and the development of gunpowder led to a series of social, political and intellectual transformations throughout Europe. But the most prominent development of the fifteenth century was that intense flowering of art and culture known as the Renaissance. Consideration of the great achievements of the lost civilizations of Greece and Rome caused the intervening 'Middle Ages' to be viewed as a period of stagnation and decline. The defining characteristics of the Renaissance were a renewed interest in classical learning and language, scientific investigation and a conspicuous revolution in artistic styles and techniques. At the heart of these developments lay 'humanism', an intellectual movement that pervaded every branch of scholarship and the arts, and which placed Man at the centre of scholarly and artistic endeavour. Specifically in painting and sculpture, humanism promoted an interest in anatomy, portraiture and the expression of individual character. Leonardo was

PIGMENTS

A key part of any apprentice's training was to understand the source and selection of pigments; the colours available to a painter were dependent on the pigments he could find and afford. It was vital for all concerned that the drawbacks of certain pigments be fully understood. For example, one pigment used by many artists was ultramarine, which was created from the naturally occurring mineral lapis lazuli. This rare material, more precious in weight than gold, could be found in Afghanistan.

A poor man's alternative was German blue, made from the mineral azurite, but this was not considered to have the luminosity of true ultramarine. But lapis lazuli and some other blue pigments had their drawbacks for fresco artists. When painted in wet plaster, the alkalinity of the lime would alter the colour, giving it a green hue. This meant it had to applied to dry plaster, which over time was more prone to be deterioration than true fresco where the pigments were an integral part of the support. The high price of this mineral had

led to the practice of painting the Virgin Mary's cloak with natural ultramarine, the most expensive colour available to the painter. Even today, the Virgin Mary can usually be easily identified by her blue dress, in much the same way that the Roman Caesars wore purple because being made from crushed sea snails, it was the most expensive colour available to them.

Berries, wood, rocks and clay could all be used to obtain an array of colours, although they formed a much more restricted, 'earthy' palette. The

to live his whole life in this social and cultural milieu, which was almost exclusively the domain of the ruling classes. Although these pursuits are rightly seen as the defining characteristics of the age, they were largely the preserve of a very restricted group of scholars, artists and wealthy patrons, and the overwhelming bulk of Europe's population lived in a world which remained largely untouched by these developments.

Renaissance Italy was split into numerous rival city-states, many of which sought foreign alliances to increase their local power. For most of Leonardo's lifetime, Italy was a battleground for the imperial aspirations of the great European powers, notably France and Spain, which sought to control the small independent states of Italy. These prolonged wars, although ruinous to Italy, helped to spread the ideas and achievements of the Italian Renaissance throughout Western Europe. Florence was one of the many turbulent city republics in northern and central Italy, and its successful wool and banking trade meant it was also one of the most powerful. In Florence, commercial wealth, combined with civic pride and a self-conscious awareness of the city's cultural heritage, created favourable circumstances for artists. An important aspect of artistic patronage was the competitive ethos of wealthy families in artistic and architectural commissions. Of particular importance was the Medici family, whose members dominated the city from the early fifteenth century. Of modest origins, they accumulated immense wealth as merchants and bankers, married into the most important families in Europe, and later produced three popes. While the democratic constitution of Florence was outwardly maintained, the Medici exerted real control over government. Their lavish patronage of the arts, literature

painter's choice of colours was also restricted to where he lived and worked. An artist in Venice had many more pigments at his disposal than one living in the provinces. Venice's thriving port saw the influx of a great range of materials from far afield and these products, crushed and blended with oils or egg yolk, ended up on the palettes of the Venetian artists Those painters working near cities that manufactured lead crystal glass or near ceramic centres would have been well supplied with lead-tin yellow, a by-product of these industries. It was used with caution as it was a toxic substance. Lead was also commonly used to create both white and red hues. This required immersing sheets of lead in vinegar and then burying them in dung to create a chemical reaction on the surface of the metal. This could then be scraped off, mixed with a binder and used as paint.

The preparation of the paints was an arduous task, often carried out by the painter himself or his assistant. But occasionally they could be bought ready-prepared from an apothecary or from certain monasteries. Particularly important for fresco painters – as it determined the stability of the pigment in the plaster – was to ensure that the raw materials were ground to a very fine powder to create the smoothest paste in the chosen medium of egg or linseed oil – although the use of oil (either linseed or walnut) as a binding agent didn't achieve prominence until the end of the fifteenth century.

and scholarship reflected their personal tastes and interests, but also served to emphasize the wealth and prestige of the dynasty.

Ser Piero da Vinci enjoyed a good reputation and was well connected with important Florentine capitalists, including the Medici. Around 1467, he apprenticed the adolescent Leonardo to a personal friend, one of the city's most distinguished artists. Andrea del Verrocchio (1435–88) owned a highly successful business, which fed the conspicuous consumption of Florence's merchant class. Verrocchio himself was primarily a sculptor, but his studio received a wide range of commissions. The excellence and fame of its productions, and especially the presence of Verrocchio himself, made this workshop the place to be in Florence for young artists of the day. Leonardo's fellow apprentices included Pietro Perugino (1446–1523) and Domenico Ghirlandaio (1449–94).

As one of Verrocchio's many assistants, Leonardo was immersed in a world of painting, drawing and sculpture. He would have learned a variety of crafts, from the basic technique of grinding pigments and preparing panels to the advanced processes of bronze casting and copper soldering. The latter process was employed by Verrocchio's workshop in 1472 when he was commissioned to make the copper orb for the lantern of the dome of Florence Cathedral and it is highly likely that the young

The Annunciation
c.1472–74, Uffizi, Florence
It wasn't until Leonardo had reached the age of twenty that he produced his first major individual painting and even that was riddled with flaws. *The Annunciation* was commissioned by the nuns of the convent of Monte Oliveto just outside Florence, but it now resides in the Uffizi Gallery in the heart of the city. It shows the moment when the Angel Gabriel appears before Mary to announce that she is to be the mother of God. Towards the end of the fifteenth century, a preacher from Lecce called Fra Roberto Caracciolo had outlined what he identified to be the five successive emotional states of Mary

during the moment of the Annunciation, based on a study of St Luke's gospel. These were:
1. *Conturbatio* (Disquiet)
2. *Cogitatio* (Reflection)
3. *Interrogatio* (Inquiry)
4. *Humiliatio* (Submission)
5. *Meritatio* (Merit)
   Leonardo's *Annunciation* seems to hover somewhere between reflection and inquiry, Mary having been told by the angel: 'Fear not, Mary: for thou hast found favour with God. And behold, thou shalt conceive in thy womb, and bring forth a son, and shall call his name Jesus.' Mary's response, according to Luke, was 'How shall this be, seeing I know not a man?' X-rays have revealed that Leonardo struggled to resolve certain parts of the

painting, reworking the architectural background behind Mary in order to create a more balanced perspectival space and also repositioning both the angel and Mary, whose right arm is overstretched to reach the elegant bookstand in front of her, which is rendered with the most acute attention to detail, based on parts of the tomb that Leonardo's teacher Verrocchio had recently built for Giovanni and Piero de' Medici in the Old Sacristy at the church of San Lorenzo. This more than makes up for the clumsy composition which suggests that the Virgin has three legs, even if it is simply her robe falling over the back of her chair which seems to have splayed at

an odd angle. The angel's wings are painted with meticulous care, the result of Leonardo's studies of birds, which suggest a desire to scrutinize nature as closely as possible and to make painting, even of fantastical creations like an angel, more real. Close scrutiny of the painting itself shows that Leonardo's fingerprints are discernible on the right hand of the Virgin and on the leaves of the marble lectern, as he used all the means at his disposal to make things real, to obliterate brushstrokes in the smoothest possible finish and emphatically to leave his mark.

Leonardo was involved in the making and installation of the work. In addition, the apprentice would have been expected to produce graphic studies from nude and draped models, sketches of plants and animals, and to scrutinize the achievements of other artists, in order to learn the rudimentary principles of composition, perspective and the use of colour. The earliest evidence of Leonardo the painter unsurprisingly appears in collaborative pieces in which he, along with his master and other apprentices, contributed to different sections of a painting, principally in various pictures of the Madonna and Child and a work called *Tobias and the Angel* (now in the National Gallery, London). In the latter, Tobias holds a delicately depicted fish bound, almost puppet-like, with string while the angel has a wispy little dog at its feet. Both details are widely believed to have been painted by the young Leonardo, whose early talent for portraying animals as well as background landscapes was well documented. There is a story that Verrocchio was so impressed by his apprentice's ability that he not only employed Leonardo as the principal painter for the studio but angrily swore to give up this branch of the arts altogether. True or not, what remains clear centuries later is that the young Leonardo was finding his own style in a studio environment which was not always conducive to his personal idiom.

His first major works came to fruition some time between 1472 and 1474. The first was a commission from the convent of Monte Oliveto outside Florence and resulted in Leonardo's version of *The Annunciation*. The subject and composition are traditional but certain elements are original and eccentric. Mary's legs are poorly drawn and her left arm is elongated in an elegant bid by the artist to co-ordinate the spatial relationship between figures, objects and landscape. We know from X-rays that Leonardo redrew, corrected and repainted numerous areas of the picture but we can also see how skilfully he handles individual detail, not least the robes of both the Virgin and the angel and the extraordinary wings painted from intricate studies that Leonardo had made of birds, which had little or no precedent in Italian art. No less meticulous but considerably more ethereal is the tiny harbour scene shimmering beyond the Tuscan cypress trees. Notwithstanding a certain awkwardness in the picture, it shows the scope of Leonardo's ambition, an expansive and curious vision which seemed determined to observe the natural world at close quarters in order to make art more real.

Around the same time as Leonardo was wrestling with *The Annunciation*, he also produced what is now believed to be his first portrait, a serene image of a young Florentine bride-to-be called Ginevra de' Benci. The sixteen-year-old daughter of a wealthy banking family is painted against a wooded landscape which gently billows in the breeze and gives the rather serious young woman added zest. Immediately behind her head are juniper ('ginepro') bushes, a visual pun on her name, which is enhanced on the back of the panel itself where Leonardo has painted an heraldic scroll of juniper, laurel and palms with the motto 'VIRTUTEM FORMA DECORAT', or 'Beauty adorns virtue'. The work is both an emblematic portrait and a sensitively observed visual one, where the painted flesh is smoothed by Leonardo's fingers to reduce discernible brushmarks and breathe life into inert pigment.

The popular image of Leonardo da Vinci is based on a later sketch by the artist, usually taken to be a self-portrait, though there is no direct evidence that this is the case. In this lined and heavily bearded figure, the earlier Leonardo eludes us. According to contemporary accounts, the youthful Leonardo was a tall, handsome man, something of a dandy, who dressed in refined clothes and kept his hair carefully groomed. He was known for his gracious and amenable, if somewhat eccentric, manner. In 1476, while still at Verrocchio's studio, he was denounced for homosexual offences and tried along with four other young men. He was eventually acquitted after three hearings spread over two months, possibly through the agency of his father's influential friends, but the case was a traumatic one. Florence was a reasonably tolerant place in the 1470s and 1480s, but according to the strict letter of the law, homosexuality carried the death penalty. The threat of being burned at the stake, combined with the stigma of being publicly accused of what was perceived as sexual deviancy, must have had a strong impact on Leonardo. There has been endless speculation about his sexuality and the consensus, from the Florentine gossips to Freud, is that `Leonardo's dominant sexual impulse was homosexual'. This seems to have had much less of an impact on his art than it did for painters like Michelangelo or Caravaggio but, given the moral climate of his time and an almost universal public prurience, it helps explain Leonardo's occasionally secretive nature in the decades

THE FLYING MACHINE

Leonardo was fascinated by mechanics and engineering – and dived deep into the realms of possibility. For example, he reasoned that it was well within Man's capabilities to rule the skies. To him, it was a question of mathematics: by using the laws of physics that kept birds and bats in the air and applying them to the human form, an artificial machine could, he argued, be created that would replicate the flight of a bird. The quantity of his sketches of mechanical wings and flying machinery is testimony to his obsessive nature.

His artificial wings would be operated by systems of pulleys, levers and pedals involving both the arms and legs of the pilot. It is not entirely clear from his annotated drawings how the machines were to be propelled. But by using one of his best-known drawings, we can assume the pilot had to push down with one or both of the feet to create the downbeat of the wings while the arms operated another machine at the same time to facilitate an upwards motion.

His inventions came up against many barriers. The materials available to him – wood, leather, bamboo, metal,

that followed. This was, after all, a man who often wrote in code in his notebooks and whose writing needed a mirror to decipher it. He was also left-handed, which was considered an aberration in fifteenth-century Italy, but efforts to 'correct' it, according to the cultural norm, were fiercely resisted by Leonardo. Perhaps he wrote from right to left simply to avoid smudging. This was one area of his life where, from an early age, he was proud to fly in the face of convention.

In his mid-twenties, Leonardo left Verrocchio's workshop. His father's ties to the Medici may have helped Leonardo to establish a reputation in Florence as an artist in his own right. Certainly Lorenzo de' Medici, *Il Magnifico* (1449–92), gave Leonardo permission to work in the Medici Gardens in the Piazza San Marco. This housed the Medici's

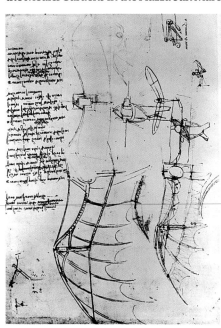

Design for a flying machine, c.1505, Royal Library, Windsor Castle

ropes and cloth – were strong but too heavy. A twentieth-century recreation of a machine based on his drawings weighed an incredible 650 pounds, far too heavy for one man to operate manually. Linked to this problem was the power needed by the pilot to manoeuvre and control such heavy wings. Leonardo looked to larger birds that relied on air currents and so turned his attention to gliding, which involved a reassessment of his original ideas.

By the time of his death in 1519, Leonardo had invented three different types of flying machine: the ornithopter, a machine based on the wings of a bird; the helicopter, which used a revolving rotor on a vertical axis; and a glider, which had a fixed wing attached to a frame.

No definitive flying machine seems to have been designed by Leonardo, although some argue he most likely built and tested out his ideas. But inhibited by the weight of the materials, human flight in the fifteenth century was an impossible dream. Man would have to wait over 400 years before successfully taking to the sky.

phenomenal collection of antique sculpture and served as a kind of postgraduate academy for young artists who were able to study and sketch the work of the classical masters. In addition, Leonardo came in contact with the illustrious circle of scholars patronized by the Medici, which doubtless stimulated the young man's passion for many fields of learning, notably mathematics and mechanics. These interests were by no means at odds with his artistic endeavours. In fact, throughout the rest of his life, scientific investigation was a central part of Leonardo's creative mindset, requiring an intricate study of nature. He developed the habit of drawing subjects from every conceivable viewpoint, filling page after page with drawings of every type: studies of hands, torsos, cats and horses in motion, architecture and machinery. The collection of notes and sketches that he produced over the next four decades ran to more than 20,000 pages, of which nearly half have been preserved. These offer some clues to the extraordinary workings of his mind. They suggest an imagination so restless that he could never focus on one idea for very long. Some pages are a chaotic jumble of drawings and notes, in which a geometrical calculation, a human hand, an astronomical theory and a flower all compete for space. Vasari's account of Leonardo's life is often more a hagiography of a divinely inspired, universal genius than a serious biography, but his description of Leonardo's infuriating tendency to shift the focus of his attention in an instant is a telling one: 'But the truth is that Leonardo's splendid and exceptional mind was hindered by the fact that he was too eager and that his constant search to add excellence to excellence and perfection to perfection was the reason why his work was slowed by his desire.' (*Lives*, 291).

Leonardo's meticulous studies began to crystallize in his first great masterpiece, an unfinished work of originality and confidence. the *Adoration of the Magi* was commissioned in March 1481 by the monastery of San Donato a Scopeto, near Florence, for which Leonardo's father was notary. Leonardo was contracted to complete this altarpiece in less than thirty months, but, like so many of his works, it remained incomplete. The setting is made up of several narrative episodes, yet they are all somehow brought together by Leonardo's composition. A vast array of more than sixty figures demanded an incredible range of gestures and facial expressions, variously conveying awe, incredulity, bewilderment, devotion, contemplation and curiosity. These are the result of Leonardo's meticulous studies of anatomical form and movement. It's as if he was trying somehow to explore the human condition in all its guises in one single work. The simple triangular composition in which the Virgin and Child are surrounded by the ageing Magi leads into a highly complex perspective system, a multi-layered backdrop of buildings and battles, of trees and clouds against which a labyrinth of incident and energy unfolds. The tight architectural framework of earlier artists from Giotto to Piero della Francesca has been shattered and a new pictorial vision has broken free.

Towards the end of 1481, and with the *Adoration of the Magi* of course unfinished, Leonardo chose to leave Florence. His reasons for abandoning this centre of wealth and patronage are unknown. He may have felt pessimistic about his career prospects; earlier that same year, when the Pope had invited some of the best Florentine painters to Rome to decorate the walls of the Sistine Chapel in the Vatican, Leonardo had not been selected. He may also have felt frustration at the bookish nature of the Medici court. Initially, it would doubtless have stimulated Leonardo's mind, but his intellectual restlessness may well have been constrained by the small intellectual élite patronized by the Medici, whose dominant interests were classical literature, grammar and philology. These were men with whom the artist would have enjoyed little sympathy. Leonardo was almost entirely self-taught and struggled to read Latin. He believed nothing unless he saw it with his own eyes and in his notes one often senses his contempt for the fabled Florentine humanist scholars, who relied almost exclusively on classical learning for their knowledge.

Whatever his reasons, by April 1483 Leonardo was in Milan, where he would spend the next seventeen years. Milan was a very different city from Florence, notably because the latter had played by far the most significant and conspicuous role in the major artistic developments of the previous two centuries and was much more conscious of, even preoccupied with, its own heritage and achievements. Although Milan never rivalled Florence in its wealth and sophistication, the northern Italian city was a place of some cultural significance, especially under its benign despots, the Sforza family. Ludovico Sforza (c.1452–1508, r.1494–99, and who was regent for his young nephew at this time) was one of the wealthiest and most powerful princes of Renaissance Italy. Known as *Il Moro* (the Moor) because of his swarthy complexion, his lavish spending on the arts and sciences briefly made Milan a glittering cultural centre, attracting influential figures to his court, including the architect Donato Bramante (1444–1514).

Leonardo had written to Ludovico to advertise the many services he could perform, adding in conclusion 'in painting I can do as much as anyone, whoever he may be'. But it was probably more his potential as a military engineer and inventor that appealed to his would-be patron. Leonardo hoped above all to become a member of the Sforza court, with a permanent salary which would enable him to pursue his personal interests more freely. But he was not accepted into Ludovico's court immediately. Instead, he established himself as a painter in Milan and founded a workshop, which prospered and attracted numerous pupils. Leonardo's first known commission in Milan was the so-called *Virgin of the Rocks*, an iconic work founded on controversy (it now hangs in the Louvre). For two decades, the *Virgin of the Rocks* was at the centre of a dispute between Leonardo and his clients, the Confraternity of the Immaculate Conception at the church of San Francesco Grande in Milan, who were highly dissatisfied with the finished picture. Leonardo took on the commission in April 1483 and agreed to complete it in seven months, but instead seems to have taken more than two years. Moreover, he completely ignored the details of the commission, which typically had

Leonardo da Vinci on Colour and the Perspective of Colour

'Of colours of equal whiteness that will look brightest which is against the darkest background. And black will display itself at its darkest against a background of greatest whiteness. And red will look most fierce against the yellowest background, and accordingly all the colours will do this surrounded by their directly contrary colour. A direct contrary is a pale colour with a red, black with white (although neither of these is a colour), blue with a yellow such as gold, green and red. The colours that go well together are green with red or purple or mauve, and yellow with blue. Black clothing makes the flesh of images of people appear whiter than it is, and white clothing makes the flesh appear darker, and yellow draperies make it appear more colourful, and red clothes make it display paleness.'

specified (in the way that an architectural commission would do today) exactly what kind of painting was required, right down to the pigments to be used as well as the details of composition and background. Leonardo had already begun to develop a different conception of the artist from the medieval notion of the glorified craftsman to the more modern one of creative genius. His confidence was such that he took a technique first explored by Northern European painters, that of creating form almost entirely through tonal modulations, through the contrast and interplay of light and shade, and revolutionized it. This gave rise to the Italian term *chiaroscuro*, meaning light and shade, which Leonardo also used to create an atmosphere charged with tension between each of the four figures. Mary, Christ, John the Baptist and an angel are pushed perilously close to the darkness which in turn emphasizes the light in the foreground, giving them a dramatic ethereal glow. The whole scene is bathed in a magical atmosphere akin to twilight, a moment when everything is on the verge of change, and this eeriness is reinforced by the fantastical, rocky, womb-like landscape which threatens to envelop all before it.

Oddly enough, it was not the startling originality of Leonardo's conception of light, dark and atmosphere which displeased the Confraternity, but the composition, which placed more emphasis on John the Baptist than on the figure of Christ who is blessing him. The picture was rejected and eventually sold (ending up in the Louvre), and Leonardo and two assistants made a second version which now hangs in the National Gallery in London. This picture, painted some time between 1491 and 1495 and barely changing the initial composition, is brighter, less mysterious and more monumental, a sign that Leonardo was evolving his own style and was important enough to have his own assistants. Within ten years or so, at least twelve copies of the original *Virgin of the Rocks* had been made in Italy, as well as quilted altar covers and tapestries. In spite of his limited output, Leonardo's reputation was burgeoning rapidly.

Consequently, Leonardo's hopes were realized and he became a permanent fixture at the Sforza court. His duties there were not onerous, which enabled him to pursue more fully his endless, meticulous, obsessive quest for knowledge. In 1489, Ludovico commissioned a colossal equestrian statue of his father, Francesco Sforza. This project occupied Leonardo for many years, but ultimately progressed no further than a clay model for the horse. Many of Leonardo's detailed studies of equine anatomy may relate to this project. Later, he decorated certain rooms in the Castello Sforzesco. But this period is more outstanding for Leonardo's intellectual curiosity and scientific investigation. During his

time in Milan, he designed countless new machines and contraptions, from parachutes to looms to clocks. He began to study human anatomy in greater depth through autopsy, eventually dissecting numerous corpses. Leonardo also made a number of profound discoveries in human biology, including correct deductions about the nervous system and blood circulation. In addition to his ongoing mathematical investigations, he commenced studies of aeronautics and submarine navigation, as well as a variety of architectural schemes, principally a projected dome for Milan Cathedral which was never realized.

Even his official work in Milan greatly appealed to his sense of ingenuity and his desire to experiment. He designed elaborate costumes and complex stage sets with special effects for performances at the court. To celebrate an important visit, he once made a mechanical lion whose breast opened up and showered lilies. Leonardo spent much of his time planning an ideal new city, but he also drew maps, designed irrigation schemes, heating systems and engines of war. Like so many of his ideas, very few of these plans ever came to fruition. In his twenty years in Milan, Leonardo completed remarkably few works of art. To the eternal frustration of his contemporaries, who felt that he constantly frittered

The Last Supper
1495–97, Convent of Sta Maria delle Grazie, Milan
In spite of the ghostly appearance of the work, itself a monument to Leonardo's desire to experiment and achieve a lasting technical perfection in fresco painting, *The Last Supper* still has an extraordinary presence. It is so precisely composed and painted that it resembles a latter-day hologram flickering in and out of vision. Even today it looks as if Leonardo has managed to create another room beyond the refectory in which the work is sited. This is enhanced by the semicircular lunettes painted above *The Last Supper*, which originally contained the Sforza coat of arms to remind all who saw it who had commissioned the work and had ruled absolutely.

The painted vision is an elevated one: the viewer looks up in awe at a scene which, if rendered strictly according to the laws of nature, would be almost invisible since the most one would see would be the underside of the table. Leonardo subtly tilts it forward to reveal the drama unfolding in a deep illusionistic space. The scene centres on Christ in every way possible. Each of the disciples either has his eyes or hands pointing towards their Lord and Master who has just revealed that one of them will betray him. Christ is framed by three windows behind him and seems to illuminate the table, its contents and the surrounding figures himself.

The twelve figures are broken up into four groups of three, order imposed by Leonardo on an image of unprecedented expressiveness. Each figure is emotionally connected to the others in his group (with the exception of Judas, who is slightly pushed forward and thereby isolated by Peter who whispers manically in the ear of John, to the immediate left of Christ as we look at it) but is, at the same time, depicted as feeling something entirely personal. It is almost as if Leonardo is producing a case study in human response to tragedy. In turn, the work can also be read as a diagram by the artist–scientist who was analysing the workings of sound waves and their impact: 'Those who are nearer understand better,' scrawled Leonardo in his notes for *The Last Supper*, and 'those farther away hear poorly'.

The work was immediately hailed as 'miraculous' and 'divine', though it quickly began to deteriorate. But copies were made and artists as significant as Rubens and Rembrandt in the north, Caravaggio in the south, and even, much later, Andy Warhol out west, drew direct inspiration from the work. It remains Leonardo's most monumental and significant artistic achievement, even as it continues to fade away.

away his time, Leonardo would often start a work, leave it unfinished and move on to something else. Even Leonardo himself appears to have found the restlessness of his own mind incompatible with the realization of his ideas. He often wrote long lists of all the things he had to do and the people he wished to consult. He was in a constant battle against time, acutely aware of it passing him by.

Leonardo's period in Milan did, however, produce a masterpiece of singular fame. In 1495, Duke Ludovico commissioned a mural in the refectory of the Convent of Santa Maria della Grazie. Completed in 1497, *The Last Supper* became Leonardo's most famous work among his contemporaries. The painting that survives today is the merest shadow of the original creation, in large part due to Leonardo's experimentation in new materials. Nevertheless, it is still possible to discern its beauty and sophistication.

The work is set at the end of a long wall in the refectory of the

Mona Lisa
c.1503–05, Louvre, Paris
No painting could live up to the fame that now surrounds the *Mona Lisa*. It is a phenomenal work of art, the most familiar picture in the world, but one that has become increasingly difficult to see clearly. Its power and Leonardo's achievement are the result of an ambitious attempt to bring the face to life by depicting a changing expression. Hovering between melancholy and wry amusement, Mona Lisa is on the verge of breaking into a smile. This is achieved through the technique of *sfumato*, where outlines are slightly blurred, notably around her mouth. Leonardo also accentuates the idea of change through the way he paints the dream-like landscape behind. It too seems alive but belongs to a different timescale, where the process of evolving from one state to another takes thousands of years. Look, though, at the horizon line either side of Mona Lisa's head and you see that Leonardo has skewed it. The two sides don't match and this helps to deceive the eye into thinking that the face itself is moving in some way.

This is partly why the picture caught the imagination of those who saw it from the outset. Vasari raved about it. As early as 1525, six years after Leonardo's death, the picture was valued at 100 *scudi*, a vast amount for a painting in the early sixteenth century. Much has been made of her sphinx-like face and there's no doubt there is something of an unfathomable mystery to the work, which struck a chord with nineteenth-century Romantic poets and painters, not least the American Walter Pater who helped mythologize the painting in the United States: 'Like the vampire, she has been dead many times', Pater wrote in 1873, 'and learned the secrets of the grave; and has been a diver in deep seas, and keeps their fallen day about her, and trafficked for strange webs with eastern merchants; and, as Leda, was the mother of Helen of Troy, and, as St Anne, was the mother of Mary.' In a way, she became a springboard for individual flights of fancy: Everywoman rather than a specific early sixteenth-century Italian noblewoman. But there are other reasons too for the fame of the *Mona Lisa* which are more mundane: the painting is one of relatively few completed works by the overriding genius of the Renaissance, itself still perceived as the bedrock of Western culture; the painting was part of the Louvre's collection when the gallery was opened in the nineteenth century, soon after the French Revolution, the first great public museum of art. Within four decades, photography had been developed and the *Mona Lisa* was among the first art postcards. Rapidly, her face was seen in the far-flung corners of the world and, as international tourism became more widespread, the art pilgrimage to Paris became popular. Parodied by artists like Marcel Duchamp and utilized by advertisers and souvenir maunfacturers, the *Mona Lisa* became something more than just an oil painting on a wooden panel. It became both a commodity and a celebrity in the age of mass production, mass media and mass tourism, where fame is virtually a self-perpetuating phenomenon.

Dominican monastery where the monks ate. Looking up from their tables, it must have seemed as though another dining hall had been added. Leonardo's greatest achievement was to consider what *The Last Supper* would really have looked like and then to try to recreate it. He has captured the very moment when Christ says, 'One of you will betray me' (Matthew 26, 21–2). Each apostle is reacting with shock and disbelief and asking the question 'Lord, is it I?', creating a scene of heightened psychological drama, while at the centre Christ sits serenely, resigned to his fate. Never before had this sacred episode appeared so lifelike. Leonardo trawled the streets of Milan to find suitable characters to transform into disciples via his sketchbooks. He sought models for certain body parts with one 'Alessandro Carissimi of Parma' providing 'the hands of Christ' according to one of the artist's notebooks. In turn, while working on the picture itself, Leonardo famously spent days simply staring at the painting. 'Often I have seen and observed him myself,' wrote the contemporary Milanese chronicler Matteo Bandello in 1497,

> he used to climb on his scaffolding early in the morning because *The Last Supper* is somewhat high and off the ground: from sunrise to sunset, forgetting to eat and drink, he would go on painting. Then, for three or four days he would not touch his work, but for one or two hours a day he would stand and merely look at it, examine and judge his own figures.

The Last Supper is, in effect, a synthesis of much of Leonardo's wide-ranging studies and theories on optics, architecture, perspective, anatomy and colour. Looking up at the ghostly forms of the work today, it becomes clear that Leonardo's whole creative life was based on the need to understand in order to recreate; to grasp the fundamentals of the world around him in order, as he put it, to produce 'a second world of nature' which was his definition of painting.

The work is also a monument to Leonardo's overzealous experimentalism. In his quest to find an alternative to the quick-drying fresco process which necessitated the artist completing the section of painting before the plaster had dried, he devised a method which involved working on a dry surface, using his own mixture of pigment and materials to seal the paint on to the wall. But even before he died, the vast panoramic picture was showing signs of deterioration. Its fame and influence, however, spread rapidly, with Leonardo credited with the invention of a new approach to painting that was dextrously controlled, spatially more sophisticated than anything before, monumental in its vision and as optically real as art could ever be. It heralded a new phase in the history of Western art, known as the High Renaissance.

Leonardo's more immediate reward was less grandiose than a place in the pantheon of art history. In April 1499, Ludovico presented him with a vineyard just outside the city, but Leonardo's career in Milan came to an abrupt end soon after, thanks to the vagaries of Italian politics. Later that year, King Louis XII of France (1498–1515) decided to make good his own hereditary claim to the Duchy of Milan and to eject the Sforzas. Within a matter of months the French had occupied Milan and Duke Ludovico was in a French prison. The Gascon bowmen of Louis XII reputedly used Leonardo's model for the equestrian statue of Francesco Sforza for target practice. Louis XII was as eager to acquire Leonardo's services as he was Ludovico's other possessions. Indeed, he was so impressed with the artist's work that his engineers tried in vain to remove the entire wall bearing *The Last Supper* for transfer to France. Leonardo chose for the moment to remain with the Sforza family, who now moved to Mantua, where Leonardo produced a delicate pastel portrait of the great patron Isabella d'Este, whose family gave refuge to the Milanese exiles. After a brief period in Venice as an architectural consultant, however, he decided to return to Florence.

The Florence to which Leonardo returned was very different from the one he had left behind seventeen years earlier. The Medici had been expelled in 1494 and the city was now a republic once again, in which, initially, ostentation was viewed with suspicion. But Leonardo had also changed. Preceded by the fame of *The Last Supper*, his varied talents were in demand. Leonardo's real passion, however, remained his research. He constantly tried to postpone commissions in order to focus instead on his studies, leading one contemporary to comment that 'he is so obsessed with geometry that he can no longer tolerate the brush'.

During the summer of 1502, Leonardo took up a new challenge when he entered the service of Cesare Borgia (*c.*1475–1507) as a senior military architect and general engineer. Cesare Borgia was the notoriously vicious and ambitious captain-general of the papal army. He was the illegitimate son of Roderigo Borgia, by then Pope Alexander VI (r.1492–1503), whom history records as one of the most depraved individuals to have worn the papal crown. At twenty-seven,

Leonardo da Vinci on the Vision of the Painter

'The Painter is Lord of all types of people and of all things. If he wishes to see beauties that charm him it lies in his power to create them and if he wishes to see monstrosities that are frightful, buffoonish or ridiculous, or pitiable, he can be lord thereof … If he wants valleys, if he wants from high mountain tops to unfold a great plain extending down to the sea's horizon, he is lord to do so … In fact, whatever exists in the universe, in essence, in appearance, in the imagination, the painter has first in his mind and then in his hand.'

Cesare was one of the most feared men in Italy, and the inspiration for Machiavelli's manual for would-be despots, *The Prince*. His aim was to carve out a kingdom for the papacy from the disparate city-states of central Italy. While working for Cesare, Leonardo travelled extensively throughout central Italy, producing hundreds of maps which are now seen as the precursors to modern topography. The death of Pope Alexander VI in 1503 put an effective end to the Borgias' territorial ambitions, and Leonardo returned to Tuscany to participate in various schemes to divert the River Arno around Pisa, with whom Florence was currently at war. The idea was to deprive the smaller city of its water supply and cut it off from its harbour. Excavation work began on two eight-mile channels and a vast wooden barrier the following summer but was abandoned as the weather worsened, workers were attacked and money ran out.

Around this time, however, Leonardo was awarded a highly prestigious commission by the Florentine government, or *signoria*. This was to be a large-scale mural in the Sala del Gran Consiglio in the Palazzo della Signoria (later called Vecchio). It would be twice as large as *The Last Supper* and was to depict an historical scene, the Battle of Anghiari (1440), in which the Florentines had inflicted a surprise defeat on the Milanese. Leonardo's younger rival in Florence, Michelangelo Buonarroti

Apocalyptic Scenes of Destruction
c.1517, Royal Library, Windsor Castle
Although he produced barely a handful of finished masterpieces in oil paint, Leonardo left in excess of 20,000 sketches and drawings. These are at the heart of his creative being, where Leonardo's curiosity, experimental zeal and phenomenal imagination merge together and often run riot. This particular group of studies produced towards the end of the artist's life, broadly relates to a series known as the *Deluge Drawings* in which Leonardo explored the destructive forces of nature. Cloudbursts, raging storms and hurricanes were depicted with scrupulous attention to detail and a visionary leap of imagination. And so it is in this drawing, but there is a biblical dimension too, from Old Testament prophecies of doom and destruction to St John's Book of Revelation. Likewise, Dante seems to have inspired the plunging pit within the mountain at the bottom of the page. Skeletons are piled high and explosive clouds rain fire on the world below.

Scholars have noted the close connection between these drawings and the images graphically conveyed in the sermons of Savonarola, the Dominican preacher of fire and brimstone who was himself burned at the stake in Florence in 1498. Leonardo, cynical about self-professed mystics and men of God who relied on irrational fear, seems to be challenging the idea of divine punishment by making it more real, but is also using the Apocalypse as a trigger for his own imagination. Leonardo the scientist and Leonardo the artist dovetail in these sketches and likewise in his notes at the top of the page which read as follows:

On clouds, smoke and dust and flames of a fired furnace or fired kiln. The clouds do not show their convexities except on those parts exposed to the sun, and other convexities are imperceptible through being shadows. If the sun is in the east and the clouds in the west, then the eye interposed between the sun and the cloud sees that the boundaries of the convexities composing these clouds will be dark, and the clouds which are surrounded by this darkness will be light.

Technical observation and free association combined in the mind of a man who saw the pursuit of all knowledge as one and the same process.

(1475–1564), was commissioned at the same time to paint a similar battle scene on a facing wall, the Battle of Cascina, an episode which had taken place sixty-five years earlier. This double commission served to highlight the antipathy between the two artists; effectively, the room itself was the scene of a battle by brush. Predictably, the unusual temperament of both these artists meant that neither work was ever completed. Although nothing remains of this fresco, it is, ironically, Leonardo's best-documented work. Had it been completed, it would have measured up to eighteen by seven metres. As with *The Last Supper*, however, Leonardo demonstrated both his inexperience and mistrust of conventional fresco painting. He experimented with the consistency of the stucco, a type of plaster applied to walls to provide a painting surface. He tried to make up a preparation he had read about that Pliny the Elder had produced some 1,500 years earlier, which he thought would enable him to work more slowly and methodically. This technique, however, required heat in order to dry it out. Fires were lit in the hall, but the excessive size of the chamber did not allow an even temperature and, as a result, part of the paint surface melted. Leonardo eventually abandoned this monumental project in 1505.

The remaining preparatory sketches and later copies of *The Battle of Anghiari* suggest that it was to have been an extraordinarily violent scene. The centrepiece, called *The Struggle over the Banner,* remained on show for a few years. This was the ideal opportunity for Leonardo to display to the Florentines on a grand scale the visual and emotional effects of which he was capable in his art. In the brilliantly drawn entwined bodies of the men and the horses, Leonardo made use of his studies of human and animal anatomy and movement. The sketch perfectly conveys the seething chaos, violence, anger and drama of war. Perhaps if it had been completed, *The Battle of Anghiari* would have become Leonardo's most famous work. Instead, as often happens in the history of art, it is a relatively mysterious and far less prestigious commission for which he has become best known: an intimate portrait of a serene and smiling woman.

There is still dispute as to who the *Mona Lisa* actually was. Various illustrious sitters have been proposed, including Isabella d'Este, but the available evidence seems to point to Lisa Gherardini del Giocondo, the third wife of Francesco del Giocondo, a successful Tuscan merchant. 'Mona', or 'Monna', is short for 'Madonna', or madam, and an inventory of the estate of Leonardo's heir (a painter called Salai) lists a portrait of a lady described in the margins as 'La Gioconda'.

In spite of the somewhat murky appearance of the painting, due in part to the varnishing which has helped preserve the work, it is still an image which comes to life before our eyes. It is the culmination both of Leonardo's portraiture, which began with Ginevra de' Benci, and of his quest to create life from painting, to produce a 'second nature'. The painted flesh of the *Mona Lisa*, particularly her hands and face, give the impression of being alive below the surface through a technique known as *sfumato*. This involved the softening of outlines almost to the point of blurring them, which helps suggest movement and is much closer to the way the eye perceives things. Previous painters had managed to convey life and expression but never to this degree. Instead of giving us a static image, Leonardo's *Mona Lisa* is in the process of changing her expression. We see the split second where melancholy moves into a smile, her mouth flickering around the edges, her lips slightly trembling, her distantly gazing eyes beginning to twinkle. There is something sphinx-like about her face and the picture has an unfathomable quality seen in the *Virgin of the Rocks*. But the key to the painting is time: from the micro-second to the lifetime of a human being to the grander passage of time played out in the weathered rocks and valley carved out by the river in the background. As various art historians have recently pointed out, Leonardo drew strong parallels between the human body and the natural world, one as a microcosm of the other, and this seems central to the *Mona Lisa*: 'In that man is composed of water, earth, air and fire', Leonardo wrote in one of his copious notebooks, 'his body is an analogue for the world: just as man has in himself bones, the supports and armature of his flesh, the world has the rocks; just as man sees in himself the lake of blood, so the body of earth has its oceanic seas.'

By 1506, Leonardo had become a well-known figure internationally. Indeed, he was so much in demand that he was even at the centre of a diplomatic incident. Leonardo obtained temporary leave from the Florentine republic to return to Milan in order to complete certain projects left unfinished due to the fall of his patron. In Milan, he once again came into contact with the French, who repeatedly asked the Florentines to extend Leonardo's leave. This led to a series of exchanges between the Florentine and Milanese governments, each laying claim to his talents. The matter was finally concluded with a stern letter from the King of France himself, asking that Leonardo stay in his service in Milan. Artistically, Leonardo's second period in Milan saw the consolidation of recent work. Large-scale sketches begun in Florence were transformed into another celebrated painting which now hangs in the Louvre, *Virgin and Child with St Anne*. The serenity of the *Mona Lisa* and its rugged background are combined with a more monumental handling of the figures which owes a good deal to Leonardo's detailed studies of antique sculpture, rekindled after several brief trips to Rome.

It is a more classical picture than his previous work, ordered rather than enigmatic but still vibrantly alive. With the unofficial title of '*peintre et ingenieur ordinarie*' bestowed on Leonardo in a letter from the King of France to the Florentine *signoria*, he continued to devote himself to broad areas of invention and study. He wrote treatises on the theory of painting and on hydraulics. He worked on the construction of the Adda and Martesana canals. His anatomical exploration flourished, in collaboration with the famous anatomist Marcantonio della Torre (1481–1512), and he produced a wealth of drawings detailing his studies in cardiology and embryology.

Yet again, Leonardo became a victim of the Italian peninsula's relentless wars. The Holy League was a disparate collection of powers organized by the Pope, whose only common goal was to end the French presence in Italy. In June 1512, the combined forces of Spain, Venice and the papacy invaded Milan and ejected the French, nominally restoring the Sforzas. The war also saw the return to power of Leonardo's former sponsors, the Medici. From 1513 to 1516, Leonardo was in Rome, where he found a new patron in Duke Giuliano de' Medici, now head of the Florentine state and the brother of the Medici pope, Leo X (1513–21), who gave him a generous monthly salary and lodgings in the Vatican Palace. Here Leonardo again came into contact with Michelangelo, and also with Raphael (1483–1520). While in Rome he pursued his work, drawing up plans to drain the Pomptine marshes, and recorded his various ideas on the art of painting. He also entertained his contemporaries with imaginative if bizarre games, as he had at the court of Milan. On one occasion he used a concealed blacksmith's bellows to inflate an animal gut until it filled the room completely, terrifying his audience. Despite these boyish pranks, now in his old age, with his eyesight and health deteriorating, Leonardo seemed to grow increasingly lonely, frustrated and resentful. He accused one of his assistants of spying on him and interfering with his work. He was later banned from working on dissections at the hospital of Santo Spirito, where he was accused of black magic. It was a period of crisis and exasperation. Although he executed a number of paintings, almost all of which are now lost, he received no large commissions, perhaps because of his appalling track record of works left '*non finito*'. One of the few paintings he managed to complete and which survives today is often hailed as his last masterpiece. *St John the Baptist* (1513–16, Louvre, Paris) is an unusual portrait of an ascetic who lived in the desert. In a dark and clinging atmosphere, St John points the way to heaven, a disquieting, half-male, half-female figure with a slightly diabolical quality. But here, the *sfumato* effect has been overdone. The figure has a lifeless quality and the work seems over-mannered, even slightly mawkish.

Two events persuaded Leonardo to leave Italy altogether. In 1516, his patron, Giuliano de' Medici, died. Perhaps more significantly, however, the Pope awarded an architectural commission Leonardo had long sought to Michelangelo. Leonardo finally accepted a long-standing invitation from the French and took up the offer of François I (r.1515–49) of a retreat without obligation at the Château de Cloux near Amboise. At the French court, the ageing Leonardo seems to have been a central if lonely figure, constantly involved in intellectual debates but with few close ties. Francis I was said to have 'fallen in love with Leonardo's great abilities' and to be 'taking pleasure in listening to his conversation'. But another contemporary described how Leonardo could 'no longer colour with the sweetness that was his custom' and from Leonardo's own notes it is clear that by the end of his life he was more frustrated and disappointed than ever, having fulfilled so few of his life's impossibly ambitious plans. He died at Amboise on 2 May 1519, aged sixty-seven, and is buried in the nearby monastery of Saint-Florentin.

Leonardo is now hailed as the embodiment of the Renaissance, a 'universal man' who made forays into new intellectual territories yet was intensely frustrated by how little he understood. There is something admirable and irritating about his life's work but certain things stand out above all. One is the range of his imagination. It is perhaps overstating the case to claim that he was the first modern scientist, but it is certainly not an exaggeration to say that he grasped a bigger picture than anyone history had hitherto produced. He brought the rigours of scientific study to his art and the creative imagination central to painting to the study of the natural world. Finally, as the venerable E. H. Gombrich pointed out, Leonardo made few if any claims to greatness. Instead, it is his humility and wisdom which stand out most strongly:

> Seeing that I can find no matter of much use or delight, because men born before me have appropriated to themselves all the useful and necessary subjects, I shall do what the poor man does who comes late to the fair: since he cannot provide himself with any other stock he picks up all the things which the others have seen but rejected as of little value. These despised and rejected goods which were left behind by many buyers I shall load on my feeble donkey and shall carry them not to big cities but to poor villages and distribute them, taking such a price as the wares I offer may be worth.

3.

Dürer
1471–1528

Albrecht Dürer of Nuremberg towers over the artists of the Northern Renaissance. His greatest accomplishment was to introduce the techniques and styles of Italian Renaissance painting to Germany. His was the first recorded pilgrimage of a German artist south of the Alps, and as a result of his travels, Dürer's work straddled two worlds. From Italy, he brought back dazzling ideas of colour, light, composition and perspective, which he incorporated into a northern tradition of portraiture and meticulous design, to produce profound and original results. His achievements are vast. Dürer is renowned for his zoological and botanical drawings, which rank among the most intense and closely observed studies of nature ever produced. He excelled in portraiture and was the first artist to produce an independent self-portrait. But he is probably most famous for his engravings and woodcuts. The print remains an undervalued art form, but it led to the dissemination of ideas and images whose impact was comparable to that of mass media in the twentieth century. And Dürer was its first internationally recognized master.

Albrecht Dürer was born in May 1471, in Nuremberg in southern Germany. One of at least seventeen siblings, he was the third son of a goldsmith who had moved to Nuremberg from Hungary in 1455. At the time of Dürer's birth, Germany was a vague geographical expression. The whole of Central Europe lay within the boundaries of the Holy Roman Empire, a vast and disparate collection of kingdoms and principalities, bishoprics and free cities, all under the nominal rule of the Holy Roman Emperor. This title was in theory elective, but had recently become hereditary within the Austrian Habsburg family. Political power was therefore fragmented, and art and culture were regionalized, each province having a multiplicity of lordships and its own traditions, customs and dialect. German artistic culture, nevertheless, possessed certain unifying characteristics. Most significantly, it remained firmly rooted in its medieval traditions, in which altarpieces were the prevailing form of painting and sculpture was dominated by the requirements of church decoration. Artistic production was carried out in craft workshops, in which artisans plied their trades under the supervision of a master. Their social status was effectively that of any other tradesman, though the more technically demanding crafts, such as engraving and goldsmithing, could command higher prices. All aspects of artistic production were heavily regulated by the trade guilds, which jealously guarded the privileges and economic status of their members.

Nuremberg was an imperial free city in the region of Franconia in southern Germany. It was proud of its municipal self-government, which it shrouded with a fictional classical heritage – above its gates hung the imperial eagle and the words 'The Senate and People of Nuremberg' (*Senatus Populusque Norimbergensis*). It was a prosperous city due to its position on an important crossroads of trade routes between Germany and Italy and between France and Eastern Europe. These communications also connected Nuremberg with the wider cultural world. During the fifteenth century, the city experienced both economic and cultural prosperity. Woodcarvers, glass decorators, gold- and silversmiths, engravers and jewellers all thrived; Nuremberg became renowned for its outstanding carved and painted wooden altarpieces

OIL PAINTING

Jan van Eyck, the Netherlandish painter who worked between 1422 and his death in 1441, is often considered the link between the egg-based medium of tempera and the advent of oil paint. He is frequently acknowledged as the father and inventor of oil painting.

However, information on his life and techniques is sketchy. Vasari, in his Lives of the Artists, suggests that van Eyck founded the medium, which was then developed by another artist, Antonello da Messina. According to Vasari, the latter's formula and painting technique were preferred by Italian artists.

But without van Eyck, these developments would not have been possible.

Van Eyck's earlier works were carried out in tempera, which is water soluble, and then finished with a protective layer of varnish, which had to be dried in the sun in summer or in front of the fire in winter. But the varnish was very viscous and deeply coloured, and the heat damaged the original painting underneath. So van Eyck began to experiment with concoctions using linseed and walnut oils as they could dry quickly in the shade.

The formula he used is not known, but the oil had to be boiled and was used with other specific ingredients to keep discoloration to a minimum, and to improve drying time and texture. Vasari mentions that in old age van Eyck passed on his secret to his favourite pupil, Rogier van der Weyden, who in turn divulged the recipe to other painters.

After finding the formula for the perfect varnish to protect the tempera paintings from the atmosphere, it may have been by accident that van Eyck stumbled upon the idea of mixing the paint on his palette with the varnish. It may have occurred when he added a small detail to a varnished work as it was drying and found to his surprise that the paint

and stained-glass windows. The city was also a centre of scientific and technological discovery, including developments in clocks – the pocket watch was invented there at the beginning of the sixteenth century – musical instruments, nautical and astronomical equipment, and printing presses. Nuremberg therefore supported a large merchant class – moneyed, cultured and literate – which, in turn, attracted scholars, artists and craftsmen.

From about the age of eleven Dürer joined his father's workshop, where he learned the various techniques of engraving. When he was still apprenticed to his father, Dürer revealed a precocious talent in drawing. This is most clearly illustrated in his earliest *Self-portrait*, aged thirteen. The method is silver point, a technique involving coating paper or parchment with a preparatory substance, such as a mixture of glue and white lead. The paper is then engraved with a silver stylus. The image results from a chemical reaction between the silver and the prepared coating. The process means that no errors can be corrected, and the technique requires a great certainty of hand. The inscription reads: 'This I drew, using a mirror; it is my own likeness, in 1484 when I was still a child.' This is a remarkably sensitive self-portrait, especially for a boy of thirteen. Dürer was already conveying a sense of personality, an uncanny ability to render something of the psychological – as well as the physiological – make-up of his sitters.

In a short biographical account written during the last three

---

mixed readily with the oil-based varnish. The technique in the early stages was not perfect and needed refining before the full benefits of oil painting were apparent: For the first time, colours could be blended with great ease, realistic shadows could be depicted and chiaroscuro could bring faces and objects to life. None of this was possible with tempera paint.

It was also possible to create glazes by thinning the paint with quantities of boiled oil. Van Eyck's background in the stained-glass industry must have alerted him to the fact that a building up of transparent layers over a light ground would increase the luminosity of the mixture of colours used. This technique was often used with stained glass. A green produced by a thin layer of yellow glass and one of blue would have a more brilliant effect than just one layer of green. Van Eyck embraced this glazing method, as did many northern painters who followed in his wake. The jewel-like qualities that they achieved in the fourteenth and fifteenth centuries is testimony to the rigorous following of this technique.

But although using oils meant that for the first time tiny details could be depicted with great accuracy, this in itself became a handicap. Some painters felt compelled to use the medium to show minute details in all areas of the work which, ironically, undermined the realism inherent in the medium because it failed to reproduce as the eye actually perceived.

Although it was in northern Europe that the technique of oil painting was first mastered, the full potential of the medium was only fully realized in the Italian Renaissance which developed a more scientific approach to art as well as combining manual skill with intellectual rigour.

years of his life Dürer recalled:

> My father took special pleasure in me because he saw that
> I was diligent in striving to learn. So he sent me to school,
> and when I had learned to read and write he took me
> away from it, and taught me the goldsmith's craft. But
> when I could work neatly, my liking attracted me to
> painting rather than goldsmith's work.

At fifteen, Dürer joined the workshop of Michael Wolgemut
(1434–1519), the pre-eminent artist of Nuremberg. In Wolgemut's
workshop, the young Dürer learned to make woodcuts and book
illustrations, and assisted his master in producing altarpieces and
stained-glass windows. He also began to produce his own oil paintings,
the most accomplished of which were portraits of his parents produced
in 1490, already surpassing his teacher in their meticulous naturalism.
In the same year, having finished his apprenticeship, Dürer began a four-
year period of travel, seeking employment, worldly experience and to
establish a name for himself beyond his home town. It was, in effect,
a rite of passage which took him to other parts of Germany and the
fringes of France and Switzerland, where he made his living as a
journeyman craftsman, and picked up new skills from different masters.
He had planned to offer his services to Martin Schongauer of Colmar
(c.1453–91), the most famous copper-engraver in Germany, but he had
recently died. Other members of the Schongauer family, however,
provided him with employment as a designer of woodcuts in Basle,
then a famous centre of the book trade.

It was probably through this employment that Dürer came into
contact with copies of the Italian masters. Engravings and pictures

THE AGE OF THE PRINTING PRESS

The printing press with movable metal type was first used in Western Europe in the mid-fifteenth century. Johannes Gutenberg of Mainz, Germany, is thought to have been the founder of this particular technique, although there is evidence to suggest that the Dutch and the French could have discovered this method first.

The technique, called letterpress, involved a special type of sticky, oil-based ink which differed from the water-soluble substance used in previous printing processes. The page was printed using hundreds of individually cast metal letters (or combinations of letters) that would form the text of a page. The relief surface of the letters, placed face up, was then inked and the paper, often dampened first, was pressed on to the letters by a screw mechanism. After enough impressions had been taken the blocks could be reorganized for subsequent pages.

By Dürer's time, paper was widely available, which made mass production of printed material a viable option. In addition, the demand for reading matter was increasing, due to the growing literacy of the middle classes. (Luther and the spread of the Reformation would have been severely hampered had it not been for the printing press. Many of these ideas were disseminated by great quantities of published pamphlets.) Those who were illiterate still benefited from story-tellers who would travel

printed from copper plates were important means of disseminating artistic ideas and images. Prominent in earlier Italian engravings was the celebrated painter Andrea Mantegna (1431–1506), who had made his name in Padua and Mantua in the middle of the fifteenth century, was influential in the continued development of perspective in painting and whose work Dürer certainly knew. These images fascinated him and fuelled his imagination about Italy. Dürer desperately wanted to do what none of his German contemporaries had done: to go to Italy and study the new theories that made Italian painting seem so much more advanced. In 1494, he embarked on a journey over the Alps that would ultimately lead to Venice.

Although he had already experienced Italian art at a distance, little could have prepared Dürer for what he found when he arrived at the city on the Adriatic. Venice at the end of the fifteenth century was fabulously wealthy. Patronage of the arts was strong and the desire to compete with and surpass the achievements of other Italian cities, notably Florence, was even stronger. In certain respects, the power base of the Italian Renaissance was shifting north. Broadly speaking, Italian art and artists could boast distinct achievements that a German artist might admire and wish to learn from and imitate. Since the early fifteenth century, Italian painting had benefited from scientific studies that served to enhance its purpose of increased naturalism. Painters had studied and experimented with perspective which, they believed, could be achieved in art through mathematical calculation. Detailed studies in anatomy, botany and geology better equipped the painter to present the world as it really was. These developments were supported by scholarly enquiry into classical models and precedents, to which Italian artists had greater

from village to village reading from published material at the marketplace. Most of the works of this time in Germany had a religious content, Bibles and Psalters were the most common. There was an explosion of printed matter between 1450 and 1500, with 6,000 separate works being printed. The distribution was varied. Books were sold at fairs; other works were sold directly to wealthy citizens.

Printers also used images alongside text, and woodcuts were a perfect counterpart to the letterpress technique. Unlike copper engraving, which could only be used a limited amount of times before wearing out, woodcuts could withstand continuous use. Printed woodcuts can be dated back to the 1420s, possibly even earlier. Before movable type, there were woodblocks – each page, usually a picture and text, printed from a single carved wooden block. Woodcut was increasingly used by printers to embellish books from the 1450s and in Germany, where the woodcut was more popular

than anywhere else, it was most often used with text. Germany led the way in the quantity and the quality of illustrated printed books until the turn of the century.

Dürer's prints were made by the relief method, that is, the same method used for letterpress: images could be incorporated into the text and the entire page printed at the same time. This meant that the method was ideal for the publication of Bibles and the illustration of prayers and scriptures.

access. Furthermore, artists north of the Alps would have envied not only the talents of Italian artists, but also their status. In the public perception Italian painters, sculptors and architects had transformed themselves from tradesmen and craftsmen into creative geniuses – admired, wealthy and of social standing.

Venice was home to a group of artists, led by the aged Giovanni Bellini (c.1435–1516), who had already incorporated Renaissance ideas about perspective, composition and perfect form into their work, and were now experimenting with colour and light as integral parts of recreating human life in paint. For Dürer, the training and techniques that he saw in the workshops of Bellini and other Italian artists reinforced what he had come to learn and strengthened his desire to reinvent the art of painting in Germany.

Dürer returned to Germany with renewed vigour, his *Wanderlust* temporarily satisfied, and settled back in his native Nuremberg, where he immediately established an artist's workshop along the lines of those he'd seen in Venice. Having married the daughter of a coppersmith, Agnes Frey, who had a background not unlike his own, Dürer began his career in earnest, producing prints, both woodcuts and engravings, as well as paintings and designs for stained-glass windows. His abilities were quickly recognized and he began to receive commissions from wealthy clients. The Elector of Saxony, one of the most powerful princes of Germany, became his patron in 1496 and Dürer duly painted a striking portrait of the boggle-eyed aristocrat which now resides in the

'St John swallows the Book'; one of fifteen woodcuts forming Dürer's Apocalypse, 1497–98

Gemaldegalerie in Berlin. Although at this point in his career Dürer's largest source of income came from traditional commissions, such as painted altarpieces, as well as from portraits, it was through his prints that he made his international reputation.

Printing presses had been developed in western Germany by about 1450, and spread rapidly across Europe within a generation. Woodcuts, however, predate even printing, possibly originating in the later fourteenth century. They were made by marking on a block of wood the areas that should stay white. The wood was then sent to a carpenter, who gouged out the whitened areas, and the block was then inked and the image printed. In the fifteenth century, with the invention of the printing press and the growth of literacy throughout Europe, the woodcut was in increasing demand. The vast majority of woodcuts were made to illustrate religious publications – Bibles, prayer books and devotional pictures. It was possible to make hundreds of copies from one block, and because they were made of inexpensive materials, woodcuts could be more experimental. For Dürer, the production of prints had distinct advantages over commissioned paintings. Prints were very much quicker to produce and, being cheaper, achieved far greater circulation. They found a ready market among the bourgeoisie, for most of whom paintings were too expensive. This new literate class provided a market for increased book production. Prints also offered an opportunity to tackle secular subjects and break away from the more restricted themes of traditional German painting. In addition, the techniques and training of the engraver that he had received from his father meant that Dürer was eminently suited to this medium.

Dürer's decision to publish his woodcuts himself was a radical departure from the precise division of trades enforced by the trade guilds. He probably produced the illustrations at home on his own press and then printed any accompanying text at the press of the famous printer Anton Koberger, who was his godfather. Print production required Dürer to train and organize staff, passing on certain techniques he had begun to pioneer and thus freeing himself from the mechanical side of operations so that he could devote more time to design. In his lifetime, Dürer produced around a hundred engravings and twice as many woodcuts. His most famous creation came early in his career, in 1498, with the publication of the *Apocalypse*, a series of fifteen woodcuts of the Book of Revelations. These woodcuts were published in a larger format than was usual, with the illustrations printed across the entire right-hand page with text on the opposite (and therefore also the reverse) page. This was the first book ever produced totally independently by an artist acting alone and without a commission. It was an immense achievement, combining technical expertise with artistic creativity and imagination. The scenes are exquisitely rendered, a mass of tightly controlled lines where every mark counts. They are also visually complex, often harrowing and sometimes bizarre, produced more in the spirit of the Book of Revelations than as literal illustrations. Ultimately, of course, Satan is incarcerated and the New Jerusalem is built, but Dürer's most powerful images are ones of violence and destruction. The Four Horsemen of the Apocalypse rampage down upon feeble humanity, bringing plague, war, hunger and death. Figures are tortured in vats of boiling oil and multi-headed monsters threaten to devour babies or abduct women. Dürer's horrific vision of Doomsday was rooted in a long German tradition which flourished in the Middle Ages, but it was very much a product of its age. It was published at an opportune moment as the end of the century loomed and apocalyptic speculation was rife about the possible end of the world in 1500. This, together with popular discontent over the state of the Roman Church, made the book extremely popular with the public. It was published simultaneously in German and in Latin and within fifteen years it had been reprinted three times and was sold across Europe.

In spite of the success of his prints, painting remained a major preoccupation for Dürer. It was considered to be a vastly superior visual

Four Horsemen of the Apocalypse
1497–98, woodcut
The series of fifteen woodcuts that Dürer made illustrating the apocalyptic visions of St John marked the artist's coming of age and signalled a major change in the way that graphic art was perceived and produced. The last book of the New Testament, the Revelation of St John, was written when the saint was in exile on the island of Patmos and describes the last days of the world before the Day of Judgment. This struck a resonant chord in Dürer's world three years before the turn of the century, when apocalyptic

pronouncements were rife.
The *Four Horsemen of the Apocalypse* has become the best known of the series, heralding as it does the judgment of God descending on mankind. The image comes from the sixth chapter of the Book of Revelations, which describes the opening of the first four seals. With each comes a horse and rider signifying plague, war, hunger and death. Dürer depicts his horsemen swooping from left to right, staggered to reveal one drawing a bow; another brandishing a sword; a third holding a pair of scales; and finally, in the left-hand foreground, Death itself followed by a

hell-like cloud of darkness which threatens to overwhelm everything. The horses thunder over the hapless sinners who plead for mercy. In the bottom right-hand corner is a farmer who holds his hand protectively in front of his face, but to no avail. In the bottom left-hand corner, as if to catch whatever the horsemen miss, a monstrous creature with vast jaws devours all in its path. It is a horrifying image whose only hint of redemption is the angel hovering above the massacre pointing onwards as if to the next scene.
Dürer creates the image through a labyrinth of

tiny lines, but with no extraneous mark whatsoever. It is an extraordinary accomplishment, deft and dynamic, and one which helped to elevate print-making to the status of ine art. It is also a vividly memorable image whose impact has continued to play on the imagination of artists and even film-makers. The celebrated Russian film-maker Andrei Tarkovsky drew on Dürer's apocalyptic image extensively in his film *My Name is Ivan* in 1962, where the horsemen appear as a symbol of the German army wreaking havoc in Russia during the Second World War.

art form and painting commissions paid well. The control that Dürer exerted in his prints fuelled that in his canvas and panel paintings, but a greater range of expression was possible using oil or tempera and nowhere was this more apparent than in his portraits. In 1499, he produced one of his most striking works when he was commissioned to paint the portrait of a young accountant for the Grosser Ravenburger Handelsgesselschaft, a commercial company in Nuremberg. The *Portrait of Oswolt Krel* is psychologically charged in a way that had rarely if ever been attempted before. It shows a disturbed-looking figure, clenching his fist and staring sharply off to his left. He seems racked by an inner turmoil which suggests he is about to erupt. Krel had been recently jailed for a verbal attack on a Nuremberg citizen during the performance of a Shrovetide play. He is recorded as having been pugnacious and temperamental and Dürer conveys this through his gaze, his expression and his taut body language. In turn, he augments the idea of a fiery individual by setting the portrait against a vivid red backdrop. The landscape to the right of the figure adds a more lyrical feel and perhaps shows that Dürer was broadly sympathetic to Krel. Certainly it is not a judgmental portrait, more an image of searing psychological insight, as if Dürer is able to scratch well below the visual surface of his sitter. Likewise, but with obvious advantages in this regard, he applied the same methods to depicting his own image in a series of pioneering self-portraits that reveal both his artistic talents and pretensions.

Having begun to chart his own appearance as early as 1484 in silver point, Dürer produced a revealingly melancholic self-portrait sketch on his travels, some time around 1491. This ink drawing shows him gazing out from behind his hand in a manner which is inquisitive and full of teenage angst. In 1493, he produced the first recorded example of a pure self-portrait in oil paint in the history of Western art. The picture, which now hangs in the Louvre, shows a foppishly dressed twenty-two-year-old, growing in confidence, a man rather than a boy, on the eve of his marriage. He holds a thistle in his hands, twining its stem around his thumb nonchalantly, a symbol which may refer both to his imminent marriage and, as some scholars have argued, to Christ's Passion. This devotional idea – of Christian love and self-love – finds its fullest expression in the third and final painted self-portrait, from 1500, which shows Dürer as an imitator of Christ himself. It is a hypnotic image, from its penetrating gaze to the mirror-like touch with which Dürer handles paint. Identifying with Christ and his struggle was a central part of the Christian faith, but there is more than a touch of arrogance about this particular image. Partly Dürer may have been illustrating the belief that the power of the artist comes directly from God, and that – as an artist –

it is his God-given duty to reflect this by creating art. However, the idea of the artist as a divinely inspired earthly creator also parallels God's role as universal creator and suggests the beginnings of a new conception of the role of the artist in Northern Europe, which became immensely powerful over the next few centuries, culminating with the Romantic movement.

From the time when he painted his Christ-like *Self-portrait*, Dürer's art shows the application of mathematical theories of perspective and proportion. Later in his career, in 1525, Dürer published the *Manual of Measurement*, a book of mathematical theory that includes practical advice on drawing with the help of various devices. He tried to interpret the human form in diagrams, by measuring the ratios between the different sections of the body, and this was developed still further in his epic treatise, *Four Books on Human Proportions*, published posthumously in 1528. The inspiration came from classical writing on art which had stressed the importance of '*harmonia*' and '*symmetria*'. Dürer's own painting drew praise along classical lines when, in 1500, the Nuremberg humanist scholar Konrad Celtis (1459–1508) wrote a series of epigrams likening him to the two most celebrated artists of ancient Greece, Phidias and Apelles. The revival of classical inspiration and ambition, itself the bedrock of the Florentine Renaissance which had begun a hundred years earlier, was finally beginning to flourish north of the Alps.

The humanist quest for knowledge inspired Dürer to turn his attention to the natural world around him and to explore it in minute detail in hundreds of drawings which he produced from around 1502 onwards. Using watercolours, together with the precision he'd mastered as an engraver, Dürer's image of *The Great Piece of Turf* shows a microcosmic view of a meadow with a wide variety of plants at different stages of growth seen against a low horizon. The plants include yarrow, dandelion, plantain and meadow grass. Although the subject may at first seem like a random juxtaposition of flora, it is actually a carefully planned composition in which Dürer illustrates the entire process of growth and decay. In turn, it acted as a study in observation and naturalism that he was able to use in his larger, more macrocosmic paintings. This scientific approach to art and the desire to understand the natural world as far as possible in order to produce art parallels that of Leonardo da Vinci, whose work, like Dürer's, was subsequently used in the study of natural science.

Even more vivid, and certainly striking the popular imagination, are Dürer's studies of animals. As European travellers and explorers ventured further afield, new and seemingly exotic species were being discovered and Dürer's drawings of animals like monkeys, rhinoceros and lions were among the first to be made. Some were produced from stuffed animals,

others simply from written or even verbal reports alone. Closer to home, though, were creatures such as squirrels and hares, to which Dürer also turned his attentions. His watercolour drawing of the *Young Hare*, made in 1503, has become an iconic image. Every hair of the animal seems to be individually realized with delicate gradations of light and tone conveyed through a multitude of different lines and brushstrokes. Even its eyes glint and a window seems visible on its pupil, a device used in human portraiture to suggest a mirror of the soul. Animals, like mankind, are God's creations, Dürer seems to say, and all are worthy of profound scrutiny. The *Hare* is also a good example of Dürer's important role in the democratization of art, making pictures available to the masses. It was quickly produced as a print and sold widely. Its popularity as an image on the wall of numerous households continued to escalate and in the age of mass reproduction in the twentieth century, it was endlessly recreated.

Since the death of his father in 1501, Dürer had been responsible for maintaining his family. He employed his younger brother in his workshop and his wife and mother to sell copies of his prints at fairs and markets. With this increased responsibility came illness. In 1503 he was struck by what was thought to be a disease of the spleen (it was more likely to have been appendicitis). This complaint convinced him that he was suffering from melancholia as a great deal of 'black bile' was removed from his spleen. According to widespread medieval medical theory, melancholia was one of the four humours or elements which constituted man: black bile, bile, blood and phlegm. An imbalance of

Self-portrait

1500, Alte Pinakotek, Munich

This is the third and final surviving self-portrait in oil by Dürer and is by far the most accomplished and the most provocative. For the first and last time in Western art, an artist depicts himself full-on in the guise of Christ. Many artists had identified with their Lord and Saviour and depicted themselves carrying the cross, thereby empathizing with the suffering of Christ. However, no one had taken the strict frontal view established by the Byzantines for the depiction of Christ and used it in the creation of a self-image. The result is an hypnotic picture, closer to an icon than a traditional portrait.

Dürer creates an idealized image of self where his features have been slightly modified, as if morphed with those of Christ Himself. His nose is less pronounced – it is smaller and without the slight curve shown in previous images – and his hair, which was blond, is painted brown. He is wearing a fashionable fur-collared coat which he draws together with his right hand in a gesture which also reads as one of solemn benediction.

The composition of the painting seems broadly pyramidal, but is more complicated than first meets the eye. The triangular form of his head and hair is also mirrored by a triangle whose apex runs down from the forehead to the beginning of the collar, which also creates a further triangular image. The structure is therefore closer to a Star of David than a simple pyramid.

Dürer's eyes are penetratingly painted, with a small window visibly reflected in each iris. This alludes to the classical adage that the 'eye is a window to the soul' and emphasizes a vision which looks inwards as well as outwards.

The work has a Latin inscription which translates as 'I, Albrecht Dürer of Nuremberg, painted myself thus in indelible colours at the age of twenty-eight years'. It makes clear his intention to attempt to immortalize himself, as well as pay homage to his faith and the God-given talent that he has as an artist.

any of the four humours would lead to the excessive development of a temperament or humour: melancholy (black bile), choleric (bile), sanguine (blood) and phlegmatic (phlegm). Dürer would have been well aware of the Aristotelian idea that all truly creative men suffer from melancholy. He may also have known something about the contemporary Neoplatonic philosophy expounded in Florence, in which melancholy relates to Plato's theory of creativity as a 'divine frenzy'. The sketched self-portrait made when he was twenty suggests an air of melancholy, but the idea was most forcefully expressed in a copper engraving produced in 1514. This heavily allegorical arrangement, entitled *Melencolia I*, has been much debated, but probably represents the life of the secular scholar, the man of knowledge surrounded by the attributes of geometry, architecture, mathematics and astronomy. The 'I' in the inscribed title suggests an autobiographical involvement and the isolated figure, struggling for self-knowledge, became the embodiment of the notion of the artist as lonely genius which flourished, almost to the point of parody, in the nineteenth century.

Possibly spurred on by an outbreak of plague, in 1505 Dürer travelled to Italy again, visiting Venice, Bologna, Padua and, in all probability, Florence over the next two years. By this time he was known in Italy as Germany's greatest printmaker, and Italian nobility, even the Doge of Venice, admired Dürer's work. He was flattered by this attention, but was angered that some Italians exploited his prints and paintings by selling their own copies of his designs. Dürer's letter to a friend describes these mixed emotions:

I wish you were here in Venice. There are so many nice

Adam *1507*
Eve *1507,*
Prado, Madrid
These two pictures are independent paintings in their own right, but were produced as a pair soon after Dürer returned from his second trip to Italy in 1507. He had made a copper engraving on this theme back in 1504 as well as some preparatory studies for a painting, but his work here is bolder and far more confident. The works exemplify his study of human proportions and a quest for the perfect human form, appropriately used to depict the biblical version of the first human couple. Adam holds a branch from the Tree of Knowledge and looks yearningly towards Eve, who, in the other painting, looks back at him with a seductive glint in her eye as she succumbs to temptation and plucks the apple from the mouth of the snake. The two figures are linked by desire and by the Tree itself, which helps to create a depth of field in the pictures. They are carefully modelled and dextrously depicted in motion. These are considered to be the first life-sized nudes in the history of German religious painting and blend together a heady a mixture of idealized beauty, innocence and eroticism.

On the portrait of Eve is Dürer's now characteristic Latin inscription, hung from the branch of the tree, which translates as: 'The German Albrecht Dürer made this 1507 years after the Virgin gave birth'. The works were uncommissioned but were soon acquired by Bishop Johann V of Bresslau. Influenced originally by the work of Masolino in the Brancacci Chapel in Florence, Dürer's visions of Adam and Eve became influential, serving as models for various artists, notably for German painters such as Lucas Cranach and Hans Baldung. Their importance and value were augmented when they were acquired by the great Spanish collector King Philip IV a century after they were created.

fellows among the Italians who are my companions more and more every day, so that it warms my heart: intelligent, educated, good lute players, flautists, connoisseurs of paintings and many noble minds ... On the other hand, there are also among them some of the most false, lying, thievish rascals, the like of which I would not have believed lived on earth.

Most poignantly, Dürer summed up the difference in status and ethos between of the Italian and the German artist: 'here I am a lord, at home a parasite. How I shall shiver for the sun.'

As during Dürer's first Italian trip, the work of Giovanni Bellini continued to have a strong impact on the German artist's work, in particular the altarpiece that Bellini had created in the church of San Zaccaria in Venice, painted in 1505. This work inspired Dürer's own Venetian altarpiece, *The Feast of the Rose Garlands*, painted the following year. The work was commissioned by the German Brotherhood of the Rosary for the chapel of San Bartolomeo, the Venetian church of the German community. In his use of sharp light and rich, luminous colour, and in the relaxed postures of the figures, which represented significant departures from the conventions of German religious art, Dürer shows how much he owed to Bellini. Indeed, the angel playing the lute in the foreground of the dramatic scene has been considered an explicit tribute to Bellini himself. But Dürer continued to synthesize styles and to assert his own artistic presence. As if to emphasize this, a self-portrait of Dürer appears in the backgound of the painting, holding a scroll bearing the date, Dürer's characteristic monogram and a note that the work took five months to complete. Another kneeling figure is recognizable as that of Jacob Fugger, the wealthy German banker, who was Dürer's host for much of his time in Italy and who helped Dürer to sell work and to gain

HEAVEN AND HELL

The time leading up to the Reformation in 1517 was a turbulent one for those living in Germany, full of religious, social and political disharmony. The legacy of the plague was still affecting the population and fear of a terrifying and widespread new disease, the so-called French disease, syphilis, was taking its toll. In the ever-expanding cities and the countryside there was also famine – a result of drought and bad harvests. Activity in the heavens such as meteors and comets flying across the skies frightened people. Natural disasters were thought to show the rage of an angry God. Consequently with so much discontent and instability, people feared for their salvation and believed in an imminent Second Coming which would make way for an age of peace. The year 1500 was thought by some to be the year when literally all hell would break loose.

It was a time of religious fanaticism and pilgrimages, particularly in the countryside, of individuals who toured the land castigating the Pope, the Emperor, priests and the landed nobility for exploiting the poor, as well as inciting fear and hysteria among the masses with accounts of their terrible visions.

other commissions. By the time he returned to Nuremberg, he had enhanced his reputation from a printmaking maestro to that of a major painter in Italy and had paid off all his debts in the process.

Dürer's status was rising in Nuremberg too. In 1509 he bought a large house in the shadow of the vast castle which dominated the geography of the city. He also became a member of Nuremberg's Grand Council. Although the post held little real power, it was a sign of his growing prestige. Commissions were also plentiful, partly as a consequence of the Venetian altarpiece which had attracted wide commendation from the German community in Italy and beyond. Within two years of his return, three major ecclesiastical contracts had been agreed and realized: a three-panelled altarpiece for the Dominican church of St Thomas Aquinas in Frankfurt; a single-panelled altarpiece of *The Adoration of the Trinity* for the private chapel of a Nuremberg merchant, Matthaus Landauer; and a large, complex painting called *The Martyrdom of the Ten Thousand* for the Elector of Saxony, Frederick the Wise. The work was intended for the chamber of relics in the Wittenberg castle chapel and showed the legendary ten thousand Christians martyred on Mount Ararat by Oriental princes on the orders of the Roman Emperor Hadrian. At the centre of the painting stands Dürer himself, together with the humanist scholar Conrad Celtis, who was also highly regarded by the Elector. They watch the horrendous slaughter, dressed as if in mourning. The image is therefore devotional, commemorating relics and martyrs, and a memorial to the humanist Celtis, who had just died.

Frederick the Wise's patronage was superseded within three years by that of the Holy Roman Emperor himself, Maximilian I (r.1493–1519), who designated Dürer as a court painter in 1512 and awarded the artist an annual pension of 100 florins in 1515. Dürer had recently produced imaginary portraits of the Emperor Charlemagne which prompted Maximilian to commission one of himself in 1519, but Dürer's first and most ambitious project for the Emperor was a series of woodcuts glorifying the deeds of the emperors, culminating in the triumphs of Maximilian himself. *The Gates of Honour*, finished in 1515, was a series of 190 woodcuts by four other artists and Dürer himself, who oversaw the entire project. The design created a vast triumphal arch filled with tiny heroic episodes, which were both self-contained and part of a vast monument. The work was architectural in design and conception but almost scientific in its detail. It also illustrated how much the imperial court appreciated the propagandist potential of printmaking.

Within two years of the completion of *The Gates of Honour*, Maximilian needed all the propoganda he could muster as the Catholic

foundations of Western Europe began to fragment into the religious turmoil known as the Reformation. At the root of this upheaval was a long-standing discontent with the worldliness, abuses and corruption of the Catholic Church. The protests came from diverse social levels: from humanist scholars, from many clergymen themselves and from the wider populace, both the urban bourgeoisie and the rural peasantry. The failure of the Church to address these problems and reform itself from within eventually resulted in schism, at first little different from earlier ruptures, but ultimately a permanent and radical split. The principal agent was the Augustinian monk Martin Luther (1483–1546), Professor of Theology at Wittenberg. Luther combined his extensive theological and scriptural knowledge with his violent disgust at the abuses in the Church. What began as a programme of ecclesiastical reform eventually led to a radical theological revolution. Above all, Luther rejected the role of the Church as the intermediary between Man and God, and argued that Man's salvation could be determined solely by his personal faith. The increased independence offered by Lutheran doctrines, together with the tantalizing prospect of sequestrating church lands, had a great appeal to

The Four Apostles
1526, Alte Pinakhotek, Munich
This is Dürer's last known oil painting, begun soon after Nuremberg had joined the Reformation and when he was clearly wrestling with both the theological and political impacts of Lutheranism. Initially, it seems as if Dürer has produced two flanking panels for a three-part altarpiece, but records show that this was how he intended the work to be, an uncommissioned pair of paintings donated to his native city as a monument to himself and to a broader moral struggle. It shows, from left to right, St John reading his gospel; St Peter holding the keys to the Church; St Mark holding a manuscript, also suggesting his gospel; and

St Paul gripping his sword and book of epistles. St Mark was an evangelist, not an apostle, and so the picture is incorrectly named. It is also given the title *The Four Holy Men*. St Peter, the first pope and the rock on which the Roman Church was built, is pushed into the background, while St Paul emerges as the embodiment of muscular Christianity, a dramatic convert to the faith who took the word further afield than any of the early followers of Christ and who was central to Luther's reforming theology. In addition, the opening verses of St John's gospel are clearly visible: 'In the beginning was the Word, and the Word was with God and the Word was God.' These words are taken

directly from Martin Luther's translation of the Bible from Latin to German in 1522 and certainly indicate Dürer's sympathy for the Protestant cause. Underneath the figures, though, runs an inscription which reads as follows: 'Let all worldly rulers in these dangerous times take care not to give heed to human temptation as if it were the word of God. For God wishes nothing added to his Word, nor taken from it. Take heed of the admonition of these four excellent men, Peter, John, Paul and Mark.' It is a clear warning that in reforming the Church no one should lose sight of the fundamental principles of Christianity nor veer away from the Word of God. In this respect Dürer seems to be fearful of the growing

impact of extremists on both sides of the religious divide. In 1526, when the work was completed, it was far from inevitable that Europe would be terminally divided into Protestant and Catholic Churches. Indeed, Luther himself preached vehemently against the fanatical behaviour of certain Protestant sects.

The paintings themselves fell victim to a certain form of religious extremism a century after they were produced. The Catholic Bavarian Duke Maximilian I took them to Munich in 1627 and had the inscriptions sawn off, returning the 'offending' texts (as he saw them) to Nuremberg. It was only in 1921 that the inscriptions were reunited with the images.

many German princes. Ecclesiastical reform therefore very quickly acquired a political dimension that would lead to the many European religious wars of the following century.

Art played a significant role in the religious controversies of the period. Some works were used as tools to teach the ideas of Protestantism; others were cited as examples of the idolatry of the Catholic Church. Luther and the other reformers regarded religious images as blasphemous idols, and condemned many examples of traditional religious painting as masks behind which the devil lurked, hoping to lure souls to damnation. The Reformation therefore transformed artistic developments and sensibilities in Germany in a way that would have baffled and alienated many artists. There was a sudden ban on sacred paintings and by forbidding devotional images Luther provoked a move against altar paintings. By 1530 altarpieces and wooden altars were no longer produced in Germany. The Reformation stifled art in its traditional forms and prompted the departure of artists to other countries which remained sympathetic to Catholicism, notably Spain and Italy.

In 1519, seemingly as a result of the Lutheran crisis, Dürer suffered a nervous breakdown. Ultimately, while appearing reluctant to take such a radical step as the Reformers, he accepted the truth of their aims and message. Indeed, he called Martin Luther 'that Christian man who has helped me out of great anxieties'. In 1520, aged fifty, Dürer, his wife Anne and their maid travelled to the Low Countries, partly, perhaps, to recuperate but also for more prosaic reasons. Maximilian had died the previous year and there was a dispute over Dürer's annual pension which the Nuremberg Council now refused to pay. Dürer therefore sought reconfirmation of the deal from the new emperor, Maximilian's grandson, Charles V (r.1519–56). Dürer's diary from this period records the banquets and carnivals they attended on their way. When he finally arrived in Antwerp, he was greeted like a visiting dignitary. He attended the coronation of Charles V and met a host of influential artists, including Jan Gossaert and Lucas van Leyden. He also became acquainted with the leading European humanist writer and philosopher Erasmus of Rotterdam, as well as various diplomats and power brokers at the imperial court. His art had won him a central position among Europe's cultural élite. But the journey began the slide into ill health that led to his death. The report of a beached whale prompted Dürer to travel into the marshes of Zeeland, a coastal province of the Netherlands. He missed the whale, which had been washed back out to sea, and caught malaria.

On returning to Nuremberg, Dürer began his last painting. The *Four Apostles* (completed in 1526 and now in the Alte Pinakotek in Munich) was another of Dürer's works that was not commissioned. It is also a painting whose antecedents may be found in Dürer's engravings. It comprises two panels which were originally planned as the wings of a traditional triptych for an altarpiece, but the changed attitude towards religious art ushered in by the Reformation meant that the main central panel was never constructed. Dürer gave it to the city of Nuremberg and insisted that the work should be 'preserved in public place as a memorial to him and should not be allowed to fall into foreign hands'. He was reimbursed with 112 florins. This painting was created during the early stages of the Reformation and although both Protestants and Catholics have attempted to interpret the piece to their own advantage, it seems to reflect Dürer's dislike of the ongoing conflict which had become more pronounced in the artist's life as Nuremberg had joined the Reformation in 1525.

The paintings show St John, St Peter, St Mark and St Paul. Some scholars have identified the saints as Nuremberg citizens. *The Four Apostles* (as it came to be incorrectly known), according to Dürer's calligrapher, again represents the four humours from traditional medieval medicine – sanguine, choleric, phlegmatic and melancholic. The four men are drawn with profound feeling and insight, each one graphically portraying a different mood or emotion. The inscription running along the bottom begins, 'Let all worldly rulers in these dangerous times take care not to give heed to human temptation as if it were the word of God.' Some have argued that the image is clearly pro-Reformers, as the melancholic St Paul, whose writings were fundamental to Lutheran theology, is shown in the foreground dominant over St Peter, the 'first pope'. When the paintings were taken to Catholic Munich in 1627, the inscriptions were sawn off.

Dürer's last two years saw the publication of a treatise on fortifications, mirroring Leonardo's interest in the subject, as well as the completion of his *Four Books on Human Proportions*, a summation of his artistic and philosophical theories, which demonstrates how completely the German artist had understood and developed the achievements of the Italian masters. But Dürer never completely recovered from the malaria he contracted in Zeeland. Finally, undone by his relentless curiosity in the natural world, Dürer died on 6 April 1528, aged fifty-six.

4.

Michelangelo
1475–1564

On a hot July afternoon in 1564, a requiem mass was celebrated at the church of San Lorenzo in Florence. The interior was draped in black and festooned with paintings and sculptures recently produced by members of the Accademia del Desegno to commemorate the life of the man they described as 'head, master and father to us all'. Michelangelo's death reinforced the overriding purpose of his life – to elevate the status of the visual arts from an artisan's trade to one of the liberal arts pursued by men of intellect, vision and social standing. He enjoyed a fame previously unmatched by an artist in his own lifetime and was the first artist to have a biography written before he died. In fact, by 1553 there were already two books charting his creative achievements as a sculptor, painter, architect and poet. His work was almost immediately acknowledged as among the most significant ever produced and although it was invariably commissioned to proclaim the glory of dukes, cardinals, popes and, of course, God, Michelangelo's art sowed the seeds of an idea which flourished in later centuries and which still dominates our thinking about art today, namely that painting and sculpture could exist and be understood as pursuits in and of themselves.

Michelangelo Buonarroti Simoni was born on 6 March 1475, in the small town of Caprese, near Arezzo, about fifty miles south-east of Florence. He was the second son of Lodovico di Leonardo Buonarroti Simoni, a Florentine official or *podesta* who oversaw the administration of various hill towns. The Buonarroti Simonis were reputedly descended from dukes and had been respected small-scale bankers in Florence for three hundred years. Michelangelo later described his family as 'of very noble descent', which was not the case but reflected an inherited obsession with status and rank. In accordance with the common practice of the period, Michelangelo was handed to a wet-nurse. Appropriately enough for one destined to be a great sculptor, his first years were spent with a family of stonecutters, among the olive groves and cypresses of the small village of Settignano, east of Florence, in a valley exploited for centuries for its marble quarries. Michelangelo would later claim that he drank in a love of sculpture at the breast of his wet-nurse. At the age of two or three, Michelangelo was reclaimed by his family, who had returned to Florence and were living in the Santa Croce quarter of the city, in the shadow of the great church decorated by Giotto a hundred and fifty years earlier.

Biographers suggest that Michelangelo was an intelligent, introspective and sensitive child. His mother died when he was only six. Like all the sons of ambitious Florentines, he was sent to a grammar school in the city, but to his father's despair, Latin scholarship was superseded by his desire to draw. Both his biographers, Giorgio Vasari and Michelangelo's one-time assistant Ascanio Condivi, fuelled the myth of the suffering young Michelangelo by suggesting that his father beat him in order to discourage his lowly aspirations to become an artist. In what became almost a commonplace in the biographies of later artists, Michelangelo is reputed to have shown admirable stubbornness, fortitude and single-mindedness in his quest to be an artist; so much so that in the spring of 1487, the obstinate twelve-year-old was apprenticed to the leading artistic workshop, that of painter Domenico Ghirlandaio (1449–94). Under Ghirlandaio, whose reputation had been made at the recently built Sistine Chapel in Rome, Michelangelo learned the essentials of fresco painting, studying earlier masters such as Massaccio and Giotto and helping with the preparation of pigment and plaster for a series of paintings in the Tornabuoni Chapel at the church of Santa Maria Novella, depicting the life of the Virgin. He was also given the opportunity to draw from nude models, beginning his life-long artistic passion for the human body. The earliest surviving drawings by Michelangelo show an acute eye for observation and a growing feeling for physical presence in the rendering of figures. He certainly learned the rudiments of drawing, of cross-hatching and thickened contours, from Ghirlandaio, but already there were precocious signs of an individual talent in his work which seem to have strained relations between master and pupil. The apprenticeship was for a three-year period, but after only one year in the workshop Michelangelo sought inspiration elsewhere.

Through his circle of young Florentine craftsmen, notably his friend Francesco Granacci, who had also been an apprentice to Ghirlandaio, Michelangelo met the ageing sculptor Bertoldo di Giovanni. Bertoldi had been a pupil of the pioneering Florentine sculptor Donatello, the artist who had, among other things, created a powerful and sensual sculpture of David which would strike a chord with his pupil's pupil at the beginning of the sixteenth century. Now approaching his seventies, Bertoldi ran a sculpture studio and was also in charge of the Medici family's celebrated sculpture collection. This was kept in the Medici Garden near the Piazza San Marco, where young craftsmen could go for pleasure or study. Bertoldi brought him into contact with Lorenzo de' Medici (1449–92), who had dominated the city of Florence both politically and culturally for the previous two decades. His court was the focal point for leading humanist poets and scholars as well as young artists, including the illustrious Leonardo da Vinci, who had been associated with it a decade earlier. Like Leonardo, the young Michelangelo was profoundly influenced by both humanist learning and classical art. In particular, the Medici court, or 'academy', as it was nicknamed, fostered Michelangelo's primary interest in sculpture; he was later, rather disingenuously, to declare painting fit only for women and the idle. The impact of Roman and Greek sculpture owned by the Medici is clear in one of Michelangelo's first attempts at carving marble. *Battle of the Centaurs* is a relief which he did at the age of seventeen. It was intended to portray the conflict in Greek legend between men and centaurs, an allegorical struggle between reason and passion. In concentrating on the upper parts of the centaurs, however, it now reads as a seething mass of naked men in combat. Spatially, the work is unresolved, with the figures ambiguously staged against a flat background rather than subtly emerging from the stone, but as an exercise in representing dynamic form, it is strong. Human anatomy is carefully observed and tightly rendered in a complex pattern of intertwined bodies. The resulting sense of power and violence that is generated from the carved marble, tinged as it is with eroticism, anticipates the central concerns of much of Michelangelo's best work.

Although Bertoldo died in 1491, his young protégé's skill was enough to persuade Lorenzo de' Medici to give him a room in his palace and a generous salary of five ducats a day. Still in his teens, Michelangelo found himself at the very heart of the Florentine court, but this period was brief. Within a year Lorenzo de' Medici had died, and two years later the Medici had been expelled from Florence altogether. The immediate cause of their fall was that perennial bane of Renaissance Italy, foreign invasion; in this instance, the French army led by Charles VIII. The underlying cause, however, was financial; even before Lorenzo's death, the Medici Bank had collapsed and with it the family's political power. Furthermore, the Medici regime had been undermined from within by the activities of a Dominican friar, Girolamo Savonarola (1452–98). Since 1489, Savonarola had been claiming to be the mouthpiece of God, condemning Florentine decadence and Medici tyranny in equal measure. When the Medici fled in 1494, their palace was ransacked. Florence was declared a republic, but cultural and artistic life momentarily floundered under Savonarola's violent and puritanical regime. He outlawed carnivals and enforced strict religious observances. Secular books, paintings that made 'a whore' of the Virgin, cosmetics, silks, games and all manner of luxuries were consigned to 'bonfires of the vanities' in the city's open spaces.

After an unsettled period, Michelangelo eventually arrived in Rome in 1496. The ancient imperial capital was just beginning to give up its buried artistic treasures, as the ancient 'grottoes' yielded statues of staggering quality and sophistication, and paintings of hitherto unimaginable beauty. Michelangelo already possessed a good knowledge of classical sculpture from the Medici collections. He had earlier copied a second-century Roman *Sleeping Cupid* so convincingly that an unscrupulous art dealer sold it on as genuinely antique. Michelangelo was lauded for his skill when the fraud was eventually exposed; it was the purchaser of his copy, Cardinal Riario, who became his first patron in Rome. In 1496 Cardinal Raffaele Riario, a powerful vice-chancellor of the papal court, commissioned a statue of the Greco-Roman god Bacchus for his vast new palace near the Campo de Fiori. The subject is classical, but much of Michelangelo's treatment of it is not. Rather than suggesting the poise and balance central to antique art, the figure is precariously posed, almost staggering. His belly is distended, his chest and shoulders slightly stooped and he gazes in adoration at the cause of it all, namely the cup of wine which he clutches in his right hand with – if not quite the desperation of a latter-day drunk – little or nothing of the grace associated with Roman sculptures of the god of wine. In addition, and even more startlingly original, is the fact that the sculpture is created

MARBLE

Many different materials were used in the Renaissance to create statues or to decorate the interiors and exteriors of buildings. Bronze, stone, gold, silver and naturally occurring substances like coral, eggshells or animal tusks were prized for their beauty and often their scarcity. And, of course, there was marble. There were a great variety of types of marble available in Italy, the quality and colouring dependent on the region from which it was quarried. Veiny, coloured marbles could be found in northern Italy, in the lower areas of the Alps, while black or red marble could be found near Verona.

One type particularly admired by sculptors was that found in the Carrara region, a mountainous area north of Pisa. It had been much admired by artists since the first century BC for the density of its structure. And it was this fine 'grain' that lent itself to precision cutting and a highly polished finish. Carrara marble was expensive. Like all quarried materials, it was difficult to transport over long distances. It was labour-intensive, requiring skill to quarry the stone. But because patrons wanted it, as much as sculptors liked working with it, Carrara marble was always in demand.

Often the sculptor's work would begin in the quarry itself, choosing the right slab for the commission, attempting to select the highest-quality marble, of the right size and dimensions, and visualizing the statues hidden within.

to be seen from a multitude of viewpoints with no one position revealing all. Behind Bacchus is a cheeky little satyr stealing grapes who is hidden from both the Roman god and the spectator until one moves around the work. Like the satyr itself, the sculpture plays a mischievous game of hide and seek which flew in the face of classical orthodoxy. In turn, Michelangelo's delicacy of touch in producing the body of the main figure, as well as the detailed rendering of the garland of vine-leaves, is still breath-taking, but contrasts with the much coarser finish of the hair and faces. Add to this the still-visible drill holes at various points in the work, notably to create the eye-sockets of the animal skin trailing behind Bacchus, and you realize just how radical, violent and staccato-like the work would have seemed to an eye trained by an idealized classical notion of beauty. Not surprisingly, perhaps, Riario rejected a work which certainly suggested the dangers of drink but also hinted at a more subversive way of treating the human form. Rather than imitating classical sculpture as Riario wanted Michelangelo to do, he had competed with it and thereby committed a cardinal sin, at least in artistic terms.

Throughout his life, Michelangelo maintained a detailed correspondence with his father and four brothers. He also effectively supported the whole family financially. His letters to his family during his stay in Rome suggest that despite a growing number of commissions, he found this time difficult and uncertain. Rome was nominally ruled by the Senate, a pale shadow of the ancient institution, for in practice the city was commanded by the papal court, which also ruled over considerable territories beyond. The papacy was at the centre of the economic and political life of Rome, but the city was vulnerable to the frequent elections of new popes and to the factional rivalries that consequently simmered away. During Michelangelo's early years in Rome, the ruthless Borgia family was in control with the despotic Rodrigo Borgia ruling as Pope Alexander VI (r.1492–1503), and his illegitimate son Cesare establishing the family's control over large swaths of northern Italy. The Borgia court was violent and corrupt, and incessant rumours of poisonings, murder and intrigue led Michelangelo to comment to his own family that 'they sell the blood of Christ by handfuls here and have closed the road to all goodness'. His father's concerns for his son were, however, slightly more mundane: 'Live with moderation and do not go without, and above all', he continues, 'keep yourself from hardship because in your trade if you were to fall ill – God keep you from it – you'd be a lost man.' Lodovico then adds that Michelangelo should keep his head 'reasonably warm and never wash: have yourself rubbed down and don't wash'.

Michelangelo's first period in Rome was bolstered by the emergence of another father figure whose assistance extended well beyond the realms of advice about personal hygiene. Jacob Galli, an educated Florentine banker, helped the young artist with lodgings and, more crucially, with commissions. After Riario's rejection of the *Bacchus*, Galli bought the work, commissioned another version of Cupid and acted as broker and financial guarantor in various contracts for sculpture made from expensive marble. The most important of these commissions was for a *Pietà* for Cardinal Jean Bilhères de Lagraulas, the French Ambassador to the Holy See, who wanted a sculpture of the Virgin holding her dead son for his own tomb in the church of St Petronella. The contract stipulated that the finished work should be so well crafted that 'no living artist could better it' and Michelangelo stuck by the terms of the agreement in producing a masterpiece which has rarely, if ever, been surpassed in the history of devotional sculpture. It is the only existing signed work by Michelangelo – the band across the Virgin's breast bears the inscription: 'MICHELANGELUS BUONARROTUS FIORENTINUS FACIEBAT' ('Michelangelo the Florentine made this'). Some scholars have suggested that the fact that the inscription disappears behind the Virgin's cloak emphasizes that the artist was stressing the impossibility of ever totally finishing a work which aspired to perfection, but Vasari had a simpler and more amusing explanation. He maintained that Michelangelo once overheard a group of visitors saying that another

Holy Family (Doni Tondo)
1503–04, Uffizi, Florence
This picture of the Holy Family was Michelangelo's first completed masterpiece in painting. It was produced to commemorate the wedding of Agnoli Doni (hence its name) and Maddalena Strozzi in Florence on 31 January 1504. The circular format was common enough in the late fifteenth century but Michelangelo's handling of the subject was not. The composition is rigorously divided with the figures of Mary, Joseph and Jesus separated from the background by a narrow wall or sill. Languid, sensual, slightly out of

focus and in marked contrast to the Holy Family are a group of nude men relaxing in the sun. They are both the forerunners of Michelangelo's extraordinary *ignudi* on the ceiling of the Sistine Chapel and a counterpart to the cartoon of nude soldiers surprised by the enemy that he produced for his unrealized painting of the Battle of Cascina. Here, though, they function as symbols of classical perfection in a pagan world which preceded the Christian one. On the threshold of ancient and modern worlds is John the Baptist, the harbinger of Christ, carrying his

traditional, prophetic cross across his shoulder and gazing upwards at the figure of Christ at the apex of the picture.

In the foreground are the monumental figures of the Holy Family, sculptural in feel but rendered with a subtle painter's touch that is close to perfection in its finish. No brushstroke is discernible, just a polished lustre and a dazzling use of white, particularly on the Virgin, which stresses her centrality in the Catholic tradition. The muscular grace of the Virgin begins to dissolve the distinction between male and female figures in Michelangelo's art in which the human

body is transformed into something approaching an ideal form.

The gaze between Mary and her son is particularly charged, a little like the space between God and Adam in the Sistine Chapel. Both Mary's eyes are visible but by the laws of nature only one should be; and Michelangelo also tilts her face back in order to emphasize the connection between mother and son. In doing so, he distorts the image in his quest for pictorial power over naturalism and establishes his credentials as a great experimental artist in the making.

artist from Milan had carved the statue (a sculptor called Cristofero Solari) and that he returned at night to carve his name and thereby re-establish his authorship in bold, uncompromising letters.

The *Pietà* is a staggering work, sublimely carved, serene in its effect even if the dazzling lustre of its polished surface was intended to be seen in candlelight. Michelangelo was twenty-four when he made the work and the sculpture itself seems suspended in a state of eternal youth. He portrays the mother of Christ as if younger than the son who lies across her lap. When asked why, according to Condivi he answered: 'Don't you know that chaste women keep their freshness much better than those who are not chaste? Even more so a Virgin whose body has never been troubled by the slightest immodest desire ... As for Jesus, He grows old because He has been incarnated as a man.' The sculpture is dominated by a powerful sense of calm. The Virgin is not racked with grief as is so often the case with this image. Instead, she is lost in deep meditation and, with her left hand held out towards the viewer with its palm facing upwards, she seems to be inviting the viewer to join her in contemplation. It is a gesture which also emphasizes that Michelangelo's version of the *Pietà* is a profound vision of resignation to divine providence, realized through a restrained and beautiful poignancy rather than heavy melodrama.

In 1501, succumbing to his father's pleas, Michelangelo returned to Florence just after his twenty-sixth birthday, leaving behind the intrigue of the Borgia court. Michelangelo had left Florence in the grip of Savonarola. The religious fanatic had himself succumbed to revolution; first excommunicated, then deserted by the populace, he was eventually burned at the stake. As the Florentine republic recovered from the rule of the zealous preacher, opportunities for artists and craftsmen returned. The rich families who had cautiously kept a low profile after the fall of the Medici once again sought the prestige and status that artistic and architectural patronage offered. Moreover, there was a general desire to enhance the visible status and symbolism of the republic, which resulted in a major project for Michelangelo.

In 1504, the commune of Florence commissioned a statue of David. The contract stipulated that Michelangelo was to carve one giant male figure to stand on one of the cathedral's buttresses. It was mooted that he produce a composite work from a number of pieces of stone but subsequently he was allowed the vital freedom of carving from a single block of marble on which work had already been started in a botched exercise by Donatello's assistant Agostino Duccio about forty years earlier. More recently, and not entirely convincingly, it has been suggested that Leonardo da Vinci had botched the marble, a theory fuelled by the antagonism that Leonardo felt for his younger rival and which was reciprocated. Motivation, though, was never a problem for Michelangelo on this, his most prestigious commission to date. The preparatory drawings for the statue seem to confirm his passionate identification with the subject. 'As David overcame his Goliath in the flesh with the sling,' he wrote in his sketchbook, 'so Michelangelo will overcome his giant in marble with the bow.' At over four metres high, the *David* established Michelangelo as the supreme sculptor of his time. It is an imitation of antique Greek sculpture with Christian overtones created to glorify republican Florence. Once again, Michelangelo ignored convention and abandoned the traditional image of David as simply a victorious warrior; instead, his David appears deep in thought and shows signs of both controlled strength and anger, two qualities considered civic virtues in Renaissance Florence. It also suggested the idea of perfect, flawless male beauty and subsequently became the most admired male nude in Western art history.

Initial reaction was one of awe tempered by a small number of stone-throwers who hurled missiles at *David* as it was slowly transported over four days on rollers from the cathedral workshop to the Piazza della Signoria. Reasons suggested for this protest vary from a pro-Medici faction who resented the colossal republican monument to post-Savonarolan moralists who took umbrage at nudity on so large a scale. Both groups would have been incensed by the decision made by a board of artists and officials, who carefully chose to site *David* beside the main entrance to the seat of government, the Palazzo della Signoria, replacing Donatello's sculture of *Judith and Holofernes* as the most prominent symbol of tyranny vanquished. It became *the* symbol of republican Florence and its struggle as an independent city-state in the face of the powerful despotic forces which surrounded it, from Medici-led coalitions to the armies of various European monarchs. *David* stood, as his replica does today, as the guardian at the gateway to Florentine political life; a monument to political struggle, to those small states under threat from the larger forces of tyranny.

In 1505, Michelangelo had a personal battle to fight when he found himself in direct confrontation with Leonardo da Vinci. Both artists had been commissioned by the Florentine state to decorate the walls of Sala del Gran Consiglio in the Palazzo Vecchio. Here, in what was effectively the seat of government, the republic commissioned a more private symbol of its power and aspirations, an interior counterpart to Michelangelo's great monument just outside the gates of the palace. Unlike *David*, however, the project was never realized, but its artistic impact was still considerable. With what had become a traditional mixture of religious and secular imagery, the chamber was to have an altarpiece by Fra Bartolomeo oppposite the loggia under which the eight members of the *signoria* sat together with their elected leader, the *gonfaloniere*, Piero Soderini. On either side of the loggia were to be two vast mural paintings, measuring nearly seven by seventeen and a half metres depicting former triumphs on the battlefield and painted by the two most illustrious artists of the city. Leonardo was to commemorate the Florentine victory over the Milanese in 1440 at the Battle of Anghiari while Michelangelo depicted a scene from a victorious campaign against Pisa in 1354. In his *Battle of Cascina*, Michelangelo eschewed the more usual depiction of warfare, and chose an episode in which the Florentine soldiers learn of the enemy approach while they are bathing in the Arno. In their scramble to dress and arm themselves, Michelangelo demonstrates his capacity to depict almost every aspect of the male body in action. The scene is dramatic, full of taut gesture and detailed expression and an intensity previously unseen in two-dimensional Western art. It was to function as an allegory of the need to be prepared as well as celebrating eventual victory over a rival against whom the Florentines were currently at war. It was also a means of showing what Michelangelo could do in the face of competition from his artistic rival, Leonardo. Neither work was ever finished, not least because of the scale of the project and the fact that the republic ended within ten years. But gigantic cartoons were made and displayed which functioned as a laboratory for younger artists and had a strong impact on painting throughout Italy over the next few decades. As late as 1559, Benvenuto Cellini recalled that 'Michelangelo's cartoon was placed in the Medici

David
1504, Accademia, Florence
This sculpture has become a monument to idealized male beauty, to Michelangelo himself, to Florentine republican virtue and to all who struggle in the face of tyranny. It was hewn from a gigantic block of marble that had defeated several Florentine sculptors before Michelangelo fought his own battle with the stone and won. It is now located on a plinth in the Accademia in Florence and an exact replica stands just outside the Palazzo

della Signoria where *David* was first sited. The original commission, however, was intended for one of the buttresses of Florence Cathedral and was carved to be seen from way down below. This accounts for David's oversized head and hands which seem over-prominent when viewed on an almost level perspective. But Michelangelo pays scrupulous attention to detail, notably in the face which is set in an expression of firm resolve and defiance. The eyes have a small triangular

shard of marble left in their hollowed-out pupils which is an almost painterly touch, a highlight which adds steel to his gaze. At the same time, David's stare into the distance gives the sculpture a dreamy quality enhanced by his languid pose.

Instead of showing David in the traditional pose, triumphant with a sword and the head of Goliath in his hand, Michelangelo depicts him armed with a small sling and stone, relaxed but ready to spring into action. The work was installed in the same

month that Florence went to war with neighbouring Pisa (May 1504) and it dovetails neatly with Michelangelo's planned painting of the Battle of Cascina which showed the Florentines surprised by the Pisans in battle.

Standing over four metres tall, it is a colossal work and a colossal achievement: a giant-killer as giant himself, asserting Florence's claim to be the new Roman republic and establishing Michelangelo as the dominant sculptor of the High Renaissance.

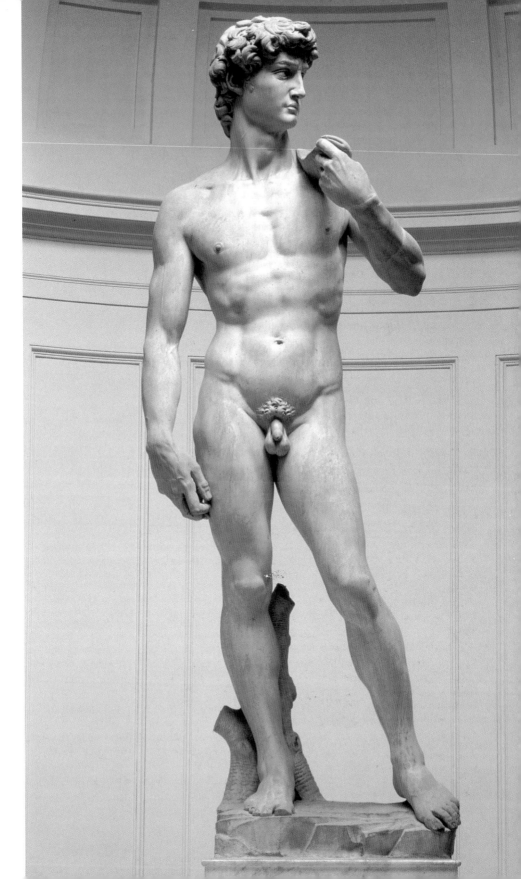

Palace and Leonardo's in the Sala del Papa and for as long as they were on show they were the school at which the whole world came to study'. Today, only a copy exists of Michelangelo's cartoon, but it is enough to see how inventive and intense the finished painting would have been.

Michelangelo had not even begun painting the *Battle of Cascina* when he was summoned to Rome by the new pope, Julius II (r.1503–13). The former Cardinal Giuliano della Rovere was a considerable political manipulator who managed to be elected pope during one of the shortest conclaves ever recorded. Julius II was also the 'warrior-pope'; as much the commander of the papal armies as supreme pontiff, he aimed to establish the papacy as a secular domain in central Italy. Aware of his mortality and the importance of posthumous fame, Julius required Michelangelo to plan and construct a magnificent tomb for him. Michelangelo devised a hugely ambitious design for a gigantic marble structure, roughly ten metres long, seven metres deep and over sixteen metres high, at the centre of which was a room housing Julius's sarcophagus. It was to be decorated with forty marble statues and numerous bronze reliefs, all detailing the deeds of Julius's papacy, both real and imaginatively embellished. His biographers give graphic accounts of how Michelangelo set off eagerly for the mountains to select the large quantities of marble he would need for the grand project. It is difficult to exaggerate the excitement of this vast commission from one of the wealthiest princes in Christendom. Michelangelo went to Carrara in the foothills of the Apuan Mountains. Since the first century, Carrara had provided Europe with a fine white marble, and with it Michelangelo hoped to imitate and better the work of ancient sculptors. He was said to have a unique gift for selecting marble, which held the key to making good sculpture; choose faulty stone and a sculpture could be severely compromised. He spent eight months in Carrara in 1505 and it is not hard to imagine him there, visualizing sculptures waiting to be released from these rocks, and dreaming, as Condivi recalls, of carving gigantic statues out of the whole mountain. He returned to these hills many times in his life and the long periods he spent in Carrara were like spiritual retreats for him, often preludes to great spells of activity. It was also perhaps here that he was happiest, alone with his beloved marble, undisturbed by the demands of impatient or ignorant patrons or needy relatives. Local legend maintains that Michelangelo's ghost still walks in these hills.

In the winter of 1505, Michelangelo returned to Rome, impatient to begin the huge project, which he felt would finally allow him to realize the full potential of sculpture. But he was denied access to the Pope for an entire week; Julius II appeared to have lost interest. In large part, this was due to the decision to build a new St Peter's, which for the present deprived the tomb of both funding and its planned location. Suspecting that his rivals, principally the architect Bramante, had deliberately sabotaged the commission, and feeling outraged and betrayed, he stormed back to Florence. The Pope recalled Michelangelo in vain, eventually writing several letters to the Florentine government, demanding the artist's return. Michelangelo stubbornly refused, leading one contemporary to voice his concerns about the consequences: 'You've tried and tested the Pope as not even the King of France would dare ... we don't want to wage war with him over you and put our state at risk!' After seven months, Michelangelo finally relented and went to see Julius at Bologna, which the warrior-pope had just captured. According to one of his biographers, when Julius asked him why he had left Rome he replied, 'Not from ill will, but from disdain!' Given that detailed letters between the Florentine government and the papal court negotiating Michelangelo's safety exist, it is unlikely that he would have dared treat his volatile and powerful patron with such conceit and the account is almost certainly one of retrospective revenge. What is clear, however, is that Michelangelo's patience with patrons declined as he aged and that arrogance was a crucial part of his creative being.

Aside from the monumental decision to rebuild the basilica of St Peter, Julius II had plans for another ambitious commission in the Vatican which involved Michelangelo. To the artist's frustration, the new commission was entirely unrelated to the tomb project that had so fired his imagination, and which was now postponed. Instead, the Pope required him to paint the ceiling of the Sistine Chapel. This important chapel in the Vatican, in which papal elections took place and where the prestigious College of Cardinals regularly celebrated mass, was built and named after Pope Sixtus IV (r.1471–84). It had been decorated by other artists, including Michelangelo's former master, Ghirlandaio, but the vault remained blank. Michelangelo had always felt that painting was a lesser art than sculpture and he argued frequently and eloquently that he was a sculptor not a painter. Indeed, he had little experience of fresco painting. He even suspected rivals of engineering this commission for him so that he would be forced to work in a medium in which he was not expert. In the end, he reluctantly accepted the challenge, little realizing the true extent of the work involved. In 1508, amid the dust and heat generated by the masses of candles that lit the dark chapel, he began the monumental task of covering a surface of a thousand square metres and painting over three hundred figures. The idea, promoted by Hollywood with a little encouragement from Michelangelo and his biographers, that he struggled alone and on his back for years on end is a ludicrous one. For a start, he drew caricature sketches for friends in which he depicted

himself comically standing, arm stretching up with a brush in his hand. It is also clear that Michelangelo had numerous assistants to build the scaffolding, mix his paints and to help him work on the frames and architectural details of the ceiling. But it is equally clear that the majority of the detailed work was Michelangelo's and that the final achievement, its impact and the subsequent power that the work has had on the Western imagination were his and his alone.

Starting above the altar and moving across towards the entrance, Michelangelo painted nine scenes from the Book of Genesis from the beginning of Creation to the time of Noah. Images depicting Christianity's version of the Big Bang were rare but Michelangelo's vision was explosive. God is presented in the guise of a muscular Greek hero, a classical sculpture brought to life who brings life to the universe. He soars across the ceiling, separating darkness from light, creating the sun, moon and planets before turning his attention to mankind. With arm outstretched and cloak billowing out behind him, he produces – as Michelangelo was metaphorically doing – the inexplicable spark of creation which brings Adam to life. The next image, which shows the creation of Eve, is directly above the screen dividing the altar from the rest of the chapel and marks the point when creation is superseded by the fall of humanity, from the expulsion from the Garden of Eden to the turmoil of the great flood. Background detail is sparse, which helps to emphasize the immense physical presence of the characters in Michelangelo's biblical drama. Prior to his work on the chapel, scenes painted by Perugino depicted episodes from the lives of Moses and Christ on the walls below. Michelangelo completed the Old Testament in visual form with episodes such as Judith beheading Holofernes and, almost inevitably, David slaying Goliath painted in the triangular spaces (or pendentives) at the corner of roof and wall. This carefully considered design would almost certainly have been devised in collaboration with Julius himself, as well as various theologians from the College of Cardinals. The organization of the scenes and the extraordinary architectural *trompe l'oeil* framing came from the sculptor–painter. On each corner of the main scenes, Michelangelo painted small pedestals on which sit single nude male figures. Here is both mystery and divine perfection, human forms which mirror those created by God in His own image prior to the Fall, after which the figures look slightly grotesque. Holding bronze reliefs which show other biblical scenes, they act as transitional figures, a kind of energized chorus, drawing our attention to the unfolding events and hovering between one painted world and the next. They, too, are without precedent in Western art. They embellish what is already a dazzling creation and add a sensual dimension which proved difficult for some later popes to accept. Towards the end of the sixteenth century, as the Catholic Church began its various inquisitions, there was talk of altering the nude figures (*ignudi*), even destroying them, but the overwhelming power of Michelangelo's creative vision was allowed to remain intact. Interestingly enough, it is only recently, since the Sistine ceiling was cleaned of centuries of candle soot and the effects of overpainted restoration, that our world has been able to see just how vibrant that vision was and that, contrary to the nineteenth-century view, Michelangelo had an exhilarating feel for colour as well as form.

Throughout the four years that Michelangelo had spent working on the Sistine ceiling, the chapel itself had been in continuous use for a small, selective Vatican congregation. When the completed vault was finally unveiled on 31 October 1512, the Roman public flocked to see it, along with visitors from further afield as word spread. Its status today as a site of artistic as well as religious pilgrimage was established within months of its completion. The Vatican, however, was about to change. On 21 February 1513, Julius II died and was succeeded by Leo X, previously known as Giovanni de' Medici. The family were back in business and for the next twenty years dominated central Italy and beyond with two popes in Rome and a re-established power base in Florence. Pope Leo was the son of Michelangelo's former patron Lorenzo de' Medici, and had known the artist since his childhood. In 1512, Florence had been defeated by an imperial coalition and forced to accept the return of the Medici. The family celebrated with a colourful array of festivals and pageants. The streets were filled with extravagant floats and processions, which included senators in togas, buffaloes disguised as elephants, men in gleaming armour and horses made to look life griffins with artificial wings. The most eye-catching part of the festivities was a giant globe out of which a naked gilded boy emerged representing the return of the Golden Age of the Medici. The child, who had been paid ten crowns to be covered in gold paint, died shortly after the ceremonies.

While other artists were employed on extravagant but frivolous artworks to flatter the Medici, Michelangelo persevered with the tomb of Julius II, who had left money for the project in his will and stated that it should be completed within seven years. In 1515, Michelangelo wrote to his brother that he hoped to finish the tomb within two or three years, but what Condivi subsequently described as 'the tragedy of the tomb' would drag on for forty years. Michelangelo suffered from the repeated legal action of Julius's heirs, and the artist would later write that he spent his youth 'chained to this tomb'. Conflicting commitments, combined with his extreme perfectionism, meant that Michelangelo would ultimately complete only five of the forty figures originally stipulated.

Two of these, the so-called *Dying* and *Rebellious* Slaves, were to have symbolized the imprisonment of the liberal arts after the death of Julius but were not included in the final tomb. Instead, after numerous renewals of the contract and many alterations, a shadow of the original design was eventually completed in 1545 in the church of San Pietro in Vincoli. Michelangelo worked on only the bottom section of the two-tiered monument, carving two contrasting niched figures – those of *Leah* and *Rachel* – who represented active and contemplative life respectively and flank the magnificent marble sculpture of *Moses*. This over-life-sized figure is almost monstrous, with its horns, serpentine beard and glowering expression. His arms bulge with muscle and veins, as if he had just hewn the Ten Commandments out of stone and carried them down the mountain. He is both mystic and man of action, the law-giver who strikes a degree of terror into the hearts of those who confront him. Some of Michelangelo's contemporaries used the term *terribilità* to describe the aura that *Moses* exuded and in turn it was applied to Michelangelo himself.

Michelangelo had already achieved greater fame in his lifetime than any previous artist, and this meant that he would be in demand for the rest of his life. A succession of popes, almost by definition old men, sought in their brief pontificates to establish a lasting legacy by commissioning works from the most famous artist of the age, hoping thereby to bask in his reflected glory. Throughout his life, therefore, Michelangelo left many commissions unfinished. Yet he seems to have worked ceaselessly and often complained in his letters of not even having time to eat or sleep. The artist himself was in part to blame; he undoubtedly accepted far too many projects, more than he could ever hope to realize. He signed contracts that were unrealistic from the start and frequently conflicted with each other, forcing him once to confess to himself that 'my mind and my memory have run ahead of me, and await me in the world to come'. Despite the massive commitment to the tomb of Julius II, he accepted Leo X's commission around 1515 to design and carve a huge façade for the church of San Lorenzo in Florence, the family church of the Medici. To a great extent, he had little choice; Leo X maintained a bitter hostility towards the heirs of Julius II and was concerned with his own family's reputation. The façade of San Lorenzo was another colossal work that was to include twenty-two statues. Although Michelangelo could enjoy the satisfaction that Leonardo was reputed to have sought this commission, by the end of 1518 he was in a state of despair and panic, describing his various commitments 'like so many knife thrusts'. This didn't stop him expressing his intense disappointment, however, when Leo cancelled the contract after three

years of complicated negotiation during which time the Pope had the growing protests of a German monk called Martin Luther to deal with. Even today, San Lorenzo has an incomplete façade of bare brick.

Papal and Medici patronage at San Lorenzo continued for Michelangelo, however, when Leo X decided to have a funerary chapel built for his family in the new sacristy to the church, a project that was to occupy Michelangelo on and off for the next fourteen years. Although the commission was initially for elaborate tombs, it expanded into a much more architectural project and established Michelangelo as one of the great architects of his time as well as enhancing his stature as a sculptor. From the simple altar to the intricate play of niche and pilaster with contrasting grey and white marble, the Medici Chapel is a masterful creation which seems to have both grandeur and intimacy and a similar intensity to that experienced when looking at one of Michelangelo's carved figures. When Leo X died soon after the project began in 1521, he was succeeded by a Netherlandish pope, Adrian VI, but there was little or no diminution of the Medici power base, nor was Michelangelo's work threatened. After less than two years, Adrian died and was replaced by Leo's cousin, the Cardinal Giulio de' Medici, as Pope Clement VII (r.1523–34). Like his predecessors, Clement took an active interest in art, patronage and the family reputation, and he duly expanded the building

Dying Slave
1513–16, Louvre, Paris
The commission to create a tomb for Pope Julius II in 1505 was later described by Michelangelo's biographer and assistant, Ascanio Condivi, as a 'tragedy', but it spawned some of the most powerful sculpture of Michelangelo's career and can also be viewed as a sculptural laboratory where ideas were generated and worked through. The *Dying Slave* or *Captive* was one of a series of figures produced for the tomb but not included in its final version at the church of San Pietro in Vincoli in Rome. The slaves, of which four exist, were created as symbols of the liberal arts imprisoned after the death

of Julius II, whose life and papacy had done so much to nurture them, or so the tomb was to proclaim.

The *Dying Slave* was conceived frontally and was made to be displayed in a niche on one of the three sides of the tomb while its brother, the *Rebellious Slave*, also created between 1513 and 1516 (soon after the death of Julius), was intended for a corner. There is a strong ambiguity in the sculpture. It could just as easily be awakening as dying and there is a wonderfully elastic tension in the figure that seems, at one moment, to be stretching, and then, at another, to be deflating as life empties out of it. The facial

expression is close to rapture and there are subtle but definite allusions to sexual as well as religious ecstasy in this, the most overtly homo-erotic sculpture that Michelangelo ever produced.

Behind the main figure is the roughly hewn body of an ape. Interpretations have ranged from the idea of contrasting beauty and the beast to that of art 'aping' nature. More interesting, though, is the graphic illustration of the process of sculpture which the animal form reveals in this the most finished of all the Michelangelo slaves. Carving becomes a way of releasing the enslaved image or form from the

stone and the sculptor's art is to bring life to inert material: 'Just as in pen and ink we find elevated, plain and middle styles,' Michelangelo wrote in later life, 'and in marble noble or lowly forms according as the sculptor's imagination is capable of drawing them forth from the block'. This idea was expressed more powerfully in the opening verse of a poem written by Michelangelo around 1536:

The greatest artist has no conception which a single block of marble does not potentially contain within its mass, but only a hand obedient to the mind can penetrate this image.

plans at San Lorenzo with the addition of a vast library bequeathed to the city. Here, above the cloisters of the adjoining monastery, Michelangelo produced a calm, ordered space but added an entrance hall and staircase up to the Laurentian Library that remains one of the most radical architectural constructions in Florence. Buried in deep recesses and with scrolls below rather than above them, the structural logic of the columns and pilasters is thrown out of the window, or rather would have been had Michelangelo not presented windows of stone, abstract blocks which punctuate the walls, topped by geometric ornamental devices that fly in the face of any previous classical design. It is a subversion of the classical language of architecture, a small dense space which has inspired architects and artists alike from Edwin Lutyens to the American abstract painter Mark Rothko. It is also considered to be the first great work of Mannerist architecture.

In 1527, Italy was again beset by foreign armies, this time with catastrophic consequences. A dispute between the Holy Roman Emperor, Charles V (1519–56), and Pope Clement VII resulted in one of the worst atrocities of the age. The Emperor's army of German mercenaries broke into Rome, held the Pope captive, and comprehensively sacked the city for ten days. The Sack of Rome had repercussions across Europe, but in Florence the opponents of the Medici saw their opportunity to expel the family again. Michelangelo's civic patriotism was now directly at odds with his patron's interests. In 1528 he was named governor of the fortifications of Florence. Understandably, however, given its recent history, Michelangelo had little faith in the survival of Florentine independence, even fleeing the city on one occasion, only to return to its defence soon after. In 1530, another shift in international alliances produced an entente between the Emperor and the Pope. Left alone, Florence passed again into the hands of the Medici. Michelangelo was forced to go into hiding, since his republican stance made him a target of the restored Medici regime. The papal governor, Baccio Valori, even ordered Michelangelo's assassination, but Clement intervened, granted a pardon and insisted that Michelangelo get back to work on the San Lorenzo project.

Like almost every other artist of his time, Michelangelo was wary of politics, but as he aged his dislike of the overt tyranny of the Medici became more pronounced. This, after all, was what his most prominent public sculpture was seen to oppose. In 1532, Alessandro de' Medici was appointed Duke of the Florentine Republic and became, paradoxically, its sole ruler. Two years later, Clement VII died and the Medici stranglehold on the papacy was released. With work at San Lorenzo almost complete, Michelangelo left Florence for Rome for the last time. There were

Interior of the Laurentian Library, 1534, San Lorenzo, Florence

personal reasons too. His father and his favourite brother had recently died and he felt an increasing anxiety about his own age and mortality. At this time, he began to write intensely affectionate letters and poems to the talented young Roman aristocrat Tommaso Cavalieri. The artist had met Cavalieri in 1532, and the two men had since developed a mutual admiration and intense attachment. Michelangelo found it increasingly hard to reconcile his homosexuality with his love of God and his deep desire for salvation in the next life. Nowhere was he able to express this conflict more clearly than in the final great completed work of his life.

The year 1534 saw the election of Alessandro Farnese as Pope Paul III (r.1534–49). Paul III was an important figure in the process of the reform and reorganization of the Roman Church and doctrinal retrenchment known to historians as the Counter-Reformation. Partly to establish the importance of the visual arts in reaffirming the threatened power of the Church, he confirmed Michelangelo's commission to return to the scene of his earlier triumph, the Sistine Chapel, this time to paint the wall behind the altar. Pope Paul appointed him 'Supreme Architect, Sculptor and Painter of the Apostolic Palace'. Michelangelo not only erased some of the earlier frescoes of Pietro Perugino (1446–1523) which covered the great wall above the altar, but also had the wall itself tilted forward at the top, to ensure that dust did not settle on the fresco during work. After detailed deliberation, the subject chosen was the Last Judgment, which certain scholars have argued was more in keeping with the concerns of the ageing artist than with a rigorous theological scheme. Certainly Michelangelo felt close affinities with the subject and is believed to have painted a self-portrait on the flayed skin held by St Bartholomew, but the work also neatly finishes off a vast historical cycle from Creation to the Day of Final Judgment.

Michelangelo laboured relentlessly on the *Last Judgment* from 1536 to 1541, surviving a nasty fall from the scaffolding and with his eyesight failing. By any reckoning, it is an astonishing work but it becomes almost mythically powerful when you realize that it is the intense physical creation of a man in his sixties. It loosely follows the traditional format of previous paintings of the Last Judgment, but merges the sections into a vast, almost tragic space in which individuals struggle for redemption around the pivotal figure of Christ. Instead of depicting Christ enthroned, Michelangelo presents Him as a muscular man of action and a young one at that. This, in addition to the mass of naked humanity seething all around him, gave the zealous champions of the Counter-Reformation ammunition with which to attack an artist whom they felt transcended the boundaries of Christian morality.

Initial opposition to the *Last Judgment* has tended to be overstated by some historians. When it was unveiled on All Saints' Eve 1541, twenty-nine years to the day since the official unveiling of the chapel's ceiling, the reaction was largely favourable and it was widely copied and engraved. Subsequently, though, after the Council of Trent, which concluded just before the artist's death, threats of censorship were carried out and an artist called Daniele da Volterra (nicknamed '*Il Braghettone*', or 'the breeches maker') was instructed by yet another Medici pope, Pius IV, to paint over the genitalia of the nude figures with loincloths. It took a rather more doctrinally conservative pope, John Paul II, to allow the work to be restored to its original state at the end of the twentieth century.

For the last twenty years of his life, Michelangelo interested himself mainly in architectural projects, developing the ideas he had conceived at the church of San Lorenzo, where sculpture and architecture were symbiotically linked. 'The elements that make up the framework of a building', Michelangelo observed in his later life, 'are akin to the limbs of the body.' Given his interest in monumental physical bodies, it is apt that the most celebrated building on which Michelangelo was commissioned to work was the largest church in the world – St Peter's in Rome. The colossal project of rebuilding the mother church of Christendom had originally been supervised by his rival, Bramante. Since the latter's death in 1514, several artist–architects had worked on the project, including Raphael. The chief problem for Bramante's successors was the size and structure of the dome, and from early in 1547, when Pope Paul III made Michelangelo the chief architect of the great basilica, he devoted the rest of his life to the problems of construction. The work was unfinished at his death, and the dome was completed by one of Michelangelo's pupils – Giacomo della Porta – between 1585 and 1590. It is indicative of Michelangelo's state of mind in his later years that he accepted no payment for his work on St Peter's. This was his personal offering to God, the atonement of an aged artist for what he came to regard as a long and sinful life.

Michelangelo's final years were extraordinarily productive and he began to develop yet another sphere of interest, that of urban planning. In order to ease the congested traffic in a city inundated with pilgrims, he helped re-route an old Roman road through a new gateway into Rome, the Porta Pia, built by him between 1561 and 1564. In addition, he redesigned the architecture of one of the most important public spaces in Rome, the Capitoline Hill. But his overriding concern in his last years was for personal salvation, at a time when his enemies and critics seemed to

---

MICHELANGELO ON THE NATURE OF SCULPTURE AND PAINTING

In 1547, Michelangelo wrote to a Florentine intellectual, Benedetto Varchi, who had recently given a lecture to the Florentine Academy in praise of Michelangelo and who had sent the manuscript to the artist and asked for his response. Michelangelo's reply is both ironic and full of insight, amounting to a rare statement about his artistic practice and theory.

I say that for me it seems that painting should be held good when it most approaches relief, and relief held worse in the degree to which it approaches painting. Therefore to me it used to seem that sculpture was the lantern of painting and that between one and the other there was the same difference as there is between the sun and the moon. Now that I have read your little book where you say that, speaking philosophically, those things that have the same end are the same thing, I have changed my opinion and I say that if greater judgment and difficulty, obstacles and toil do not make for greater nobility, that painting and sculpture are the same thing . . . I mean by sculpture that which is made by taking material off. That which is done by putting on [i.e. modelling in clay or wax] is similar to painting. Enough that the one and the other – that is, sculpture and painting – since they proceed from the same intellectual faculty should make a good peace together and leave such disputes because they take up more time than making figures.

Last Judgment

1536–41, Sistine Chapel

In order to create his vision of the Last Judgement, Michelangelo had to destroy a pair of lunettes he had painted for the roof of the Sistine Chapel, as well as a frescoed altarpiece of the Assumption by Perugino. This duality of creation and destruction runs through the work itself, which takes the subject from St John's Book of Revelation and throws it into a chaotic realm where the laws of space seem to have been abolished. Figures are gathered here and there in groups, but others emerge larger than life, isolated in their own tiny worlds. This discrepancy of scale helps to break down the traditional divisions between those damned and those saved in an image where everything threatens to merge together. The fresco has no frame and its edges seem almost arbitrary, a partial vision of a much larger whole which accentuates the idea that Christ is ending human time on this, the final Day of Judgment.

The feeling of a deep, almost infinite space beyond this world is highlighted by the rich lapis lazuli blue which dominates the painting. Colour is once again used with surprising subtlety, given Michelangelo's time-honoured reputation as a muted colourist prior to the recent restoration and cleaning of the Sistine Chapel. The flesh of the damned figures on the right is a deathly grey while the saved, emerging from the grave on the left, have a more luminous colour which brightens as they ascend towards the heavens. The Virgin has similar icy highlights to her pink and blue robes to those in Michelangelo's *Doni Tondo*, but here she is more muted, less muscular and slightly older. Christ, on the other hand, bursts forth as a muscular young man, unbearded and unlike the older patriarchs in most depictions of the subject.

The style of the painting is more brutal than the ceiling of the Sistine Chapel, its mood harsher and its impact more disturbing. Christ is surrounded by saints, Peter and John the Baptist most clearly visible on either side. Directly below are the early Christian martyrs, St Lawrence with an arm through his gridiron and St Bartholomew holding his own flayed skin on the face of which is what many have seen as a self-portrait of Michelangelo. While there is no direct evidence to support this, the image is strongly in keeping with the artist's growing and recorded terror of the 'sins of the flesh', as well as his quest for spiritual renewal and salvation.

The fusion of classical beauty and Christian iconography is writ large on this, the main wall of the Sistine Chapel. Christ himself is the most sublime expression of this duality, a Greek god fused with New Testament saviour. Hell is also the Hades of antiquity, with Charon, the mythological ferryman, beating sinners out of his boat and into a life of eternal damnation.

The harsh criticism to which the work was subjected on account of its apparently shocking nudity is partly countered by Michelangelo in a delicious if tiny detail: in the very bottom right-hand corner is the figure of Minos, the legendary king of Crete who fell foul of the gods and whose wife fell in love with a bull. Here, though, his face is depicted as that of a certain Biagio da Cesene, the papal Master of Ceremonies who had led the initial criticism of the work even before Michelangelo had completed it. Biagio's own punishment at Michelangelo's hands was severe – a man destined for posterity as a painted figure whose genitals are being savagely bitten by a large serpent. It is an image which gives wry pleasure to any artist who has been attacked by a harsh critic at one time or another.

be closing around him. Since 1538 he had been in the philosophical and theological circle of Vittoria Colonna, the Marchioness of Pescara. He dedicated many religious poems to her and admired this remarkable woman who enhanced his faith and sought to reform the Catholic Church from within. Without ever fully embracing the Protestant Reformation at a time when the two doctrinal codes did not seem irreconcilable, Vittoria Colonna seems to have encouraged Michelangelo to consider the doctrine of justification by faith alone, one of the principal tenets of Lutheranism, which some commentators see strong evidence of in his last paintings, notably the two frescoes for the Pauline Chapel adjacent to the Sistine. In both *The Conversion of Saul* (1542–45) and *The Crucifixion of Peter* (1545–49), the emphasis is on blind faith, particularly in the case of the first pope, St Peter, who grimly faces his fate. As the soldiers prepare to crucify him upside-down, he stares out at the viewer as if to remind them of the real nature of the rock on which the Roman Church was built, a far cry from the Vatican of the sixteenth century that Michelangelo had seen at close quarters for five decades.

In 1557 Michelangelo's work came under severe criticism in a posthumous tirade published in Venice by admirers of the late satirist Pietro Aretino (1492–1556), who had a personal grudge against Michelangelo because the artist had previously refused to enter into a public correspondence with him. Aretino's attack is a devastating hatchet job: 'As a baptized Christian, I am shamed by the licence, so unlawful to the soul and intellect, you have taken in expressing those ideas and that goal to which all aspects of our faith aspire.' Aretino mocks the 'Michelangelo of stupendous fame' as having produced, in the Sistine Chapel, work which 'would better suit a bathhouse than the supreme chapel'. His colouring and technique were described as inferior to Raphael's and his work was dismissed as formulaic: 'Whoever sees one figure of Michelangelo sees them all.' The dubious morality of his personal life was also censured. In spite of the stinging criticism, however, he continued to work right up to his death and left a magnificent late *Pietà* in a state of total irresolution, which struck a chord so strong in the twentieth century that some distinguished commentators hailed it as perhaps the greatest sculpture ever made, a work that is both expressionistic and conceptual to modern eyes and yet which, to its creator, would not have warranted the status of art.

Racked with regret and guilt, Michelangelo died in Rome on 18 February 1564, aged eighty-eight. According to his wishes, his body was taken secretly to Florence, where he now lies in the church of Santa Croce, in a tomb built in 1572 by the most celebrated of his biographers, Giorgio Vasari. Ironically, the artist whose work has given so much pleasure, inspiration and redemptive hope to religious and artistic pilgrims the world over had, by the end of his life, lost faith in art. This was most eloquently expressed by in one of Michelangelo's neglected sonnets:

At last my life's course, in its fragile barque
Has crossed the stormy seas to reach that port
Where all arrive and give due account
For every deed done ill or piously.
I see now how error-bound was that fond dream
That made my art an idol and a king,
A thing that men contrarily desire.
What will become of amorous dreams, so vain
And once so glad, now I approach two deaths?
One is for sure: the other menaces.
No painting and no sculpture can now soothe
The soul which turns towards that divine love,
Arms spread upon the cross to take us in.

5.

Raphael
1483–1520

Unlike Leonardo da Vinci and Michelangelo, Raphael did not have the benefit of spending his early years in Florence. Yet this product of a 'provincial school' came to be regarded in the cultivated and artistic circles of Europe as the greatest artist who had ever lived. His style is more immediately accessible than much of the drama and intensity of Leonardo or Michelangelo. Raphael was less the rebel or the victim agonizing over his fate than a synthesist and a sensualist. His art became the model upheld by the teaching academies which later flourished across Europe; and he came to represent the ideals of perfection, harmony and grace to which generations of artists aspired right until the late nineteenth century but which diminished after the birth of the modern movement. Raphael is admired nowadays, but not held in the same esteem as either of his two great contemporaries.

Raffaello Sanzio was born on 6 April 1483 in Urbino, in the Marche province, about seventy miles east of Florence. Urbino, although small and relatively unimportant compared with Florence or Rome, possessed an unusually advanced artistic culture for a provincial town of its size. Indeed, at the time of Raphael's birth, the town was at the height of its artistic development. This was thanks largely to its former ruler, Federigo da Montefeltro, Duke of Urbino (r.1444–82), a generous patron of several artists, most notably the influential painter Piero della Francesca (c.1420–92). Raphael's father, Giovanni Santi, was himself a respected artist and poet within the intellectual circles of the duke's magnificent court, but underpinned this financially precarious status with economic stability as a merchant and money-changer. It was this early privileged background that made Raphael such a sophisticated and cultured individual, who would later move easily within intellectual and courtly circles.

Raphael began to learn the rudiments of painting in his father's studio and the cultural vitality of Urbino no doubt stimulated his precocious talent. But his privileged childhood ended suddenly when both his parents died within three years of each other, and Raphael became an orphan aged just eleven. Around 1495, the young Raphael went to Perugia, the capital of Umbria, possibly under the guardianship of Evangelista da Piandimeleto, his father's pupil and friend. His foremost ambition was to become a painter. The facts about Raphael's early years are uncertain, but it is thought that he at first became an apprentice in the workshop of Pietro Perugino (1446–1523), a well-established Perugian master, known for his popular gentle and sentimental religious images, and the leading painter of the 'Umbrian school'. Perugino became responsible for Raphael's artistic and intellectual development, and Raphael's early paintings reveal a considerable debt to him. Perugino clearly taught his pupil the techniques of perspective, composition, light and colour. In addition, there are traces of more recent developments, notably some awareness of Leonardo's *sfumato*, the blending of tones to eliminate definite lines. Raphael was quick to learn and by the age of seventeen was already referred to as a 'master' in a contract for a substantial work on which he was collaborating with an artist much older than himself.

Raphael's mastery of the art of painting when he was barely out of his teens is exemplified in the painting *Madonna and Child Enthroned with Saints*, produced some time around 1503–04, which now hangs in the Metropolitan Museum in New York. The work was commissioned by the nuns of the convent of St Antonio in Perugia as an altarpiece. It shows the Virgin Mary and her infant son surrounded by saints, notably the two great male pillars of Christianity, St Peter on the left and St Paul on the right, together with two early Christian martyrs, Catherine and Cecilia. The upper portion of the painting is competent but derivative, based on the teaching of Perugino, as are the central figures of Christ and his mother, but changes are afoot. The colour is more vivid, there's a swagger to the grouping, but, above all, the male saints have a boldness about them. They seem weightier presences, full of life under their heavy robes, and are rendered with a decisiveness that hints at the emergence of Raphael's own style.

This stylistic development is further illustrated in the most innovative of Raphael's works from this early period, the *Marriage of the Virgin*, painted in 1504. The painting was commissioned by the Albizzini family for the chapel of San Giuseppe in the church of San Francesco, in Città di Castello, an ally of Perugia. Although it was clearly inspired by the works of Perugino, notably the latter's own *Marriage of the Virgin*, Raphael's style is already distinct. The composition is spacious and the group of figures cleverly echoes the curves of the temple without being positioned in a way which rigidly relates them to the architecture. Each figure is positioned fluidly in relation to the other and a sense of gently animated interaction is conveyed, rather than the more formal depiction of human figures in Perugino's work. The shape of the painting mirrors that of *Madonna and Child Enthroned with Saints*, but the two sections have become one unified whole, at the heart of which is the Virgin's ring, itself a precious relic owned by the city of Perugia, having been stolen thirty years before from nearby Chiusi. The painting was therefore religious and political, and both staked a territorial claim to a relic and established a new artistic voice in central Italy.

Despite his already considerable success in Perugia, and a growing fame in Umbria, Raphael harboured greater ambitions and recognized the need to improve his technique further. He was, of course, aware of the overwhelming importance of Florence as the centre of artistic and cultural developments, and doubtless had heard reports of the revolutionary works currently being produced by Leonardo da Vinci and Michelangelo Buonarroti.

> Because of the love he always bore for excellence
> in painting . . . he set aside his work and every personal
> advantage . . . and went to Florence.
>
> (Vasari)

In late 1504, Raphael arrived in the city just after Michelangelo's colossal statue of *David* had been erected in the Piazza della Signoria. Raphael arrived with a letter of introduction from the court of Urbino addressed to the chief magistrate of Florence. The letter described him as a talented artist and stated that he had come to spend some time in the city in order to study. As a result of his intellectual and artistic background, and his easy charm, Raphael was soon participating in the intellectual life of the city, notably the circle of Neoplatonist philosophers and poets. He also became familiar with other painters, including the slightly older Fra Bartolomeo (c.1474–1517). As at other points in his life, Raphael's background, scholarly education and courtly sophistication enabled him to move freely in élite academic and cultural circles in a way unimaginable to the more reclusive and eccentric Leonardo and Michelangelo.

It was, however, Leonardo and Michelangelo who then dominated Florentine art, and reports of their rivalry were widespread. There can be little doubt that Raphael went to see the two works that were causing a furore in Florence, the two cartoons for Leonardo's *Battle of Anghiari* and Michelangelo's *Battle of Cascina*. Although the frescoes were never completed, the cartoons became important models for aspiring artists to admire and study. The young Raphael, like his contemporaries, was probably astounded by the two vast drawings. Leonardo had depicted a violent and highly realistic battle scene full of movement and drama, while Michelangelo had drawn a more sensual group of naked bathing soldiers urgently dressing and arming themselves for battle.

Although highly accomplished by the standards of a provincial school, Raphael could see the level of achievement to which he might aspire in the work of both older masters. Through single-minded study and his considerable powers of imitation and assimilation, Raphael acquired an expertise in the most recent developments of Florentine painting, notably Leonardo's compositional and tonal innovations: he perfected the *sfumato* technique. Raphael was still young and unknown; in particular, he was not a Florentine, nor had he trained in Florence. His first commissions therefore were small-scale and predominantly of the Madonna and Child. During his time in Florence, Raphael painted at least fifteen, all the time improving his technique. After late 1506, he benefited from the absence from Florence of both Leonardo and Michelangelo, allowing him to establish his own reputation; he became increasingly admired and imitated by younger artists. Ultimately Raphael would establish the accepted formula for portraying the Madonna up to the twentieth century, not just in high art, but perhaps even more so in popular or mass-produced devotional imagery. His vision is so much a part of the iconography of Western religious painting that it is difficult to see his paintings with new eyes and to appreciate the novelty of his achievement.

A large-scale painting that illustrates the ways in which Raphael had been influenced by his elder mentors is the *Entombment of Christ*

Madonna of the Goldfinch
c.1506, Uffizi, Florence
Images of the Madonna and Child were rare in the first centuries of Christian art, but after the establishment of Mary's official title of *Theotokus* or 'Mother of God' in a papal edict of 431, they slowly began to appear. By the Middle Ages, the cult of the Virgin Mary was immensely strong in Christian worship and, consequently, devotional images of Mary and her son proliferated.

Raphael is almost universally regarded as the most potent and serene portrayer of the subject in the history of Western art.

In many respects, Raphael's subtle changes in style and assimilation of Michelangelo and Leonardo are most clearly charted in his numerous paintings of the Madonna and Child. In this picture, painted around 1506, when he had begun to establish himself in Florence, his palette is strengthened, his forms are

more volumetric and the composition is elegantly staged. The triangular format comes from Leonardo, but the mood of serenity is all Raphael's. Mary gazes down at the small figure of John the Baptist, who hands the infant Christ a tiny bird – a goldfinch, and a symbol of His future Passion. As in all images of Christ as a child, the present is framed through a knowledge of the future, but there is also a feeling of protectiveness

and love emanating from the commanding figure of Mary, the mother of God. Her son touches her toes with His feet, reaching out towards John to pet the bird. In turn, Mary strokes the back of her nephew, completing the physical chain. She appears against a lush, gently undulating landscape, a universal image of nurture and nature.

of 1507, commissioned by Atalanta Baglioni in memory of her son, Grifonetto. He had been killed in a violent family dispute in which he himself had murdered four of his relatives. There exist sixteen preparatory drawings, through which it is possible to trace how Raphael developed this painting, and in particular his attempts at mastering composition. He tried to convey some of the grief and drama by placing the figures in a seemingly confused, less graceful arrangement. In spite of the moving expressions and the beautiful landscape, he had not yet fully developed his compositional skills. It is also possible to discern how Raphael tried to learn the expressive possibilities of human anatomy in art from Michelangelo, even adapting specific figures to his own compositions.

By 1508, the twenty-four-year-old Raphael was beginning to establish himself in Florence and had received a number of larger commissions. He was working on an important commission for the altarpiece of the Dei Chaptel in Santo Spirito, known as the *Madonna del Baldacchino*, a masterpiece very much admired by Raphael's younger contemporaries. He left this unfinished, however, when in the summer of 1508 he suddenly moved to Rome. His impulse appears to have been essentially a question of patronage. Julius II (r.1503–13) had transformed the papacy into the greatest centre of patronage of the arts, learning and literature in Europe. He wanted Rome to be the greatest Renaissance city – especially as the papacy was facing ever greater threats from northern Europe. Julius was lucky – the coffers were full – and his efforts saw Florence lose its cultural and artistic supremacy to the Eternal City. Under Julius's direction, the great architect Donato Bramante was rebuilding

THE ALTARPIECE

The development of the altarpiece was an important economic boost for artists. The altarpiece effectively came about as a response to the Lateran Council's decree in 1215 that the blessing of the sacramental bread and wine of the Eucharist would 'transubstantiate', or transform, them into the body and blood of Christ. The focus of the Mass turned to the consecration of the Eucharistic elements and soon priests were required to perform Mass at least once a day. This meant

that more altars and chapels were needed to accommodate the increase in numbers.

In the early Middle Ages, the priest, when blessing the bread and wine for the laity, would stand behind the altar. The front of the altar was decorated with a painted panel, or *antependium*, to focus the congregation's attention on the celebration of the Eucharist. But gradually daily communion for the laity was phased out and could only be received with such regularity by the priest himself. This change in the consecration of the Eucharist

meant that the priest moved to the front of the altar, with his back to the congregation, concealing the image. One theory for the origins of the altarpiece was that the *antependium* was moved from the front of the altar to above and behind it to improve visibility of the image for the congregation in the nave.

Altarpieces varied in style and form depending on fashion and the personal preference of the commissioner. The single rectangular panel became more decorative, with gabled ends and

the basilica of St Peter's, while Michelangelo decorated the ceiling of the Sistine Chapel. Furthermore, the papal court sponsored an important intellectual circle of Neoplatonic philosophers and poets. This was an environment in which Raphael could flourish.

It was a period of new discoveries and inspiration. One of the most astonishing ongoing discoveries was a vast underground network of rooms and passageways, at the time thought to be the remains of an imperial bathing complex, but now known to be the ruins of the Golden House, a gigantic palatial complex built by the Emperor Nero. Like many previous artists, Raphael made his way down through narrow tunnels into the subterranean chambers. By candlelight, he could see dazzlingly colourful and intricate classical paintings covering almost every wall and ceiling. These artistic schemes later served as models for his own decorative compositions. Also of great importance were the artistic treasures excavated during this period. As Rome was dug up to make way for the great building projects of Julius II, numerous Roman sculptures were discovered. Contemporary accounts describe how statues of Hercules, Venus and Apollo were found which possessed the look of real flesh. These new classical models were vital to Raphael's artistic achievement. Their attempts to realize a beauty approaching an ideal of human perfection reinforced trends already present in his painting and, indeed, in that of his master, Perugino. Raphael's aim, likewise, became focused on rendering an idealized form of beauty which effectively reversed the dominant trend towards ever-greater realism which had hitherto prevailed in Italian Renaissance art.

Like other artists and scholars, Raphael had been drawn to Rome

---

colonnades separating narrative scenes. Sometimes the elaborate carved and gilded wooden frame would be more expensive than the painting itself.

Two- and three-panel altarpieces soon became popular and were hinged together, the side panels protecting the main painting when folded over. For smaller diptychs and triptychs, this made transportation of the object safer. It also meant that other images could be painted on both sides of the panels. At certain times in the church calendar, altarpieces were kept 'shut' and at other times reopened to reveal the main and side panels.

The main panel of the altarpiece often featured the Madonna and Child or the Crucifixion. Surrounding this scene on side panels, or sometimes within it, were various saints. Often the nominal saint of the church was depicted, as well as the patron saint of the family or individual who commissioned the work. It was also common for the saint to whom the altar was dedicated to appear on the panel. A portrait of the donor himself, or sometimes his heraldic emblem, could be worked into the composition, making the altarpiece an image unique to that particular church.

In the fourteenth century, the purpose of altarpieces shifted from a purely ecclesiastical context to a more secular one. The profusion of dedicated family chapels and private devotion made the altarpiece popular with the urban middle classes.

by the opportunities offered by the great renovation project which was unfolding, and he hoped to receive a papal commission. Rome was not as we see it today – there were no vast straight avenues, no piazzas and fountains. Instead, it was a jumbled mass of scattered medieval buildings, churches and antique ruins, among which cattle grazed. At the heart of Pope Julius's vision was the complete overhaul of the buildings of the Vatican, which he planned to transform into the grandest palace in Europe. Finding the decorative arrangements of his hated predecessor, Pope Alexander VI (1492–1503), intolerable, Pope Julius decided to use another suite of rooms on the floor above as the papal apartments. Julius had commissioned a team of artists to redecorate these rooms and work was already in progress. Raphael's involvement probably came as a result of the recommendation of his fellow Urbinese artist, Bramante. Raphael initially worked alongside the other artists, but Julius soon recognized his supreme talents and dismissed all the others, ordering their works to be erased.

In 1509, Raphael became a salaried painter of the papal court. Thereafter, he began decorating the new suite of rooms or *stanze* in the Vatican that now bear his name. The first room he decorated was a library, later known as the *Stanza della Segnatura* because it became the room where the popes signed and sealed documents. The overall design and composition were Raphael's most ambitious project yet.

The inspiration for the decoration of the room came essentially from four of the standard classifications of a Renaissance library: theology, poetry, philosophy and law (canon and civil). The theme of the piece is the historical justification of the power of the Roman Catholic Church through Neoplatonic philosophy – the glorification of the ideas of Truth, Goodness and Beauty, the most elevated forms of knowledge. Some scholars believe the idea for the decoration was carefully prescribed by the Pope himself, but it is clear from the development in his preparatory sketches that Raphael also played an important role in the conception of the design. This was a pivotal commission in Raphael's career as it led him to rationalize his drawing process significantly. The enormous size of the project forced him carefully to plan and break down the preparatory process into a number of steps. It also gave Raphael an opportunity to experiment with composition on the grandest of scales in the grandest of settings.

Aside from the celebrated *School of Athens*, depicting Plato and Aristotle at the centre of their intellectual universe, Raphael created a series of works which celebrated the pursuit of knowledge and learning. Christian and pagan systems of knowledge are brought together in a room where the Judgment of Solomon and the calculations of Pythagoras jostle, side by side, for our attention. Opposite the *School of Athens*, and presented as a Christian counterpart, is Raphael's fresco known as the *Disputata*. Over forty preparatory drawings exist for this work, which shows the glittering heavens above with Christ enthroned and a gathering of popes, cardinals, saints and theologians below. Christ is surrounded by a golden sphere. Below him, and descending, is a white dove set against a smaller golden halo; down further still is a round golden frame in the middle of which is a tiny white circle, the Host, which, in Catholic liturgy, contains the 'real presence' of the body of Christ. This diminishing descent of the discs is a procession which is visually balanced and theologically central to the sacrament of the Eucharist. This is what is being discussed by the earthly gathering of Christian wise men, the mysterious transformation of bread into Christ's

The School of Athens

1510–11, *Stanza della Segnatura, Vatican, Rome*
This fresco was the most celebrated in Raphael's highly ambitious scheme to decorate the papal apartments in the Vatican. It is housed in the *Stanza della Segnatura*, formerly a library where documents were signed. To the right is a fresco depicting the poet's pantheon of *Parnassus*; to the left is *Jurisprudence*, and opposite is the *Disputata*, a dramatic theological debate and in certain respects the Christian counterpart to the pre-Christian *School of Athens*.

Although set in classical Athens, ostensibly in the Academy created by Plato at the end of the fifth century BC, Raphael mixes modern figures amid the ancient philosophers, sages and scholars in a work which celebrates the rational search for truth. The backdrop is a magnificent architectural creation, an exercise in geometric proportion by the young artist of which Pythagoras would have been proud. Figures are arranged in a deep space centred on the father of Western philosophy, Plato, and his pupil, protégé and eventual rival, Aristotle. Both men are framed by the distant arch and are backlit by the sky as if to emphasize the scope of their minds and intellects. Plato holds a copy of the *Timaeus*, his attempt to explain the origins of the universe, while Aristotle brandishes a copy of his *Ethics*. They debate the nature of truth, with Plato pointing upwards to a higher realm and Aristotle gesturing downwards to the world he inhabits. Mysticism and empiricism, idealism and behaviourism, two fundamental philosophical traditions, are encapsulated in two small gestures.

A host of other key figures are recognizable, from Socrates, who holds forth to an intense group to the right of Plato, to Pythagoras, earnestly writing up his theorems in the bottom left-hand corner of the picture, oblivious to the plagiarist who looks furtively over his shoulder and takes notes. One might expect to find modern philosophers depicted but instead Raphael paints men of art and architecture: Plato is given the features of Leonardo, while Euclid, beavering away at his calculations on a blackboard on the floor in the right-hand foreground, has the face of Donato Bramante, architect of St Peter's Basilica, whose work has echoes in the barrel-vaulted ceiling above. Slumped in the middle of the steps is the brooding figure of Heraclitus, but with the face of Michelangelo, no less. This was a later addition, perhaps a year after the rest was completed, and pays homage to Michelangelo's monumental creation on the ceiling of the Sistine Chapel which Raphael saw for the first time in 1512, as well announcing Raphael's intention to take on board and surpass the achievements of his rival. Finally, on the extreme right-hand edge of the fresco, clad in a coffee-coloured hat and white cape and glancing out towards the viewer, is Raphael himself.

Knowledge, the picture proclaims, is a continual quest, passed down through the ages, developed, disputed and expanded. Classical heroes in the quest for truth, Raphael seems to be saying, were philosophers, mathematicians, astronomers and the like. In High Renaissance Italy, though, they were artists first and foremost.

body symbolizing redemptive sacrifice. Raphael depicts nearly life-sized figures orchestrated in a space that fills the viewer's field of vision and, in so doing, makes one of the great mysteries of Catholic faith more real than perhaps it had ever seemed before.

With the *Stanza della Segnatura* completed by 1512, Raphael emerged as the main rival in Rome to Michelangelo, then working on the vault of the Sistine Chapel. It seems that relations between the two had never been good; Michelangelo claimed, 'everything he knows he learned from me'. Thereafter, Raphael's importance increased with a commission to decorate the other *stanze* in the Vatican. There followed the *Stanza di Eliodoro* (until 1514), which saw the end of Raphael's quest for poise and harmony in his monumental work. Instead, in these paintings, dynamism moves centre stage. From the drama of Heliodorus being blinded for trying to steal the treasures of Jerusalem to the blindingly bright image of the angel freeing St Peter from his chains, Raphael generates a feeling of urgent action verging on melodrama.

Three years later, in 1517, he had completed yet another room – the *Stanza dell' Incendio* . After his death, the *Stanza di Costantino* was painted according to his designs. Also part of this complex is the so-called Loggia of Raphael, a long, second-floor gallery overlooking a courtyard. Originally designed and commenced by Bramante, it was completed and decorated by Raphael and his pupils. It is notable for its 'grotesques', detailed and elaborate miniature drawings, many copied from antique models during visits to the subterranean Golden House of Nero. It is important to appreciate that Raphael's completion of these works was achieved by a considerable workload being placed upon his pupils. Raphael was essentially the designer; many of the paintings in the other *stanze* are not by his own hand. Raphael was even criticized in some circles for his excessive reliance on his studio, but this practice demonstrates an important difference between himself and Michelangelo. While Michelangelo, the temperamental loner, was

---

NERO'S GOLDEN HOUSE

In the late fifteenth century, a small hill alongside the Coliseum in Rome revealed one of the most significant finds in archaeological history. Beneath vines and trees were uncovered the remains of one part of the infamous 'Golden House' of the first century AD Roman Emperor Nero. His complex of buildings covered a 200-acre space in central Rome and contained a palace, lake, gardens, temples and entertainment sites. One building on the Oppian Hill was used for elaborate dining and for exhibiting the works of art Nero had commissioned, bought and requisitioned throughout his empire. The walls were beautifully frescoed – under the lead of the artist Famulus (one of the few Roman artists we know by name) – with architectural fancies, garden scenes, mythological tales and elaborate coloured patterns.

On Nero's death, much of the Golden House had been destroyed – the lake, for example, was drained and covered in concrete, becoming the base for the Coliseum. The

prepared to accept any number of commissions, no matter how unrealistic the terms, Raphael, charming and urbane, was more of a practical businessman, and a consummate careerist.

Always well dressed, well groomed and in good spirits, Raphael had become a central figure of élite Roman society. His biographer and friend Giovio describes the 'marvellous sweetness and the particular beauty that we call grace' that he possessed. According to another biographer, Vasari: 'All who worked with Raphael lived united and in harmony, their ill humours disappearing when they saw him.' Vasari goes on to describe how all those who met him were 'conquered by his courtesy and tact, and still more by his good nature, so full of gentleness and love that even animals loved him.' These accounts undoubtedly exaggerate, but Raphael must have been deeply charismatic to provoke such responses. Wherever he went, Raphael surrounded himself with a long trail of almost fifty admirers, students and friends, prompting Michelangelo to mock him as 'a sergeant with his troop'. Raphael responded to the insult by calling Michelangelo 'The Hangman' on account of his dour and reclusive manner. Following the death of other painters such as Giorgione in Venice and Botticelli in Florence, Raphael became the only artist, apart from the ageing and erratic Leonardo, still perceived to be capable of challenging Michelangelo.

Having established himself with the success of his monumental masterpieces in the Vatican Palace, Raphael was soon running a successful workshop in Rome. He had little difficulty in making influential friends and securing commissions. As well as being an accomplished artist, he was a gifted entrepreneur. The meticulous organization of his workshop became legendary, as did the efficiency and quality of service he provided for his ever-increasing number of clients. He employed a highly skilled group of assistants who took over the work from him wherever possible, leaving him to devote his attention to only those projects he chose. There was, for instance, a great demand for

---

building on the Oppian Hill was eventually turned into a bathing complex by the Emperor Trajan. To achieve this, he destroyed the second floor and filled the ground floor with the rubble and soil. In doing so, he accidentally saved the frescoes for posterity. Thus, when, in the late fifteenth and sixteenth centuries, people began digging down through the ceilings of Nero's rooms, they were amazed – having removed the rubble and soil – by the vitality and beauty of the artwork they uncovered. Coming at a time when interest in Italy's classical past was in the ascendant, this discovery caused enormous interest. Artists flocked to gaze upon frescoes that seemed to have been painted only the day before. Among those artists was Raphael – whose signature, it is claimed, is on one of the ceilings to this day. Certainly the influence on his work is clear from a glance at the patterns he employed in the loggia of the Vatican. Thus, direct copies of a man considered by some to be the Antichrist – Nero – line the walls of the spiritual home of the Catholic Church.

small-scale paintings and portraits by Raphael from private buyers, but very little time for him to do them. Unlike his contemporary Leonardo, who was loath to allow anything to leave his workshop that did not receive his careful attention, Raphael ensured that all his students were taught to draw and paint in a manner almost indistinguishable from his own, so much so that there is still considerable debate today as to whether certain works are by Raphael or by some of his most accomplished pupils. In this way, he was able to take on a vast number of commissions and run a hugely profitable business. In another shrewd business move, Raphael employed an engraver, Marcantonio Raimondi, to make prints of many of his works and in this way his images became widely distributed. In some cases, it is thought he even created images solely for this purpose, as with his famous *Massacre of the Innocents*, which became very popular in its time.

Raphael's exuberant and extrovert personality also expressed itself in the seedier side of early sixteenth-century Rome. In stark contrast to the sweet and pious Madonnas that had first made him famous, Raphael was reputed to possess an insatiable and legendary appetite for women. In a letter to his uncle he once mentioned his fruitless quest for the perfect wife, and in another letter he complained about 'the famine of

'Cartoon for the Taperstry of Miracolours Draught of Fishes', c.1515–16, Her Majesty the Queen, a loan to the Victoria and Albert Museum, London

beautiful women' in Rome. He never married, but often kept a mistress. Raphael had no problem satisfying his lust in Rome. Prostitutes were freely available at a set price fixed by the government, and the vast number of clerics meant there was no shortage of courtesans. These practices were shared by many of his closest friends and associates. In view of Raphael's obvious passion for women, it is not surprising that some of the female figures in his works were celebrated in their time for their astonishing beauty.

In 1511, a year before he completed the *Stanza della Segnatura*, Raphael produced a fresco depicting the nymph Galatea. While it is possible to discern in some of Raphael's female types, notably in *La Fornarina*, a model (in this case possibly one his mistresses), Raphael's highest aim was to portray a more idealized image. In his depiction of female beauty, he therefore abandoned the faithful portrayal of nature that so many fifteenth-century artists had striven for and instead deliberately used an imagined type of beauty. This was the case with the *Galatea*. When asked by his friend Castiglione where he had found the model for the beautiful creature in this famous painting, Raphael replied that having been unable to find a sufficiently beautiful woman in Rome, he had been forced to resort instead to 'a certain idea that sprang from his mind'. The *Galatea* was commissioned by Agostino Chigi, 'the Magnificent', a fabulously wealthy banker from Siena, who dominated trade with the East. Chigi was one of Raphael's most important patrons. At his villa and gardens beside the Tiber, he lavishly entertained popes, ambassadors, artists and scholars. Stories of his legendary wealth include a riverside dinner at which, after each course, the silver plates and bowls were cast into the Tiber. The *Galatea* was painted in a loggia on the ground floor of Chigi's villa, now known as the Villa Farnesina. It represents the sea nymph Galatea, who hears the love song of Polyphemus as she rides across the waves. The scene was inspired by verses of the humanist poet Angelo Poliziano (1454–94), and visually the influence of Botticelli's *Birth of Venus* is clear. Again, the fresco shows Raphael's supreme skill at composition, on a much smaller scale than the Vatican *stanze*; he manages to create a perfectly harmonious composition of freely moving figures. Raphael achieves constant movement throughout the picture – yet it is not restless or unbalanced. Indeed, the painting is perfectly harmonized, each movement in the picture balanced by a counter-movement (for example, the sea-gods in water: one on either side of the image blowing their horns and a pair in front and behind). Yet at the same time, all the lines converge on the face of Galatea at the centre of the picture. *Galatea* is a great example of the sensual but remote, almost unattainable beauty, for which Raphael became famous.

Architecture was considered the foremost of all the arts and Raphael must have been delighted when, in 1514, the new pope, and Medici family member, Leo X, appointed him architect of the new St Peter's Basilica. Bramante's death in that year had created a vacancy which was now filled by his Urbinese compatriot. Bramante had demolished much of the old basilica, dating back to the fourth century, and laid plans for a much vaster structure surmounted by a dome of immense proportions. 'What church is worthier than St Peter's, which is the foremost church in the world?' Raphael wrote proudly to his uncle in Urbino. He also reported with characteristic confidence that he now had possessions worth 3,000 ducats, with a substantial income from the Pope, 'so I shall not lack for as long as I live, and I am sure I shall have much more from others'. At the papal court, Raphael attained the status of the arbiter of taste and culture, a role that was perhaps a factor in Michelangelo's return to Florence at this time. Raphael also began to develop a wider reputation. Leo X commissioned him to design tapestries to hang in the Sistine Chapel. The designs were sent to Flanders for weaving, where they were instrumental in disseminating contemporary Italian ideas in northern Europe, but more specifically in spreading the international fame of Raphael himself.

This project was so miraculously executed that it makes anyone who sees it marvel to think that it was possible to

Portrait of Baldessare Castiglione
1514–15, Louvre, Paris
The diplomat and courtier Baldessare Castiglione (1478–1529) became a close friend of Raphael, who painted his portrait with intimacy at the same time as establishing the sitter's credentials as a man of sophistication, elegance and charm. Castiglione had served as a diplomat for both the courts of Urbino and Mantua before serving as the Mantuan Ambassador to the Pope in Rome, which is where he met Raphael. From 1508 he worked on a treatise on the nature of the ideal courtier, producing both a portrait of a particular court (that of Urbino in 1506) and a more generalized handbook on manners and etiquette. The book, published at the end of his life in Venice in 1528, was accessibly written, as if to emphasize his overriding moral imperative: 'never be tedious', and became immensely influential in European courts over the next two centuries. In stressing the importance of being a balanced, responsible citizen, Castiglione helped to popularize the moral philosophy of classical writers like Aristotle and Cicero and also helped broaden the appeal of humanist writers whose scholarship underpinned a good deal of the Italian Renaissance.

Raphael produced an image of poise and seemingly effortless sophistication – qualities recommended by Castiglione for the ideal courtier. The painting became a mirror of not only the man's features but also his aspirations and advice. Colours are muted, as a courtier's clothes should be; a beautifully orchestrated combination of blacks, browns, greys and whites, offset by the faintest flicker of red on the lining of his fur robe. Dominating the painting are Castiglione's soft blue eyes, looking off into the distance, a sign of a man who sees more than most. Fur and velvet, cotton and a touch of gold with his medal make for a richly textured work, with Castiglione's copious beard and monumental hat disguising the fact that he was bald and, by all accounts, rather ashamed of it.

have woven the hair and beards and to have given such
softness to the flesh with a thread.

(Vasari)

Generally, during this period, Raphael devoted much of his attention
to architectural projects. In 1516, he was appointed Curator of Roman
Antiquities and commissioned to catalogue and preserve Roman ruins,
and also to draw up an archaeological map of the city. Raphael felt a
particular passion for the preservation of Rome's ancient monuments
and in an impassioned letter to Leo X he berated past rulers who
had carelessly defaced and destroyed ancient temples and statues.
Raphael became universally accepted as the expert on antiquity at
the papal court.

Despite his importance and status, however, it has to be admitted
that Raphael realized very few of these projects, and the reconstruction of
St Peter's seems to have floundered under his direction. Raphael certainly
lacked the much broader range of Michelangelo; it was in painting that
his talents lay and upon which his posthumous fame is based. His skill
was rarely better demonstrated than in a number of intimate portraits of
friends and associates. The most successful and celebrated is his portrait
of Count Baldassare Castiglione (1478–1529), painted in 1515. Castiglione
was, much like Raphael himself, the quintessential courtier, and author
of *Il Cortegiano*, or *The Book of the Courtier*, a popular handbook on the
virtues, manners and conduct of the ideal courtier. Castiglione had spent
much time at the ducal court of Urbino and was a close friend of the
Duke. This connection with his native city might explain Raphael's close
attachment to this man, a closeness depicted with elegant dexterity in
the portrait itself.

A similar intimacy also developed in Raphael's portraits of Pope
Leo X. He painted Leo several times, including his image in some of the
historical scenes in the *stanze*. In 1518 Raphael painted the remarkable
Portrait of Leo X with Cardinals Giulio de' Medici and Luigi de' Rossi. The
rapport between the two men transcends the usual formalities of official
portraiture. Here, Raphael's great patron is depicted with two of his
cardinals, also his nephews, one of whom, Giulio, was himself a future
pope (Clement VII, r. 1523–34). The picture was displayed at the wedding
celebrations of Leo's nephew, Lorenzo de' Medici, Duke of Urbino, in
September 1518, and later hung above a door in the Medici Palace. With
the intricate detail of the Pope's velvets and damasks in their various rich
tones, Raphael conveys pomp and power but also shows a man alone, in
spite of the presence of those around him. It is an unguarded moment,
with Leo lost in deep contemplation and, in spite of a steely expression
on his face and all the trappings of his great God-given office, looking

vulnerable. This, therefore, is so much more than a powerful portrayal of papal supremacy. It shows the human face of a troubled man. It was commissioned a year after Martin Luther began his open breach with the Roman Church, and it was Pope Leo's efforts to raise money for the building of St Peter's that was the catalyst for that fatal schism. The Reformation attacked devotional art and spawned a new, more puritanical tradition of image making. Within the Catholic Church, it generated the brashness and bravado of the Counter-Reformation style known as the baroque; art as a bolster and propagandist's tool for an institution determined to fight back. Nowhere, though, in the history of post-Reformation art is there such a telling combination of determination and vulnerability as there is in Raphael's portrait of the Pope unwittingly at the eye of the storm.

Still in his thirties, Raphael had acquired an unprecedented position in the cultural life of the papal court, and a growing international reputation. The future appeared to promise only increased stature and wealth, but Raphael's life was to be short. One of his biographers records that it was ultimately Raphael's womanizing exploits that were his undoing. According to Vasari, 'He secretly attended to his love affairs and pursued his amorous pleasures beyond all moderation.' On one occasion 'he happened to be even more immoderate than usual' and returned home with a violent and unabated fever. Too proud to confess the true nature of his illness, Raphael was given the wrong treatment by doctors. He was bled and grew faint and weak. He died after a seven-day fever on Good Friday, 6 April 1520, his birthday. He was only thirty-seven years old. It is hard to say whether he died from venereal disease or was suffering from the pitfalls of sixteenth-century medical practices. In accordance with his status at the papal court, Raphael was buried with outstanding honours. His corpse lay in state in the Vatican beneath his last, unfinished major painting, the *Transfiguration*, and then received the unprecedented honour of burial in the Pantheon – a fitting tribute to one who so admired the classical world.

6.

Titian
c.1487–1576

After the phenomenal achievements of Florentine artists and architects in the fifteenth century, there was a shift in creative power over the next century as the cultural force shifted north-east to Venice. Here, in the republic on the sea, a new style and attitude to painting flourished, led by an artist who dominated Venetian and indeed European art for nearly seventy years: Tiziano Vecellio, known to English speakers as Titian. Colour and light became the dominant means through which a more sensual, hedonistic art was nurtured. He helped to pioneer new techniques in oil painting; indeed, by concentrating on oil on canvas he played a major role in defining the modern concept of painting. He later introduced a previously unimagined freedom of expression and physical vitality into his paintings, which seemed to celebrate the act of painting itself and which pointed the way for the development of the medium over the next few centuries. Titian was not only the greatest painter of the High Renaissance in Venice, but his work was sought and owned by many of the most powerful people in his world, making him perhaps first truly international artist.

Titian was born at Pieve di Cadore, a small town in the southern Alps, about sixty miles north of Venice. His father Gregorio di Conte dei Vecelli was from a respectable if not wealthy family of lawyers and administrators. Titian's exact year of birth is unknown but a variety of references throughout his life suggest some time between 1487 and 1490. When he was only about ten years old Titian and his older brother Francesco were sent from the family home to Venice, where their uncle Antonio worked as a civil servant.

For centuries the Venetian republic had been one of the most powerful states in Europe, with a vast commercial empire dominating the eastern Mediterranean as far as Cyprus. Venice derived immense wealth from its monopoly of the trade in luxuries from the East, and its position as Europe's gateway to the Orient was highly valued and defended. From the early thirteenth century the Venetian republic had also expanded into its hinterland – the *retroterra* – to create a land empire that encompassed the majority of towns and cities of north-eastern Italy, known as the Veneto. By the time of Titian's birth, however, the days of Venetian commercial supremacy had already passed. From the mid-fifteenth century Venetian possessions in the Mediterranean had fallen rapidly to the expanding empire of the Ottoman Turks. More significantly, the opening of a new sea route to the Indies around Africa, followed shortly by discoveries in the New World, meant that the Venetian monopoly of Oriental trade was broken. Venice gradually ceased to be a Mediterranean power, and the city began a slow economic decline. From the beginning of the sixteenth century, Venice became increasingly preoccupied with defending and periodically extending its land empire, often being threatened by strong coalitions of imperial invaders and local enemies.

The Venetian republic differed significantly from contemporary Italian states. While other cities came to be dominated by individuals and dynasties, punctuated by brief resurgences of more popular regimes, in Venice political stability and a republican constitution were guaranteed by series of political checks and balances. The powers of the *Doge*, the head of the Venetian state, were considerably circumscribed by the Greater Council and the Council of Ten, the latter being instituted specifically to guard the existing constitution. Venice's landward expansion had resulted in the creation of a landed aristocracy, which increasingly monopolized the offices of state, but it was due to these

THE COLOUR OF VENICE

The basilica of San Marco in Venice has long been an inspiration to artists living and working in the city. Its walls and domed ceilings are covered with shimmering gold mosaic and rich images from the Book of Genesis. Giovanni Bellini, Titian's master, sought to replicate the properties of mosaic in his own painting, moved by the way light was reflected off the glass tesserae.

Not only were the Venetians influenced by their past, but the modern city itself contributed to their fascination with colour and light. Surrounded by lagoons and myriad canals, the light reflecting off the surface of the water on to the buildings gave the city a chameleon-like quality, changing its colour from moment to moment.

From the 1540s the use of colour was the primary concern for many artists working in Venice. They sought to achieve a harmonious whole by relating one colour to the next using subtle gradations of colour and tone. The overall effect was a sense of realism that had never been seen before in painting.

They often employed a limited palette especially, in Titian's case, where he is known to have used only red, blue and green in some paintings. But the saturation and intensity of colour used by Venetian artists and the modulation of tone produced results of remarkable subtlety.

The Venetians, and Titian in particular, brought about an intellectual quality as well as sensuality to colour. Titian may have been aware of Aristotle's theories, among others. The Greek philosopher first put forward the idea that the

institutions that Venice remained a republic and an independent polity until the late eighteenth century. These wealthy families were also central to the development of the artistic culture of the city, as they patronized poets and artists as a means of securing their names for posterity and embellishing the many *palazzi* of Venice and its hinterland.

Despite its relative decline, the Venetian republic was still a centre of conspicuous wealth. Its economic prosperity was based on the importation from Africa, the Levant and the Black Sea of an almost unimaginable variety of luxury products – sugar, wine, spices, porcelain, pearls, gems, minerals, dyes, peacock feathers and silks. In turn from the Veneto it exported manufactured woollens, silks, and linens, with the strict provision that all trade must pass through Venice itself. The financial and banking sectors of the Venetian economy were extremely sophisticated. The deposit bank, the fundamentals of banking law, compulsory marine insurance and the concept of a national debt all originated in Venice, which was also a major centre of printing, with many of the earliest editions of classical texts being produced in the city.

When Titian arrived in Venice in 1500, therefore, it was a perceptibly wealthy, beautiful and sophisticated city offering highly lucrative possibilities to a young artist. Titian and Francesco's uncle introduced them to the workshop of a minor painter called Sebastiano Zuccato, where they were to commence their artistic training. Described by his biographers as a very precocious young man, Titian soon left Zuccato's workshop and continued to study painting in two rather more prestigious studios, first that of Gentile Bellini (*c.*1429–1507) and then with his more talented brother Giovanni (*c.*1431–1516). The Bellini family,

primary colours could not include yellow as it was a constituent of light and not a hue *per se*. In Titian's earlier works between 1510 and 1520 there are few examples of yellow being used on its own for objects within a painting, although it *is* used to denote the brilliance of light.

Titian's great talent as a colourist enabled him to maintain the brilliance of a specific colour, yet also relate it with great sensitivity to the other aspects of the painting. Titian was the master of this technique although it was one employed by other Venetian painters. In the sixteenth century it was already said 'Michelangelo for form, Titian for colour'

beginning with Jacopo and then his two sons, had emerged as an artistic dynasty in Venice, developing a luminous style that paid rigorous attention to detail and which began to use the landscape to striking effect in what were mainly religious paintings. Landscape had a charged, slightly nostalgic character in Venetian culture perhaps because in the founding of the republic it had been forced to abandon land for sea. In poetry and literature and increasingly in painting there was a kind of pastoral reverence and this seems to have been gleaned by the young Titian from his early experiences in Venetian studios.

The development of painting in Venice had taken a slightly different course from elsewhere in Italy. Initially proximity to and closer contacts with the Byzantine East slowed down the influence of the artistic innovations taking place in other Italian cities in the fourteenth century, and Venetian painters in particular remained attached to Byzantine artistic conventions. But Venice also drew culturally upon its extensive Italian hinterland, and its immense wealth, both public and private, soon made the city one of the principal centres of art. It is to be noted, however, that few of the famous artists of the so-called 'Venetian School' were from the city of Venice, but were, like Titian, mostly natives of the Venetian provinces. By the beginning of the sixteenth century a distinct manner of painting was emerging in Venice, which differed to that of central Italian artists, with their concerns for design and draughtsmanship. The Bellini family – notably Giovanni – played an important role in the Venetian Renaissance, when Venetian painting began to display its own special characteristics – mastery of colour and appreciation with light verging on obsession. These features were themselves essential reflections of Venetian life – the light brilliantly reflected in canals and lagoons undoubtedly prompted painters to focus on capturing its peculiar qualities. Similarly, the extravagant and vibrant costumes worn at Venice's famous balls and carnivals may underlie the concern for rich, bright colours in new and exciting combinations. One further significant element of Venetian painting was the city's damp climate, which made fresco painting difficult and caused artists to favour oil painting as a medium. As a result, Venetians experimented in oils further than did other Italian painters. Around the last quarter of the fifteenth century oil painting began to replace tempera all over Italy, but oil painting on canvas rather than panel was largely a Venetian innovation, and one that Titian developed more than any other artist of his day.

Titian's earliest works on both canvas and panel are small religious or mythological pictures which show how much he had absorbed from the Bellinis but also suggest a more youthful inspiration, that of the most talented young artist in the city – Giorgione (Giorgio da Castelfranco, c.1476/78–1510) – with whom he began to collaborate and study. Giorgione introduced Titian to the new developments in Venetian art that he himself had pioneered, notably small-scale paintings of secular subjects, designed to appeal to private collectors and connoisseurs. An interest in the nude as a subject and a greater emphasis on landscape in composition, were also distinctive features. Titian's three years with this outstanding but tragically short-lived master of Italian Renaissance painting had an enduring influence on his work; indeed, to such a degree that certain paintings now attributed to Titian were once thought to be Giorgione's, and vice versa, a confusion stemming in part from the fact that Titian completed several of Giorgione's works left unfinished at his death in 1510, including the iconic and erotic masterpiece *Sleeping Venus* which now hangs in the Gemäldegalerie in Dresden.

They first worked together at the end of 1508 on what was Titian's first significant commission, the frescoes of the Fondaco dei Tedeschi, a vast trading centre (and now the central post office) recently ravaged by fire and with a large façade facing on to the Grand Canal on which Giorgione worked. Titian was given the less prestigious task of decorating the side of the Fondaco and even though only fragments of both artists' work survive, they are enough to dispel the idea – which stemmed in part from Vasari – that Titian was an inferior imitator of Giorgione at this stage in his early career. Giorgione produced a stylish, elegant scheme evident in the frescoed *Nude* which survives today in the Ca' d'Oro in Venice; Titian produced a more robust and dynamic series of images, not least a dramatic depiction of *Judith* (or *Justice*, as some believe it to be) wielding a sword and trampling on a bloody head. Titian began his work just as the threat to Venice from the League of Cambrai led by the Holy Roman Emperor became dangerous and it is best seen as an attempt to promote the idea of Venetian civic and military virtue. In years to come, the Emperor and his successors became more interested in Venetian artistic virtue, particularly that of Titian.

Over the next five years Titian produced a series of scenes set in idealized landscapes which owe a huge debt to Giorgione but also became the bedrock on which he built his own style and reputation. In both *The Flight into Egypt* (c.1509–10, Hermitage, St Petersburg) and *Noli me Tangere* (1510–15, National Gallery, London) biblical dramas unfold in paintings which begin to integrate figures and their surroundings in a way that enhances the poignancy of the scene.

In the latter, taken from St John's gospel where Christ miraculously appears to Mary Magdalene after His death and bids her 'Do not touch me' as she seeks to verify that it is her risen Lord, the way that Titian paints His shroud with a bluish shadow seems to bring the sky down to earth in the picture. Likewise, the sunlight glinting on Mary's hair is reproduced on the distant flock of sheep and on the bleached thatched roofs of the buildings in the distance, creating a powerfully unified vision of humanity and its surroundings. X-rays reveal that Titian worked out much of the composition on the canvas directly and modified line form and colour throughout the process of painting to produce what is tantamount to visual poetry.

By 1514, four years after Giorgione had become a victim of the savage plague epidemic which had swept through the city, Titian established his own workshop with two assistants, one of whom – Ludovico di Giovanni – had worked for Giovanni Bellini. By this time Bellini was an old man, and Titian's other potential rival, Sebastiano del Piombo (c.1485–1547), had left for Rome. Titian was thus fortunate in the timing of his career; the dearth of competition allowed his newly created workshop to become quickly one of the most successful in Venice. In 1516 he was commissioned to paint a new work for the high altar in the Franciscan church of Santa Maria Gloriosa dei Frari, a prestigious project which resulted in the largest work of his career and still one of the most staggering images in a city teeming with powerful paintings. The subject Titian chose was the *Assumption of the Virgin* and for two years he worked directly on to the twenty-one wooden panels assembled in the convent attached to

Assumption of the Virgin
1516–18, Santa Maria Gloriosa della Frari Church, Venice
This monumental work towers above the altar of the Frari Church. It is nearly seven metres tall and made up of twenty-one wooden panels, three centimetres thick, dovetailed tightly together but occasionally visible after nearly five centuries *in situ*. The painting shows the Assumption of the Virgin Mary, her ascent to heaven in glory after her earthly life was complete celebrated by the Church every August but not part of the New Testament. Previous versions of the subject in Venice, notably

Giovanni Bellini's painting from 1513 at the church of Santa Maria degli Angeli on Murano, depicted the Virgin as a static, hieratic figure borne aloft on a very solid platform of clouds and angels. Titian opts for an altogether more fluid affair, an image full of energy, vitality and luminosity.

The picture is effectively split into three sections: rooted to the ground but with their hands and thoughts stretching upwards are the apostles, statuesque figures which seem to stop the painting from drifting off into space; in the middle is Mary herself, gently ascending on a wispy cushion of cloud, seemingly garlanded

by angels; and at the zenith is God, a sage-like bearded man stretched across the heavens full of gravitas and gravity-defying at the same time. Each section has its own perspective and proportions. God is twisted diagonally to the scene below as if to subvert the traditional notion of static symmetry. But Titian is able to unify all the disparate elements in his painting through a carefully constructed colour scheme dominated by vibrant reds, counterbalanced by strong greens and bound together by a dazzling golden glow.

The work is framed in an elaborate marble frame or aedicule believed to be

designed by the Venetian sculptor Lorenzo Bregno, but almost certainly reflecting some of Titian's own ideas. Its aim is to keep out the strong Venetian light, to let the picture illuminate the altar which it duly does. But visit the church in the very late afternoon as the sun is sinking; as it moves behind the west windows of the church, suddenly you'll catch the dazzling light streaming in to the right of Titian's early masterpiece, complementing the warm, golden glow but, in spite of the artist's fears to the contrary, never threatening the radiance of the painting itself.

the Frari church. The subject itself was traditional enough (Giovanni Bellini had recently painted a version on the island of Murano), but Titian's treatment was innovative, even radical. The painting was full of movement and light, with each of the three sections – the apostles below, the Virgin ascending on a cloud surrounded by angels and God the Father hovering above the billowing drama – bound together by a luminous golden glow and heightened colour scheme. The friars reputedly harassed Titian for his seemingly odd proportions, notably the monumental figures at the bottom of the picture, but he explained that the work had to be viewed *in situ*, high above the altar. The guardian of the Franciscan convent who had commissioned the work, Germano da Casale, was unsure about the dazzling colour but when the imperial ambassador offered to buy the work the realization dawned that this was an outstanding painting and it was duly unveiled on 19 May 1518.

The *Assumption* was a significant achievement. A contemporary critic compared it to 'the magnitude and awe of Michelangelo, the pleasantness and beauty of Raphael and the true colours of nature.' In fact, the altarpiece made Titian the most celebrated Venetian painter of his day. Again the timing was crucial; Bellini died in the year of the commission and the old master's former patrons among the princely houses of northern Italy were looking for a figure of similar stature. Chief among these were the Gonzaga family of the court of Mantua and the Este family of Ferrara; Titian became very popular with both these families but most importantly with the latter. When Titian was in his early thirties, Alfonso d'Este, Duke of Ferrara invited him to his court, permitted him to study his phenomenal collection, paid him to purchase additional works of art and commissioned paintings directly from the increasingly celebrated Venetian artist. The most important commission he received from the Duke was the decoration of a study known as the Alabaster Room. Other famous artists had already contributed to the decoration of this room; Raphael and Fra Bartolomeo had both died before finishing their work, and Titian reworked Bellini's *The Feast of the Gods* (1514, National Gallery, Washington) to correspond to his own style. In turn he produced three large, luscious mythological scenes over a period of ten years: *The Offering to Venus* (1518–19, Prado, Madrid), *Bacchus and Ariadne* (1520–23, National Gallery, London) and *Bacchanal of the Andrians* (1523–29, Prado, Madrid).

The Bacchanalian trilogy, as they might be called, are richly coloured, formally elegant and utterly hedonistic: *The Offering to Venus* is a cherubic vision where a sea of angelic figures proffer fruit to the statuesque Venus; the *Bacchinal of the Andrians* is a sensual feast full of languid erotic energy; but best of all is *Bacchus and Ariadne*, a startling scene where two people have just clapped eyes on each other and seem to have fallen head over heels with each other. Ariadne has just been deserted by Theseus on the island of Naxos. Desolately she waves at his departing ship. Suddenly, out of the blue – a deep lapis lazuli – there's a crash of cymbals and a rush of energy as the wine god Bacchus and his entourage appear. A dog barks; serpents writhe around the body of a snake-man-cum-Laocoon figure; a chariot is drawn by leopards followed by nymphs and goat-footed satyrs. Out of the chariot Bacchus leaps – a graceful jump but one that is forever held, suspended in mid-air, a perfect frozen moment which still takes the breath away. His merry band are intoxicated by the wine but he is intoxicated by the woman at whom he stares, fixated as if his heart had stopped beating. A pagan scene has probably never been painted with such relish or gusto as this one, nor perhaps has the spine-tingling sensation of falling in love.

The success in Ferrara helped crystalize the idea that an artist could potentially promote himself successfully in numerous places. Titian was one of the first Venetian artists to be aware of the importance of public relations, hiring agents to promote his workshop internationally. He was so successful in the art of self-promotion that he was repeatedly invited to move permanently to Rome by the papal court but with characteristic good business sense he decided to continue to cement his reputation in and from Venice. Titian ran his workshop as a tight, quasi-modern commercial venture. He applied a very strict organizational regime to his business and selected all his collaborators with great care. His brother, son and various cousins all worked for him but he also attracted numerous other painters to his studio, including an artist who became one of his few credible Venetian rivals, Jacopo Tintoretto (1518–94), and perhaps even the young Domenikos Theotokopolous, later known as El Greco (1541–1614). In his later years he became so successful that he could chose exactly for whom he wanted to work, and that various patrons had to accept work only partly or sometimes barely touched by Titian himself but signed by the maestro, a practice that angered many art collectors. He also helped to introduce the notion of copyright into art by another shrewd business venture in which he charged a specially chosen engraver for permission to reproduce his paintings.

The workshop flourished in Venice in the 1520s with two commissions for the principal convent churches of the city, the Frari, where his first major altarpiece was sited, and Santi Giovanni e Paoli, where the leading soldiers and politicians of the republic were buried. In this vast church Titian produced an image of *The Death of St Peter the Martyr*, described by Vasari as 'the most complete, the most celebrated and the largest and best conceived work that Titian had produced'. The work, finished in 1530, was tragically destroyed in a fire in 1867 and only descriptions remain. There is, however, the preceding commission in the Frari which remains a work of monumental invention. *The Pesaro Madonna* (1519–26, Santa Maria Gloriosa dei Frari, Venice) was commissioned by the Venetian Bishop of Paphos on Cyprus, Jacopo Pesaro, in 1519 for his family altar. It commemorates the Battle of Santa Maura in which Bishop Jacopo successfully led the Venetian and papal fleets against the Turks, an important event in the annals of the Pesaro family. It was not completed until 1526 and recent X-ray research suggests that Titian radically rethought the composition after having painted an initial version. The painting shows the Madonna and Child surrounded by the saints Anthony, Peter, Francis and either George or Maurice holding the Pesaro family banner. In addition Bishop Jacopo himself is present in the sacred scene along with other members of his family, their piety writ large in a picture which is solemn but characteristically vibrant in colour. Where Titian really innovates, however, is in the composition itself. Such scenes were invariably frontal but here Titian rotates the central image by forty-five degrees which generates a more dynamic sense of space. In turn, there are two gigantic columns which soar upwards and out of the canvas, enhancing the sense that the painting is a mere fragment of a vast world beyond. Mary and her son are placed in front of the right-hand column but if the viewer walks to the left of the painting in the Frari the Virgin shifts centre stage, framed by the pillars but seemingly in a fluid space apart. It's an engaging, visceral and surprising experience, a monument to Titian's enduring power to startle the viewer. It also anticipates many of the central concerns of the Baroque altarpiece nearly a century later.

One of the main reasons for Titian's swift rise to celebrity was his large and varied output. From very early in his career, as well as works destined to be put in prominent public places, he painted numerous smaller works for private collectors. His international reputation was largely founded on his portrait practice which was vigorous and direct from the outset. In a work like *Portrait of a Young Man* (at the National Gallery in London, painted around 1512), Titian depicts a sitter once thought to be the poet Ariosto leaning on a ledge which is flat onto the picture plane. The man, however, is in profile, his exquisitely rendered blue silk sleeve clearly projecting over the ledge as if moving into our world. He looks slightly down his nose at us as if to tell us that he has more important things to think about than us gazing at his likeness. In later portraits Titian pays the same attention to sumptuous detail and brings his sitters to life through the glint of an eye or the nuance of an expression. He introduced the half-length portrait that had been developed in Florence at the end of the previous century to Venetian art. In a work like his *Portrait of Federico Gonzaga*, painted between 1523 and 1525 and now in the Prado, Madrid, the format permitted the appearance of the Mantuan aristocrat's dog and sword to amplify his status as humane gentleman and soldier, an image of quiet, dignified power. When used to depict women, however, Titian's sensual obsessions moved to the fore. *Flora*, painted around 1520, seems to have been designed as a trophy image for a wealthy man and, as such, can be described as an example of a courtesan portrait, which the patron commissioned for his bedroom or private study. The courtesan portrait, a half-length portrait of a woman sensually clothed, had became increasingly popular in sixteenth-century Venice. This type of painting was often hung behind curtains and displayed only to select male visitors. The figure of Flora, the protagonist of the most popular and most licentious ancient Roman festivals, was known in antiquity and during the Renaissance as both goddess and courtesan. The classical pretext for such eroticism was fairly flimsy; Flora is removed from her mythical setting by the contemporary long white undershirt she wears. Part of the eroticism stems from the dreamy, ambiguous look of the sitter and with one breast covered and the other revealed she exemplifies the duality of virtue and vice. Courtesans were high-class prostitutes, well versed in poetry, literature and music and the demand for both ordinary prostitutes and courtesans was high in a city which received numerous visitors then as now. Out of a population of around 125, 000 at the beginning of the sixteenth century it has been estimated that nearly 12,000 women were involved in prostitution. It was big business and actively encouraged by the government as a means of attracting commerce to the city. There was even a catalogue of Venetian courtesans with addresses, prices and descriptions made available to important or at least wealthy visitors.

Titian's own relationships with women have been a tad sentimentalised. Various art historians seem unable to refer to Titian's wife Cecilia without the epithet 'beloved' in front of it and although there's no reason to doubt his love the notion that he remained devastated for the rest of his life after her death in 1530 and remained alone is somewhat exaggerated. Cecilia came from the neighbouring village to Titian and they married in 1525 while she was ill and in order to legitimize their two sons. Subsequently Titian had a child called Lavinia, in all probability with a second wife whose name is unknown; he later also had an illegitimate daughter. Soon after Cecilia's death, Titian moved home, family and studio to a smart house in the Biri Grande near the Fondamente Nuove, a sign that he was now a wealthy man, living the life of a Venetian gentleman. Vasari described him as 'very kind and well

bred, and being possessed of the gentlest habits and manners'. Titian differed significantly from his most celebrated artistic contemporaries, Michelangelo, Leonardo and Raphael, in that his interest always remained rooted in painting. He did not venture into other artistic fields such as sculpture or architecture, nor was he a great intellectual. Titian himself was aware of his deficient mastery of language and once described his profession as being 'alien to forming words'. His own lack of intellectual refinement made his relationship with the distinguished poet Pietro Aretino (1492–1557) all the more beneficial. Aretino was one of Titian's most important friends, who arrived in Venice soon after the Sack of Rome in 1527 and became one of the republic's and Titian's great propagandists. He was principally famous for his published letters, which had won him many important enemies – Michelangelo among them – and earned him the epithet *Il Flagello dei Principe* ('the scourge of princes'). But he also wrote frequently, lucidly, and sometimes extravagantly of Titian's talent to the extent that Vasari claimed that Aretino made the painter 'known wherever his

Portrait of Charles V on Horseback
1548, Prado, Madrid
This is the largest portrait Titian ever painted and probably the grandest. It shows the Emperor Charles V on a black horse, clad in the armour in which he led the Habsburg army and defeated the Protestant forces at the Battle of Mühlberg on 24 April 1547. During the ensuing months the Emperor's chancellor and Titian exchanged letters devising the composition for a vast commemorative portrait. All manner of schemes were put forward but in the end Titian chose a format which had its origins in classical and Renaissance sculpture, the equestrian monument.

The association with antique art, and particularly with the statue of Marcus Aurelius on horseback which stands on the Capitoline Hill in Rome, is pronounced and establishes the military and political pedigree of the most powerful man in sixteenth-century Europe. Instead of brandishing a sword or short spear, as he would have done in battle, Titian depicts Charles holding a long spear of the type used by Roman Emperors. This enhances his classical credentials but also reinforces the controlled thrust from left to right which dominates the composition.

Once again, colour orchestrates the mood of the picture. The pinkish red of the Emperor's sash and saddle is mirrored by the plumage on his head and that of his horse. In the distance, the sun sets, casting a warm glow that fills the painting, but the dazzling reflection from Charles's armour seems to come from a different source as if to suggest that he is a self-contained and illuminating presence. No one else appears in the picture and the image is one of a man alone, riding triumphantly towards a glorious destiny, an heroic warrior, but a humane Christian one at that.

Charles also commissioned Titian to paint the portraits of various defeated Protestant leaders who took part in meetings at the Diet of Augsburg in 1547 and 1548 to establish a religious settlement.

The work is vast and does suggest a detached, remote figure. He stares into the distance, his expression solemn, his pronounced Habsburg jaw jutting out with an air of defiance. But look again and there is a faint glint in the eye that suggests human intimacy. Titian knew his subject, and conversed with him in spite of the jealousies that this provoked among other courtiers for whom the Emperor was tantamount to a demi-god. And it is this knowingness that makes the painting stand apart and which makes it more than a dextrous piece of imperial propaganda.

On another level, though, its scale and ambition struck a chord with artists such as Rubens and van Dyck in the following century and so it is that Titian can claim to be the father of a new pictorial genre, the full-length, full-blown equestrian portrait.

pen could reach and especially to princes of importance.'

It was partly through Aretino's recommendations but mainly through the introductions of the Duke of Mantua that Titian came to the notice of the most important of princes and the man who became his most prestigious patron yet, the Holy Roman Emperor Charles V. At the age of nineteen Charles Habsburg (1500–58) had become the most powerful ruler in Europe, and ultimately the founder of the Habsburg dynasty. Few if any men in history can have possessed so many titles. Generations of dynastic alliances had culminated in this one man inheriting immense and disparate dominions from Hungary to Peru. As Emperor Karl V (1519–56) he ruled over the whole of Central Europe; as King Carlos I of Spain (1516–56) he also had access to the riches of the New World. His life was dominated by near-continuous conflict with the King of France in the west and with the Ottoman Sultan in the east, while he simultaneously sought to heal the Protestant schism that had divided western Christendom. Titian first met him briefly in 1529, attended his coronation in 1530 in Bologna and within two years had been commissioned to paint the imperial portrait.

Titian's first portrait of Charles has since been destroyed but the earliest remaining image of the Emperor perhaps had a greater impact. *Portrait of Charles V with His Dog* (Prado, Madrid) was painted at Charles V's court in Augsburg in southern Germany and is Titian's earliest full-length portrait, a form pioneered by German artists in the early sixteenth century. In terms of composition Titian's painting is identical to one by the Austrian artist Jakob Seisenegger (*c.*1505–67), probably painted only a year before but with every detail, from dog to intricate robe, reinvigorated and brought grandly and warmly to life. The background is dark and Charles has the appearance of having stepped into the light which has metaphorical as well as visual overtones. He has a swagger to him, confident and with a hint of nonchalance as he holds his mastiff. Here, the picture seems to be saying, is a man in control of his world. In the end, in spite of Seisenegger's credible international reputation, there was no competition and Charles declared that he would be painted by no one else but Titian. In turn Titian was made an official member of the imperial court in 1533 and given the title of Knight of the Golden Spur and Count of the Lateran Palace. Over the next two decades, Titian produced various images of the imperial family and the Emperor himself, not least the majestic and monumental image of *Charles on Horseback* from 1548 after the battle of Mühlberg the previous year (Prado, Madrid). The painting celebrated the Habsburg victory over the Protestant princes of Mühlberg the previous year but it also mythologized Charles as a great soldier and initiated an entire genre in

European painting, the equestrian portrait. It flourished over half a century later, first under Rubens and then his pupil van Dyck but it was forged by the creative bond between Charles and Titian.

The attention of Charles V greatly enhanced Titian's international reputation and consequently the most powerful and prestigious patrons in Europe sought his services. In short, he was fashionable to the point of being the first artistic celebrity of the modern world. His client list read as a *Who's Who* of mid-sixteenth-century Europe. It already included the names of d'Este and Gonzaga but subsequently he was able to add, among others, Medici, d'Avalos, Farnese and della Rovere. The last of these were the ducal family from Urbino and in 1536 Titian painted the portrait of the Duke himself, Francesco Maria della Rovere (1490–1538), and his wife Eleonora. Two years later, Francesco Maria died and was succeeded by his son Guidobaldo. In the same year (1538) Guidobaldo della Rovere commissioned a work whose impact has reverberated throughout the subsequent history of Western art, the so-called *Venus of Urbino* (Ufizzi, Florence).

Titian was clearly inspired by Giorgione's *Sleeping Venus* (c.1510, Gemäldergalerie, Dresden), which he himself had completed. But Titian's figure, described in initial correspondence as just 'the naked woman' (the classical tag was given later), lies on a crumpled bed rather than in an undulating rural setting and she fixes her gaze without bashfulness on the viewer rather than languidly dozing with eyes firmly closed. There are various interpretations possible in Titian's painting and there are certain ambiguities surrounding the commission itself (see caption, p.150) but the sensual nature of the image and the erotic charge conveyed by the eyes, the cascading and slightly dishevelled hair and the hand concealing and enticing the viewer to look at her pudenda are unmistakable.

The *Venus of Urbino* is characteristic of a new type of secular easel painting destined for a purely private market. Although earlier artists had justified nudes with heavy classical contexts, such as Raphael's *Galatea*, no one before Titian had placed such an openly sexual image of a woman in a non-classical setting. Subsequently, he produced a handful of other Venuses, full of sensuality, but none with quite the impact of this particular one. The image is a landmark of eroticism in Western painting and came to influence many subsequent depictions of women in art. Ironically, however, by the time Titian died the entrenchment of conservative Catholic attitudes in the Counter-Reformation had imposed a censorship on erotic paintings that slowed down the demand for nudes of this kind. But it was only temporary. Over the following centuries Velázquez, Goya, Manet and Picasso are

just four of the more illustrious artists who have paid homage to and been inspired by Titian's reclining Venus.

In 1545, in his mid-fifties, Titian finally visited Rome. He was invited by the grandson of Pope Paul III – Cardinal Alessandro Farnese – and stayed in an apartment overlooking the Vatican. In a letter to Charles V, Titian wrote of his interest in the city's numerous classical monuments: 'I am learning from these marvellous ancient stones,' but the primary purpose of the trip was patronage: first, for his son Pomponio, who had become a priest and who wanted a grand living which Alessandro Farnese suggested he could provide; second, artistic patronage for himself – not least the sale of another erotic picture with classical overtones, the *Danaë*, (Gallerie Nazionale di Capodimonte, Naples), which Titian completed for the Cardinal during his stay in Rome. In turn, he painted portraits of the Farnese family, including the Pope himself. Pope Paul III (1468–1549; r.1534–49) was seventy-seven years old at the time. He spent most of his pontificate furthering the secular and ecclesiastical ambitions of his family, the Farnese, but was also the first pope to take effective steps to counter the Lutheran heresy, including the institution of the Jesuit Order (1540) and the Inquisition in Rome. Titian had first

Venus of Urbino

1538, Ufizzi, Florence

No one is sure who she is or why exactly she came to be painted, but Titian's image of a reclining naked female figure has become one of the icons of western art. We know that Guidobaldo della Rovere bought her in 1538 and that in various correspondence he refered to her as 'the naked woman'. The idea of Venus came later and gave the work an air of classical gravitas. Urbino was where Guidobaldo came from – and became duke of – and where the painting resided for nearly a century before it was moved to Florence, where it has remained ever since.

Speculation has ranged from the slightly ludicrous notion that the model might have been Guidobaldo's mother Eleonora Gonzaga (imagine what Freud would have made of that) to the idea that it was one of Titian's lovers. Certainly the intimacy with which she is portrayed suggests a physical closeness but it is more than likely that Titian was producing an idealised image of eroticism based on more general and imaginative sexual experience.

Venus stares unblinkingly at the viewer, utterly confident and with a coquettish glimmer in her eye. Both her ruffled hair and the crumpled sheet on which she lies suggest that the image is post-coital. Her hand conceals her pudenda but draws the viewer's gaze towards it.

Her skin is painted with the most extraordinary lustre. Titian was experimenting with slow-drying oils and was able to apply layer upon layer of translucent paint which came close to reproducing the texture and tone of human flesh.

There are other important details, not least the rose that she holds – a symbol of the pleasure and constancy of love; likewise the dog at her feet and the myrtle plant on the window sill are symbols of conjugal loyalty. In the background of the painting, two servant women are either putting garments and bedding into a cassone or taking them out. This hints at the most likely purpose of the painting. Guidobaldo had married four years

previously. His bride – Giulia da Varano – was still a child of thirteen or so. The picture praises the importance of fidelity, celebrates marriage, hints at the importance of running a household competently and gives a delicate but nonetheless explicit image of woman as sexual goddess. It is a painting that has inspired numerous copies and various masterpieces from Goya's *Maya* to Manet's *Olympia* and beyond. It has angered feminists as a demeaning depiction of female sexuality but has also been seen as an image of an empowered woman. It remains, however, a landmark in the history of erotic art specifically and Western painting generally.

painted him two years earlier in Bologna without his camauro (papal hat) and then repeated the same three-quarter-length pose whilst in Rome but adding the camauro this time and also the setting sun behind the ageing man. Most striking was the group portrait of *Pope Paul III with his Grandsons Alessandro and Otavio Farnese* (Museo Nazionale del Capodimonte, Naples) which shows a psychologically charged scene where the old man still plays power politics with his family, scheming with Otavio as Alessandro looks dolefully and with a certain aloofness towards the viewer. Although Titian's images of the Pope were partly inspired by Raphael's *Portrait of Julius II*, of which he made a copy, Titian's portrait is strikingly different. Instead of Raphael's precise, detailed depiction, the Venetian painter revels in colour, light and texture, with a looser brush and a more expressive effect. When Michelangelo saw the group portrait in Rome he is reported by Vasari to have praised it to Titian's face but said behind his back that 'he very much liked his colouring and style' but that 'it was a pity that in Venice they never learned to draw'. It is a myth that still endures in certain quarters but is almost entirely irrelevant. Titian's approach was not based on a classical and Florentine interest in the draughtsmanship. Instead, as work produced in the last three decades of his life shows with a vengeance, painterliness became the dominant force.

Towards the end of 1550, Titian went to visit Charles V in Augsburg where the Emperor told him of his decision to give up the imperial crown some time in the next few years and of his intention to divide his vast dominions between his brother Ferdinand, who would become the Holy Roman Emperor, and his son, Philip, who would inherit Spain, the Low Countries and the Spanish possessions in the New World. This duly happened when Charles abdicated in 1555 and coincided with Titian's own gradual abdication – of sorts – from the Venetian art world. With the exception of a few religious commissions, not least the staggering, tormented image of the *Martyrdom of St Lawrence* for the Crociferi church in 1559, Titian virtually stopped painting for Venetian patrons from the beginning of the 1550s. He was in his sixties, internationally celebrated and tired of the constraints placed on him in even the smallest of commissioned work. In turn, a new generation of younger, hungrier artists was emerging in the city, painters such as Jacopo Bassano, Paolo Veronese as well as Tintoretto. What Titian needed was enlightened, liberated patronage which gave him the freedom to create as radically as his imagination inspired him and individuals who were able to grasp what he was trying to achieve. In many respects, he found all this in the Habsburg family for whom he worked if not exclusively then certainly prodigiously over the next few years; in particular, he found a powerful and sympathetic new patron in Phillip II.

Titian painted the young King of Spain in waiting early in 1551, an image of youthful vulnerability and introspective soul searching. Two years later, Philip was confident enough to commission two pictures from Titian of what became a seven-part mythological series described as 'painted poems' or *poesies*. Beginning with a version of the *Danaë* and *Venus and Adonis* (both now in the Prado, Madrid), Titian explored the idea of painting pairs of figures inspired by Ovid's *Metamorphoses*, the Roman poet's account of the great classical myths and legends. Over the next decade, he produced images of Perseus and Andromeda, Diana and Actaeon, Diana and Callisto and the savage *Rape of Europa* together with an unfinished painting, *The Death of Actaeon,* which hangs in the National Gallery in London. Unlike the joyful bachanals of his youth, these mythological works were darker, more brooding and intense. They were ruminations on the human condition and its often brutal nature.

Diana and Callisto
1556–59, National Gallery of Scotland
This is one of the great *poesies* or painted poems produced by Titian for Philip II based on the classical myths and legends from Ovid's *Metamorphoses*. Within the series of eight paintings it forms a trilogy exploring the sensual power of Diana, a moon goddess and a huntress.

Titian's poetic metamorphosis in paint shows the saga of Callisto, the daughter of the King of Arcadia who became one of Diana's nymphs. She was seduced by Jupiter who temporarily transformed himself into a goddess in order to get close to her and Callisto subsequently became pregnant. When Diana discovered what had happened she transformed Callisto into a bear and set her hunting dogs on her but, Jupiter at last behaved

honourably, rescued her and transported her to the heavens and changed her into the constellation known as the Great Bear.

The painting shows the moment when Callisto is accused by Diana of breaking the rules, of allowing a man to seduce her. The goddess points a finger at the hapless nymph who is stripped to reveal her swollen stomach. It is a theatrical image from the gestures of the protagonists to the swaggering drapes that frame Diana and her immediate entourage but it is also a sinister image conveying the brutal power of the gods. The dog drinks at the stream but is crouched and ready to pounce; the huntresses gather their bows and arrows whilst Callisto has a doomed grimace of horror on her face. It is a frozen moment but one whose ongoing sense of action

is suggested by the fluid way in which Titian applies paint to canvas. Notably in the landscape and sky, colour is loosely applied but also among the figures there is a blurring of edges to the point where the contours and solidity of the bodies begin to dissolve. Paint is used fast and furiously in patches, dried and then applied again with fingers as well as brushes. The approach is direct, hands-on, and the visual effect hovers on the edge of focus, threatening to spiral out of control in places. Here then are the beginnings of Titian's full-blown late style, a radical, expressive approach and one which has had enormous impact on generation after generation of painters who seek to explore the fullest possibilities of their medium.

The Florentine art historian Giorgio Vasari

amended his influential *Lives of the Artists* after travelling to Venice in 1566 and seeing Titian in his studio. His revised version, published two years later, eulogized the Venetian painter but suggested that the *poesie* were 'made up of bold strokes and blobs, in such a way that seen from close up you cannot make anything out, but from afar they look perfect'. In addition, Vasari observed that 'although to many people they appaear to have been made easily, this is not the case, and the viewers are mistaken, because it is known that they are reworked, and that he returns to recolour them many times, you can imagine with what pains. This method is judicious, beautiful, astonishing, because it makes paintings seem alive and created with great artistry, disguising the labour involved'.

Figures are violated, raped by bulls, savaged by dogs or devoured by sea-monsters. Even when Diana's nymphs cavort nakedly in the woods, the spectre of death lingers. What makes the pictures so powerful and eye-catching, however, is less the subject matter – although clearly it helps – but more the way that Titian paints them. Here, colour becomes the building block for everything. Line is virtually dispensed with, as if to show Michelangelo just how far painting could move away from the rudiments of drawing. Of course, Titian used charcoal outlines on his canvas but then set about obliterating them with what his former pupil Palma Giovane described as 'masses of colour' applied with either 'a confident brush' or 'the stroke of a finger'. In this celebrated account of Titian at work, Giovane describes how he would work furiously on an image, sometimes 'producing the outlines of a beautiful figure with four strokes of the brush', but then 'having finished this foundation, he would turn the paintings up to the wall for several months'. The process was fast then slow, a layering of frenetic activity and then sometimes the rubbing out or destruction of part of the picture in order to create again. By the end of the process, according to Giovane 'Titian painted more with his fingers than his brush'.

It is a compelling idea where paint becomes something akin to clay, moulded and shaped by the hand of the painter in a painstaking process that becomes highly personal and expressive. The notion of the artist's direct and almost divine touch so strong in Romanticism three centuries later found something of its roots in Titian's later technique. The painting of *The Death of Actaeon* notwithstanding, a good deal of Titian's late work has been perceived as unfinished over the centuries because of the experimental looseness of brushstroke. Vasari wrote that some were intended to be seen at a distance and others were indeed not completed but all evidence now points to an artist who sought new, more direct and spontaneous means of painting which were right there in the viewer's face.

Titian's final years were marked by personal tragedy. An old man in his seventies may well have expected his close friends to die but the deaths of Charles V, the poet Aretino and his brother Francesco still hit him hard from the evidence of correspondence. In addition, the death of his daughter Lavinia in 1661 seems to have fuelled some notably anguished paintings, not least *The Entombment* (1565–70, Prado, Madrid) and various images of the Crucifixion where the sense of isolation and despair is acute. A more phlegmatic Titian re-emerges briefly in a late self-portrait, painted in 1567–68 and now in the Prado and continues in his moving rumination on the process of ageing, the *Allegory of Time Governed by Prudence* (c.1565) which hangs in the National Gallery in

London where past, present and future, youth, maturity and old age are depicted through three human and animal heads with Titian and a wry-looking wolf symbolizing a life almost past. Running across the top and around the heads reads an inscription in Latin which translates as: 'From the past the present acts with prudence in order not to ruin future action'.

Titian's very last work, completed after his death, was a *Pietà*, painted for the chapel of Christ in the Frari Church, the location of several of his earliest artistic triumphs. In 1576 Venice was once again ravaged by plague and the work was produced for the church on the understanding that he would be buried there. It is a dark, forbidding image; monumental, nearly life-size figures emerge out of the brooding blackness that contrasts starkly with the radiant light around the dead Christ's head. Poignantly, Titian paints himself and his son Orazio begging the Virgin Mary for protection against the plague. But neither was spared and nor were 70,000 other Venetians, a third of the city's population at the time. Titian died on 27 August 1576. The *Pietà* never made it to the Frari but the body of its creator did and Titian was buried flanked by two of his early masterpieces in a place which has become a place of pilgrimmage for modern painters.

7.

Bruegel
*c.*1524/30–69

All artists are subjected to the process of historical and critical reinterpretation, but perhaps none more so than Pieter Bruegel. His earliest biographer gave him the epithet 'Peasant' Bruegel but that was later replaced by the idea of Bruegel the intellectual, humanist and moralist. Most recently, his work has been examined in the context of capitalism and the burgeoning mercantile culture of Antwerp in the sixteenth century. In many respects his art tries to make sense of a rapidly changing world where almost every major ideology was being significantly questioned. His paintings, drawings and prints are full of intricate detail focusing on life as it is lived rather than the grander visions of Italian art with its classical and Christian heroes. Bruegel is perhaps the most humane of all the major European painters, a man whose interest in the everyday was epic in itself and whose work seems to survey a still largely medieval world from an early modern perspective.

Little is known about his life – our main source is Karel van Mander, who wrote Bruegel's biography thirty-five years after the artist's death. Among the many gaps is the date of Bruegel's birth, which is estimated as some time between 1524 and 1530. He is thought to have been born near the town of Breda in North Brabant. Brabant was one of seventeen separate provinces that comprised the Low Countries (modern Belgium, Holland and Luxembourg). The whole region was a patchwork of political privilege and cultural diversity; each of the provinces had its own parliament and was eager to preserve its independence and liberties. The south was predominantly French-speaking and Catholic, while the Dutch-speaking northern provinces had an expanding Protestant population. Flanders and Brabant bestrode this broad linguistic and religious divide. From 1551, all these provinces came under the rule of Spain, and for the rest of Bruegel's life the Low Countries were ruled by a series of regents for the Spanish King, a regime which became

The Parable of the Blind, 1568, Museo Nazionalz di Capodimonte, Naples

increasingly unsympathetic and oppressive. In particular, Philip II's (r.1556–98) disregard for provincial privileges and his intolerant Catholicism would soon provoke revolt. These provinces were nevertheless a vital possession for Spain. A highly developed capitalism and mercantile expertise meant that the cities of the Low Countries managed possibly half of all European trade, and as a consequence regional taxes were *seven* times greater than all the gold bullion of the New World.

Very early in his life, Bruegel left Breda for the nearby thriving city of Antwerp, at this time one of the great urban centres of Europe. Wealthy and prosperous, its impressive artistic and cultural achievements meant that it was often called 'the Florence of the north'. By the beginning of the sixteenth century, Antwerp had overtaken neighbouring Bruges and Ghent as the principal port of the Low Countries. The successful establishment of a sea route to the East Indies around the Cape of Good Hope, followed by discoveries and rapid exploitation in the New World, resulted in both a greater number of ships and vessels of greater tonnage. Antwerp was a perfect deep-water harbour at a time when the canals connecting Ghent and Bruges to the sea were silting up; it was reported that a thousand ships could anchor in its docks. It was also less dominated by the guilds that monopolized economic activity in other cities, and merchants were encouraged to move their warehouses there, especially those involved in the spice trade. The city subsequently became the chief banking centre of Europe. All these developments made the city an attractive location for artists and artisans – a burgeoning bourgeoisie offered a growing market for artists' talents, especially paintings as domestic adornments. As a result, it is said there were as many as three hundred artists' workshops.

Bruegel is thought to have become an apprentice to Pieter Coecke van Aelst (*c.*1502–50), who ran two successful studios in Antwerp and Brussels, of which Bruegel worked in former. Coecke had worked in both Italy and the Ottoman Empire as a painter and designer of stained glass and tapestries. He was well read and had translated architectural treatises from Latin and Italian. His wife assisted in these translations and was an accomplished painter in her own right. The Coeckes thus offered a very promising environment for an apprentice painter and Bruegel became close to the family; on one occasion he is recorded looking after their young daughter. (More than thirty years later, this girl became his wife.) Coecke was considered a leading Flemish painter of the time, painting in the Italian style of Raphael that was then popular in Antwerp. Bruegel was to follow an alternative line but Coecke's ambition and reputation were significant in the young Bruegel's development.

There were two basic types of painting style in fashion in the Low Countries at this time. The works of many of Bruegel's Flemish contemporaries, especially in Antwerp, showed the influence of Italianate forms and ideas. On both sides of the Alps, artists of the generation after Leonardo, Michelangelo and Raphael suffered from the broad consensus that, with these masters, art had attained perfection. In their efforts to imitate the Italian masters of the High Renaissance, many Northern painters produced rather artificial results. Effectively, they were Flemish artists attempting to use an Italian vocabulary they did not fully understand. This style was used extensively for church commissions and large public buildings and was considered the 'official art' of the time. Other artists were influenced more by the local Flemish tradition of contemporary, often everyday settings, represented in meticulously observed detail. Furthermore, in northern Europe these artistic concerns were subject to the effects of the Protestant Reformation, which prohibited religious paintings and brought to an end artistic traditions dating back centuries. Paintings and statues of saints and Madonnas were now regarded as idolatrous, and the spread of the Reformation was accompanied by often riotous iconoclasm, the destruction of religious images. In the Low Countries painting developed new subjects that were permissible in this changed religious climate. The long-standing traditions of painting strange landscapes and depicting peasant life were now more fully explored.

In 1550, the Catholic Bruegel is known to have worked in the studio of Claude Dorizi in Mechelen. The following year, he is recorded entering the Guild of St Luke in Antwerp, of which Coecke was Dean. He was clearly also interested in travelling south of the Alps, and soon thereafter he undertook a journey to Italy. This was not unusual; many Northern painters made similar trips, primarily to study Italian painting, which they knew only from engravings. There are few indications of his destination, but Calabria seems likely, with a stay in Naples, and subsequent journeys to Sicily and Rome. Detailed images of all these places feature in several engravings that subsequently emerged from Coecke's workshop. Of particular interest to Bruegel, however, was the Alpine scenery he experienced on this journey, notably in the Tyrol, so very different from the landscape of his native region. His drawings served as a pool of images for many of his later paintings and engravings. In marked distinction to his general disregard for Italianate influences, Bruegel's travels clearly broadened his experience and appreciation of landscape. Van Mander states that Bruegel 'swallowed all the mountains and rocks and spat them out again, after his return, on to his canvases and panels'.

During the Middle Ages, mountains were seen at best as frustrating obstructions, at worst the homes of devils. By Bruegel's time, attitudes had changed and artists and scholars were more intrigued by their size and mystery. It was around this time that the Alps were being climbed and scientifically mapped. There was a demand for paintings and prints that depicted far-away places, not just the flat landscape of the Low Countries. Distant travel for the ordinary man was dangerous and expensive, so these prints were a means of bringing uncharted territory into their homes. At a time of restricted horizons and limited travel, Alpine images might arguably have possessed as much novelty as exotic scenes from the newly discovered Americas. In 1555, Bruegel returned home and established himself in Antwerp. There, he began work with the engraver Hieronymus Cock (c.1507–70), who ran a renowned and highly productive workshop. Many of Cock's etchings and engravings were based on the work of Italian masters. The print was more than mere decoration; it was an important medium of the period for conveying information concerning other countries and recent events, though often the landscapes are not realistic. For inspiration, Bruegel looked back to Joachim de Patinir (c.1480–1524), who spent most of his career at Antwerp and was the first Flemish artist to be primarily a painter of landscapes. Patinir had raised landscape painting to a level of relative independence – a non-scientific interpretation of the world, filled with detail. Bruegel was not a mere copyist; his mountain scenes were more magnificent, higher and more precipitous. The first painting attributed to Bruegel is from 1553 and is entitled *Landscape with Christ Appearing to the Apostles at the Sea of Tiberius*. Its focus on natural detail, on a rocky coastal scene viewed from high above the cliffs, rather than on religious iconography, is a clear indicator of the path Bruegel was to pursue.

In Antwerp in the later 1550s, Bruegel enjoyed both a growing

EXPLORATION AND TRAVEL

The sixteenth century was a pivotal period in the evolution of the modern world, not least because of the strides taken to expand the possibilities for international travel and trade. As the physical horizons expanded, so too did the emotional ones. Throughout Europe, for example, a general interest in 'armchair travel' grew and with it the desire – among those who could afford it – to have prints showing the new lands and peoples that were being talked about.

The late 1400s had seen remarkable successes in exploration. Driven largely by economic ambition, sailors had been edging further and further afield – in particular, in the hope of establishing new spice routes. The Vikings may have discovered America but it was the later voyage of Columbus in 1492 that sparked the colonization of this vast continent. Shortly thereafter, the Florentine explorer Amerigo Vespucci (1451–1512), once the Medici agent in Seville – travelled there, and gave the continent its name.

The Portuguese were the most significant international explorers, not least for having navigated around the southern tip of Africa, thus opening the routes to the east (and significantly undermining the

reputation, largely based on his print-making, and a wider circle of friends and associates. These included Abraham Ortelius (1527–98), the famous geographer and compiler of the first modern atlas. His principal patron was Niclaes Jonghelinck, who over the next decade purchased sixteen of Bruegel's paintings. Through Jonghelinck, Bruegel became acquainted with Margaret of Parma's chief minister, Cardinal Antoine Perrenot de Granvelle (1517–86), who, though widely unpopular, was a generous patron of the arts. The financial security this brought allowed Bruegel to experiment in paintings which depicted proverbs or parables, or offered serious moral instruction. He took scenes and events from everyday life in the contemporary Low Countries and gave them a moral significance; occasionally, he reversed the process and took a biblical scene and recast it in the guise of a contemporary village saga, but the purpose was one and the same: in short, he produced picture sermons. This in itself wasn't original – most art of this period served a moral purpose – but where Bruegel differed from his contemporaries was in his ability to go beyond the conventional, to invest his paintings with recognizable human emotion and quotidian drama, a kind of theatre of the everyday but achieved through phenomenal powers of observation.

A perfect early example of this is *The Fall of Icarus* (Musées Royaux des Beaux-Arts, Brussels), produced some time between 1555 and 1558. It is the only mythological subject he ever painted but it reads as a contemporary parable. Having helped to manufacture wings from wax and feathers in order to escape from Crete, Icarus, the son of Daedalus, disobeyed his father and flew too near to the sun. When the wax melted, as Daedalus predicted, Icarus plummeted into the Aegean Sea. Bruegel would have been attracted to this story because it reveals the weakness and folly of man, one of his primary preoccupations as a painter. He makes Icarus seem even more ridiculous by practically hiding him in the

---

role of Venice as a middleman in the trade of goods, notably spices). The Portuguese also – almost by accident – landed in Brazil in 1500. In 1519–22, a Spanish expedition led by the Portuguese Ferdinand Magellan circumnavigated the globe.

The Spanish continued to finance ships – animated by the lure of foreign gold. Using Cuba – settled in 1511 – as a base for further conquest, Spain sent Cortéz to conquer the Aztecs in Mexico in 1520 and Pizarro the Incas in the 1530s. By 1600, a ship landed in Seville every couple of days.

The English, French and Dutch had little choice but to direct thier energies further north; gradually building colonies in North America. The English built an empire partially on the income from cloth, which was hugely popular in the Low Countries and especially in Spain and Portugal. Much of the profit from Brazilian sugar went straight to London. The key to this trade was Antwerp – core of English and Spanish trade until the crash of 1557–60, when the focus switched to Amsterdam

In 1602, the Dutch East Indies Company was born. It was later copied by the English East India Company, which marked the beginning of Britain's international and imperial ascendancy.

painting. He is tiny; all we see are his legs disappearing into the water.

The main subjects of the painting are the landscape itself and the men who work in it – the farmer, the shepherd and the fisherman. They are much larger than Icarus and are strangely oblivious to this great event. They carry on as if nothing has happened at all, unaware of or aloof from one cocky young man's ambitions. The common man and his labours on the land are seen as more important than one boy's remarkable, tragic attempt to fly. Bruegel has a deep understanding of the land dictating the nature of human existence and the notion that life continues, whatever else happens. He reinforces this message in an ingenious way. On the left edge of the painting, and almost out of sight, he shows a dead man lying under a bush – a reference to a contemporary Netherlandish proverb which translates as 'No plough stops because a man dies'.

One pictorial allusion to proverbial wisdom seems to have inspired an epic vision of many proverbs – over a hundred, in fact – crammed into a panel measuring nearly three feet by five and called *Netherlandish*

The Fall of Icarus

1555–58, Musées Royaux des Beaux-Arts, Brussels

At first glance, this picture reads as a pastoral idyll. A figure ploughs his field; a shepherd gazes up at the sky; a fisherman casts his rod into the shimmering blue sea. The landscape is serene, idealized slightly, doubtless the result of Bruegel's trip to Italy between 1551 and 1554. Look again, though, and things are not quite what they seem. In the sea, a pair of tiny legs are visible, as if a figure has just dropped out of the sky – and he has. For this is Icarus, the classical anti-hero who disobeyed his father Daedalus and flew too near the sun as they escaped from Crete with wings made from feathers and wax.

It is the only mythological painting

known to have been made by Bruegel and much of the detail is taken directly from Ovid's account in *Metamorphoses*, where he describes even the men at work as the drama unfolds. In this respect it is a literary picture, but the painter's imagination subtly shifts the emphasis. Icarus is supposed to be the central character, but is reduced to a ludicrous figure in the margins. His flailing legs are comic: they raise a smile from the viewer but not a flicker of pity or recognition from the men who go about their daily business.

In many respects, it is a clear-cut moral fable: excessive ambition will lead to disaster; moderation is a virtue, as is knowing one's place. Interestingly, Bruegel's favoured pictorial vantage point, high above the action, also has

judgmental overtones in this instance, mirroring the quiet distain of those who know their place and accept their lot in life.

Previously, commentators saw this as a sympathetic depiction of simple folk with simple aspirations, but this has recently been interpreted as a parody by Bruegel of the upper-class ideal of the common man who has no discernible ambition in an increasingly competitive mercantile culture. But it is also a picture of seemingly studied ambiguity. The sun is setting, so how has Icarus managed to melt his waxen wings? Where is his father Daedalus? (Presumably the shepherd is looking upwards at the figure but he is out of the frame.) Why do the labourers show no human pity? There may well be practical answers to some

of these questions, not least that this picture is a copy of the original. There is another, smaller version in a private collection in New York which does depict Daedalus, but the rest remains the same.

In the bushes on the left-hand side of the image, and barely visible above the horse's head, is the head of a dead man, a human corpse decaying in the shadows. 'No plough is stopped because a man dies' went the contemporary proverb. Life is harsh and wonderful at one and the same time, Bruegel seems to be saying; the landscape is serene and tough, it nourishes and it destroys; human beings are comic and tragic, they purport to live together, to seek comfort from each other, but, ultimately, they are alone.

Proverbs (1559, Staatliche Museen, Berlin). In 1500, the influential humanist scholar Erasmus of Rotterdam had published his *Adagia*, a book containing about 800 extended proverbs. Over the following decades, it was reprinted repeatedly and with numerous additions, struck a popular chord. In his painting, Bruegel sought to strike a similar chord and graphically to illustrate a vast range of human follies and foibles. Other artists had produced painted proverbs, but no one had attempted to depict so many at once. The painting is potentially a seething moral mass and mess, but Bruegel manages to compose the scene in such a way that it rings true. Perspective is accurate and each episode is bound into a pictorial whole as well as conveying its own particular message. It is as if Bruegel has created a Flemish village by the sea as a theatrical setting in which his characters can perform. Colour, particularly the striking use of reds and blues, helps unify the picture and although no one scenario stands out strongly above the others, the image of the woman in red placing a vivid blue hood over a man in the middle foreground of the painting could be claimed as the central image. Specifically, so the proverb goes, she is denouncing her husband as a cuckold; generally, the image berates the act of cheating and betrayal. To the right of the hooded cuckold, Christ Himself sits on a throne being mocked by a monk who puts a flaxen beard on the face of his saviour. All around, comedy and tragedy unfold in what now look like bizarre episodes, but which would have made immediate sense when viewed or 'read' by a contemporary audience. There is the pillar-biter – a Flemish term for a hypocrite. A man tries to shear a pig, stupidly following the example of his companion, shearing a sheep. Another falls from an ox on to a donkey, the equivalent of 'falling out of the frying pan into the fire'. A well is filled with a drowned calf floating in it – a Netherlandish version of closing the stable door after the horse has bolted. Men speak out of two mouths or sit in ashes between two stools. Daylight is carried in a bottomless basket; water is carried in a woman's hand. Like most proverbs, there is an ambiguity once one sifts around below the surface; they are open to various interpretations, however strong the initial concept seems to be. And so it is with Bruegel's paintings, where humour and menace often vie with each other for the viewer's attention in images which seem at once to celebrate human life but also hint at the futility of it all.

The quirky vision of the world encapsulated in *Netherlandish Proverbs* owed a small debt to Bruegel's Flemish predecessor, Hieronymus Bosch, which was soon to grow. Bosch (*c*.1450–1516) was from the small Dutch city of 's-Hertogenbosch. Next to nothing is known of his life, yet he left behind astonishing visions of hell, filled with every conceivable horror and torment – demons, monstrous animals and infernal machines. Deploying contemporary artistic techniques, which ranged from oil paint to perspective, Bosch conjured up all the hellish fears that preyed upon the medieval mind. The buyers of Bruegel's images perhaps had a slightly different attitude to these scenes than Bosch's audience. Increased literacy, vernacular Bibles and Reformation theology all tended to dilute popular superstition, and devils and demons were thought of in a less oppressive way than they had been a generation before. Nonetheless, Bruegel seems to have wanted to pay homage to Bosch's vision and to capitalize on the latter's popularity, which he did in a monumental sequence of apocalyptic paintings. *The Fall of the Rebel Angels* (Musées Royaux des Beaux-Arts, Brussels), painted in 1562, shows St Michael and his angelic assistants pummelling the dragon of the Apocalypse and giving various fallen angels a beating in the process. *Mad Meg* or *Dulle Griet* (Musée Mayer van den Bergh, Antwerp), produced around the same time, is an iridescent image full of hellfire and damnation in which a monstrous, demonic woman (Mad Meg) emerges from hell, having ransacked the place. She is, by implication, worse than hell itself.

The culmination of Bruegel's fascination with Bosch and the crowning image in the doom-laden sequence of paintings is *The Triumph of Death* (Prado, Madrid), one of the most epic portrayals of death ever painted, produced at the end of 1562. This is Bruegel at his Boschian best. No mortal is spared the inevitability of mortality – which is the result of sin rather than human frailty. The lovers singing in the lower right of the painting, for example, have Death joining in with a fiddle behind them; a king, bottom left, with a skeleton holding a timer behind him, tries to stop another skeleton from stealing his gold. The young, old, rich and poor are all shown at the mercy of the relentless, advancing skeletal army of Death. They cut people down *en masse* with scythes or pick them off one by one. Even the church cannot offer sanctuary; it is shown as a ruined building with a graveyard for a roof.

Once again, the vantage point is from above, a lofty image of utter depravity. It is a bird's-eye view or, better perhaps , it is God's-eye view – part of Bruegel's macabre sense of humour. There seems to be a sense of amusement gleaned from seeing the futile attempts of mortals fighting with Death. A joker tries to hide under a table but the joke, ultimately, is on him and the rest of sinful humanity. It is also thought that Bruegel was parodying the heroic battle scenes popular with the public at this time. Indeed, the dead are almost in battle formation – but the image, as is often the case in Bruegel's art, is anti-heroic.

The horrors of *The Triumph of Death* were not merely an artistic contrivance, but were in part inspired by contemporary events. The rule of Philip II of Spain had become increasingly difficult for the provinces to endure. The regency of Philip's half-sister, Margaret of Parma between 1559–67, saw the opening moves of the Dutch Revolt or Eighty Years' War (1568–1648), a momentous struggle in which the northern provinces ultimately rejected Spanish rule and established a republic. Philip's increasingly absolutist and centralizing regime was at odds with the privileges and liberties of the seventeen provinces and soon alienated the ruling political class. Social and economic factors – wars, plagues, poor harvests, flooding and drastic inflation – caused discontent among the lower classes, and made them susceptible to disorder. In addition, a loose grouping of Protestants, mainly lesser nobility and the urban middle class, found their position under Spanish rule precarious and therefore increasingly intolerable. The attempts of Margaret of Parma's regime to appease the various discontented factions proved unsuccessful. When a small group of Protestant nobles petitioned for church reform and religious toleration, Philip's outright refusal provoked rioting among the broader Protestant population in 1566 and, in particular, the widespread destruction of religious images. The efforts of the Protestant nobles to calm these disturbances were too late to avoid the full wrath of Spanish suppression. A new regency (1567–73) under the ferocious Duke of Alva saw the establishment of the so-called *Bloedraad* ('Blood Council') to execute the rebel nobles, and the full terror of the Inquisition. There followed open revolt across the whole of the Low Countries, even in the Catholic south. Bruegel's last years were filled with worsening atrocities – quasi-legal trials, casual murders, mass arrests and the sacking of cities. Although Bruegel died before the destruction of Antwerp in the 'Spanish Fury' of 1576, the deserted and charred landscape in *The Triumph of Death* was undoubtedly inspired by the context which led to the cataclysm, as well as being extraordinarily prophetic.

In 1563, Bruegel moved to Brussels. The reason for this is uncertain. Bruegel's biographer, van Mander, claims it was because of his marriage to Mayken, the daughter of his former master, Pieter Coecke van Aelst. Mayken's mother wanted Bruegel to leave Antwerp, where he had previously had a relationship with a servant girl which may well have offended the moral and social attitudes of his in-laws. But it is possible that the move was occasioned by what may have been his unorthodox religious beliefs. Some of his closest friends and associates, including many of the most influential businessmen in Antwerp, were thought to belong to a heretical sect called the Family of Love. Bruegel might well have been familiar with this sect or even have subscribed to its doctrines. The sect was very discreet and devotees were instructed to show signs of following the accepted religion to avoid suspicion, but Bruegel may have sought safety in dissociating himself. The truth is that we do not know for sure what Bruegel's beliefs were – but certainly we can hazard the guess that he sought reform from within the Catholic Church. His paintings of religious scenes give little or nothing away – he would not have wanted to experience the full force of the Inquisition – but he was an artist who constantly wrestled with moral issues in his work and rarely if ever presented simplified solutions.

After completing two paintings entitled *Tower of Babel (I)* (1563, Kunsthistoriches Museum, Vienna) and *Tower of Babel (II)* (c.1564, Museum Boymans-van Beuningen, Rotterdam) – both of which may have been attacks on princely pride as well as human hubris – he embarked on the largest of his surviving pictures, *Procession to Calvary* (Kunsthistorisches Museum, Vienna), signed and dated 1564. It depicts the traditional and moving scene of Christ carrying the Cross to Golgotha, where he will be crucified. Christ is a small figure hidden among a large crowd of over five hundred individually realized figures, illustrating

The Triumph of Death
1562, Prado, Madrid
This picture is both the culmination of Bruegel's obsession with the work of Hieronymous Bosch and an emphatic assertion of Bruegel's own apocalyptic vision as an artist. It also uses two traditions in the depiction of Death: the northern European image of the dance of death and the Italian version of the triumph of death where the Grim Reaper rides spectre-like on a pale horse brandishing a scythe. But Bruegel enhances everything and instead of one reaper there are hundreds; instead of a collection of strange hybrid monsters or fantastical creatures drawn from the depths of a morbid creative imagination such as those by Bosch, Bruegel presents an army of the most real

and chilling manifestation of human mortality – the skeleton.

The painting is highly detailed and complex, but the high vantage point (perhaps a God's-eye view) enables the viewer to see everything unfold simultaneously without losing the perspective and space which make the scene more credible.

The composition is layered with the most graphic scenes of carnage in the foreground, but the vast tomb and ruined church of the middle ground and the bleak, decimated landscape filled with gallows and burned-out buildings and ships in the distance still reinforce the idea of endless oppression when resistance is futile; in fact, it makes things worse. On the left-hand edge of the

picture, a knackered old nag, ridden by a skeleton, drags a cartload of human remains into view, drawing the eye slowly from left to right across torture and mayhem until it is confronted by the assembled cohorts of thousands of skeletal soldiers. The effect is a visual clash that seems to echo the screams suggested in the depiction of mass slaughter.

Each individual scenario is a microcosm of the whole picture where death befalls everyone irrespective of age or status. It is, Bruegel seems to be saying, a great equalizer. Justice of the harshest kind is meted out with a certain subtlety to fit the specific nature of the sinner's crime: in the bottom left-hand corner, a greedy king who has stolen

from his subjects is in turn ransacked by the skeleton who administers the death blow. Gamblers lose the ultimate bet and a pair of lustful lovers who play music together are oblivious of the spectre of Death playing a viol behind them.

As befits a dance of death, in the opposite corner of the picture to the lute-playing Lothario, two skeletons pull at ropes to ring a vast black bell, a death knell that reverberates throughout the painting, amplified by the grim gallows and gnarled trees which rhythmically punctuate the scene, together with the morbid poles with wheels on top where broken corpses are left as carrion for the circulating birds.

perhaps the indifference of Man to this momentous event, as well as Bruegel's mastery of detail and drama. Where Bruegel is most strikingly original, though, is in the contemporary figures and setting; it is treated like a modern-day execution. It has the feel of a day of festivity; no one pays much attention to Christ falling under the weight of the Cross in the middle. This would have been barely conceivable in Italy. The painting is peppered with miniature dramas; the landscape littered with wheels of torture and flesh-feeding birds similar to that depicted in *The Triumph of Death*. It is as if the human indifference or callousness shown here will lead inevitably to the carnage of the earlier painting. Some are portrayed walking away from the scene. The onlookers seem more interested in the two thieves in the cart in front, rather than Christ. Like *The Fall of Icarus*, the painting conveys a sense both that man is often ignorant and self-absorbed to the point of isolation and that life will carry on, even in the face of such a significant event.

Bruegel's patron, Niclaes Jonghelinck, who bought *Procession to Calvary*, certainly seems to have been pleased with the result. Soon after, he commissioned an ambitious series of works from Bruegel to decorate a large room in his new villa just outside Antwerp, the majority of which were completed in 1565. This new series was to run, frieze-like, around the top of the walls and depicted Man's ongoing and systematic relationship with the landscape over the course of the year. It is sometimes referred to as *The Months*, itself the term for a traditional visual sequence, originally inspired by medieval illuminated manuscripts. But no one is certain how many paintings Bruegel made. It could be that he did produce a twelve-part visual calendar but only five remain; it seems more likely that he painted six pictures, a bimonthly configuration which evoked the changing seasons in a slightly different way.

The series begins with the most celebrated of all the pictures, *Hunters in the Snow*, painted in 1565, and thought to be January, although December might well be included too. It is an image which conveys the bleakness of winter, with the hunters returning with their undernourished dogs and one fox, their sole catch; other figures struggle to lug firewood or hoist ladders up to extinguish a chimney on fire and yet the village doesn't just work or hibernate, it plays: skating, sledging, curling and ice hockey are all depicted on the frozen field turned playground on ice. The backdrop is breathtaking, a fictitious and sophisticated fusion of flat Netherlandish fields and magnificent Alpine mountains, a mixture which runs throughout the subsequent paintings.

In the following image, *Gloomy Day*, superficially at least, Man struggles more urgently with the elements, gathering firewood and repairing ravaged roofs as the storm clouds gather and billow in the distance, ready for yet another onslaught. Look again, though, and you see two men and a young boy in the right-hand foreground wearing paper crowns and stuffing waffles into their mouths, a reference to carnival time, to Shrove Tuesday, or *mardi gras*, making this an image of February or March, depending on when Easter falls. In the left-hand corner, barely discernible but there if you look hard enough, is a fiddler playing outside the tavern whilst a woman drags her child away in horror as a man leans pissing against the wall.

The spring months are missing but summer blossoms in *Haymaking*, a lush green scene with labourers carrying baskets overflowing with fruit and vegetables, whilst figures frolic in the fields as they gather up the hay. The golden glow of August or September pervades the panel depicting *Harvesters* as the wheat is scythed and figures prepare to picnic under the shade of a tree, eating some of the fruits of their labours. Finally, in the *Return of the Herd*, the leaves have fallen, the landscape has just turned from golden to brown and a herd of plump cattle are being driven purposefully from right to left across the picture and onwards towards their winter home.

Individually, the works are subtle barometers of change in mood and climate. They exist as self-contained images but, ultimately, they seem to read as a composite work of art where elements are to be experienced together, conveying a slowly unfolding panorama of human existence. Sadly this is no longer possible, but the Kunsthistorisches Museum in Vienna at least comes close with three of them hanging side by side.

Over the next two years, Bruegel continued with a loose series of large painted panels with complex compositions depicting various aspects of Flemish folk life. These relate closely to his works inspired by popular sayings and moral fables. Though these scenes were inspired more by studies of everyday occasions and festivals than by specific proverbs, they ultimately served the same purpose. The simple, artless peasants offered a better opportunity to study human actions, reactions and follies than the sophisticated urban bourgeoisie. These genre paintings, as art historians describe them, are characterized by Bruegel's perceptive observation of human nature and his wry wit. Van Mander records his preparatory method: apparently Bruegel met every day with a close friend, a wealthy Nuremberg merchant called Hans Franckert who enjoyed the artist's company, insight and sense of humour, which extended, on occasion, to Bruegel and Franckert dressing up as peasants to gatecrash peasant fairs and weddings:

> Disguised as peasants, they brought gifts like the other
> guests, claiming relationship or kinship with the bride or

groom. Here Bruegel delighted in observing the droll behaviour of the peasants, how they ate, drank, danced, capered or made love .

This anecdote immediately recalls the sort of painting for which 'Peasant' Bruegel is renowned. In 1566 he painted *The Wedding Dance* (Institute of Arts, Detroit) – a pulsating picture with 125 figures cavorting to the sound of a piper who plays his tune at the right-hand edge of the work. Groups of revellers dance, an intricate pattern of figures and colours meandering through the panel. A few drink, everyone smiles or occasionally smirks and the image is one of simple celebration. The following year Bruegel sharpened his focus, moved his vantage point closer into the scene and produced one of his most celebrated works, *The Wedding Feast* (1567–68, Kunsthistorisches Museum, Vienna).

The work is a significant departure, with the figures filling the frame rather than appearing in the distance. It involves, or even perhaps implicates, the viewer more with the unfolding scene. Music plays, peasants eat, food is served off an old door and the bride looks bemused and beatific at the same time. Much has been made of the idea of consumption, of gluttony or greed but this seems an exaggeration to say the least. Famine was rife in the 1560s and as early as 1545 an imperial

Hunters in the Snow

1565, Kunsthistorisches Museum, Vienna

This is probably the most celebrated image of winter ever produced, a chilling painting dominated by brilliant white and icy-green colours but filled with life conveyed through the briefest of black brushstrokes. It shows three hunters returning to their village, their sleek dogs somewhat undernourished and with just a single fox as the result of their efforts. They trudge through the snow, beginning their steep descent into the valley, itself mirrored by the soaring Alpine peaks in the opposite corner which both balance the picture and provide a dramatic

backdrop against which Man's struggle looks ominous if not futile. The trees emphasize their slow plod diagonally down the hill, a processional rhythm which continues to run through the picture along the tree-lined road which separates two of the three frozen fields.

Figures try to stave off the bitter cold, dragging firewood across the bridge, traipsing with horse and cart through the snow. Sometimes the attempts to keep warm are misjudged and a chimney catches fire in the far distance as two figures come racing through the fields with a ladder whilst another prepares to climb up and extinguish the flames. But the strongest image is not

of work but of play as figures cavort on the ice: lovers skate hand in hand; others race each other; an impromptu game of hockey breaks out; young and old pit their wits against each other in a curling match; dogs skid about and a figure falls over in a crumpled heap. It is a dynamic vignette depicted with the deftest of touches and economy of means. It reads as an abstract picture within a picture, a balletic image framed by snow paths and a modest but powerful monument to the human spirit.

There are no shadows visible; the sun has set and everything living, bar two of the dogs, is black, in silhouette and with no facial details visible. It is

an image of Everyman and Everywoman rather than a specific image of people and place. Space is deftly conveyed, from the bush poking out of the snow in the immediate foreground to the mountains beyond, Bruegel layers his composition and leads the viewer through. As if to reiterate the customary high vantage point, a bird soars across the scene seemingly just above eye-level, but way up above the valley.

The painting is both a self-contained image and part of an ongoing series which creates a visual calendar and a panorama of Man's relationship to the natural world.

The Wedding Feast

1567, Kunsthistorisches Museum, Vienna

This painting marks a shift of emphasis in Bruegel's approach, focusing as it does on the scene and creating a more intimate, empathetic effect with the unfolding celebrations. The wedding feast itself is a modest affair, but no less momentous for those who take part in it. The bride sits against a dark green backdrop suspended from a rope nailed to the wall. Above her head is a paper crown, marginally less elaborate than the one which she wears. Her face is bemused but also serene, a mixture of excitement, trepidation and a glass or two of wine, mead or beer. Next to her sit her parents, her father with a mildly grumpy look on his face, presumably because he is footing the bill. The bridegroom is nowhere to be seen. Convention had it that he helped serve, but there was also a proverb of which Bruegel was well aware which ran something along the lines of 'It's a poor man who is absent from his own wedding.'

There are various precedents for the subject of wedding feasts in art, not least the biblical account of the marriage at Cana where Christ turned water into wine. Likewise, patrician banquets had also been depicted but no one had ever focused so noticeably on simple people devouring food with such gusto. From the young boy in the immediate foreground relishing the idea of cleaning his bowl with his fingers to the seated guests staring intently at their food whilst they consume it, Bruegel shows a world where eating is a serious matter.

Famine was widespread in the Low Countries in the 1560s and although some art historians have claimed that this painting is an indictment of greed, these claims seem misplaced. On the right-hand edge of the picture, a monk and a nobleman are engaged in an intense discussion, perhaps on the dangers of gluttony. They show no signs of disapproval towards the guests at the feast. Above them, the wheat sheaves symbolize the harvest which has just been gathered in. Bruegel passes no judgment on the assembled multitude, nor is he over-sentimental in glorifying the life of the peasants he is reputed to have spied on. Instead, he offers a sympathetic portrayal of a contemporary ritual conveyed with the attention and interest of a latter-day anthropologist for whom every life potential is of interest.

law had been passed forbidding more than twenty people to attend country weddings in a bid to reduce widespread drunkenness. The table is duly filled with twenty figures, not including those who serve; the scene is one of controlled revelry. Certainly the figures take their food seriously and lick the bowls clean but that emphasizes the importance of food rather than overindulgence. On the wall just to the right of the bride are two sheaves of wheat, a symbol of the harvest that has just been gathered in. The feast itself takes place in a barn. This surely is a painting which sympathizes with those who have little but make the most of what nature gives them.

This is not to say that Bruegel had given up on moral lessons in his pictures; far from it. In *The Peasant Dance* (Kunsthistorisches Museum, Vienna) from the same period, a man and a woman are seen racing hand in hand towards a barn, perhaps where the wedding feast previously depicted was taking place. Tacked to the tree to their right is an image of the Virgin Mary; below their feet, two trampled pieces of straw have inadvertently made the sign of the cross. Everyone is oblivious; the message is clear but much less harsh than in *Procession to Calvary*: ignorance may be bliss, but it is not a cardinal sin. Furthermore, men and women, even the poorest ones, says Bruegel with his tongue perhaps slightly in his cheek, have the right to pleasure now and again.

In one of his last paintings, *The Parable of the Blind* (Museo Nazionale di Capodimonte, Naples), Bruegel developed his empathetic approach to making art by producing an image which reads partly as an unprecedented attempt to understand and explore the world of the blind. The overall inspiration for the work comes from two passages in the gospels (Matthew 15,14; Luke 6,39) from which originates the now standard proverb of the disasters resulting from the blind leading the blind. Here, six blind men linked by hand and stick meander haplessly towards a stream. One has tumbled in, another topples towards him and all in the end are destined for a fall. The clarity of the image, its economy of brushstroke and its muted colours hint at a bigger picture. More than the dramas of skeletal armies marching relentlessly towards their sinful victims, this is a powerful picture of potential oblivion. It seems inordinately cruel, but redemption, so Bruegel seems to be telling us, is at hand – the hand of God, no less. Starkly and simply, a church dominates the background, a clear guide for those who see not to follow blindly but to put their trust or faith in God. But is it that clear? With telling and increasingly characteristic ambiguity, Bruegel might well be warning of the dangers of those who put their trust in anyone.

In Brussels, where he lived for the last six years of his life and produced over thirty of the forty or so acknowledged paintings that remain, Bruegel himself lived well. Mayken Coecke bore him two sons, Jan and Pieter the Younger, both of whom would become painters in their own right. The civic authorities of Brussels recognized the artist's importance with certain privileges and liberties, including an exemption from the billet of Spanish soldiers in his house. He was also granted an official commission to design tapestries celebrating the completion of the Brussels–Antwerp canal in 1565, linking the two cities in which he had spent most of his life. This work, however, was interrupted by his premature death. In his final hours, he sought to leave no document that might cause his family harm in troubled and suspicious times. According to van Mander, Bruegel ordered to be consigned to the fire 'his strange and complicated allegories ... drawn to perfection and bearing inscriptions ... [because] offensive and biting, or because he repented of them, or for fear his wife might suffer harm or annoyance on their account'. Bruegel died on 5 September 1569, probably in only his early forties. He was buried in the Church of Notre Dame de la Chapelle in Brussels. Ortelius, the cartographer and one of his closest friends, wrote a touching eulogy to mark his passing: 'Pieter Bruegel was the most perfect painter of his century. No one, except a man who is envious, jealous or ignorant of that art, will ever deny'. A later Flemish artist, Peter Paul Rubens, in 1625 placed one of his own paintings on Bruegel's grave as a mark of respect.

8.

El Greco
1541–1614

The nickname 'El Greco', Spanish article combined with Italian adjective, meaning simply 'the Greek', is suitably descriptive of an artist who was born a Greek, trained in Italy and worked and died in Spain. His work is a highly individualized fusion of forms and ideas taken from these various cultures, which culminated in his characteristic portrayals of ecstatic visions, peopled by elongated, flamelike figures and expressing intense religious emotion. El Greco was a pioneering figure in the struggle to raise the profile and status of artists in Spain, but he enjoyed little of the success he desired in his lifetime. For two centuries after his death, he remained an obscure figure in the footnotes of Spanish painting, but his work became more popular in the nineteenth century, with the rise of the avant-garde in France and Germany. El Greco's idiosyncratic style, with its expressive distortions, established his reputation as a proto-modern artist; in particular, as a forerunner of the development of Expressionism in the twentieth century.

Domenikos Theotokopoulos was born in 1541 in Candia (modern Heraklion), the capital of Crete. Although he often signed his name in full, contemporaries referred to him as Domenico Greco, or, later, simply El Greco. Since the thirteenth century, Crete had been a possession of the Venetian republic, whose extensive empire stretched throughout the eastern Mediterranean and encompassed most of the islands of the Aegean. Little is known of El Greco's family, but judging by his first name, Domenikos, they must have been Roman Catholic rather than Greek Orthodox. They were apparently relatively well-connected local civil servants for the island's Venetian rulers. They could certainly afford to have Domenikos educated.

El Greco's introduction to painting and his training are obscure. It is probable that he was apprenticed to the workshop of a Cretan artist. Painting in Crete comprised a number of distinct traditions and influences; most characteristically, the Greek Orthodox Church, tolerated by the Venetian rulers, continued to patronize and foster traditional Byzantine painting as a living art form. When Constantinople fell to the Ottoman Turks in 1453, Crete became a refuge for Byzantine artists and an important centre preserving traditions which had been lost elsewhere. Although Crete remained distant from many of the artistic and cultural developments of the Italian Renaissance, Cretan artists were exposed to certain trends in Italian art and architecture. Several towns were being built in the Venetian style, and art collections on the island included works by various Venetian artists, including the illustrious Tintoretto and Titian. The origin of this synthesis of style is apparent in El Greco's first signed work, a damaged panel painting in the Church of the Dormition in the small island of Syros, to the north of Crete, showing the *Death of the Virgin* (before 1567). It's a simple image, with only a hint of perspectival depth, slightly lifting the flattened arrangement of figures painted in egg tempera on wood with a gold ground in the manner of Byzantine icons.

By the time he was twenty-five, El Greco seems to have established himself locally, probably in traditional church decoration. In a document of 1566, he describes himself as '*maistro*'. It has been suggested that El Greco may have been partly educated in Venice, where there was a Greek community of more than 4,000, many of whom were Cretans. What is certain is that he left Crete around the end of 1567 or the beginning of 1568 and went to Venice to continue his training. As the capital of a significant empire, Venice was the natural destination for an artist wishing to learn more about the great masters of Italian painting. Virtually nothing is known about his time in Venice though it has been argued, perhaps romantically, that El Greco spent some time at the workshop of Titian (*c*.1487–1576), the most celebrated and influential Venetian painter of his day.

In his later writings, often jotted in the margins of a copy of Vasari's recently published *Lives of the Artists*, El Greco stressed the importance of colour over drawing, *colore* over *disegno*, and this was strongly borne out by his mature style. He went on to emphasize the broad debt he owed to Venetian art, and in particular to Titian and Tintoretto (1518–94). From Titian he learned the expressive use of colour applied through vigorous brushwork; in Tintoretto's paintings he saw dynamic figures, dramatic use of perspective and restless, atmospheric lighting, traces of which started to creep into his earliest work made in Italy, beginning with a modest panel painting of *The Purification of the Temple* (1568–70, National Gallery of Art, Washington). In this scene, in a rare display of anger, Christ drives out the money-changers and merchants trading in the temple. The subject was not common in Italian art, but it was one that El Greco interpreted repeatedly throughout his career. Although the painting bears evidence of the work of an icon painter – it is a small piece done on board with noticeably unblended brushstrokes – it represents an early attempt by El Greco to wrestle with the complexities of Italian composition and perspective. The figures are drawn by an uncertain hand that is still trying to master draughtsmanship and the work is disjointed in its composition. Compare this picture with a painting produced a few years later in Rome of the same subject, *The Purification of the Temple* (1570–76, Institute of Art, Minneapolis) and one can see just how much El Greco's grasp of composition and perspective had improved and how much more confident and deft his touch had become. In this later version, El Greco added four figures at the bottom of the painting – Titian, Michelangelo, his friend the respected miniaturist painter Giulio Clovio and (probably) Raphael – as an acknowledgment of his sources of inspiration. Here, El Greco both acknowledges his Italian pedigree and purges or purifies his artistic past; hence, perhaps, his preoccupation with the subject chosen.

The modernist view of El Greco as a loner pushing at the conventions of pictorial form and style tends to preclude his deep involvement with the religious and political climate of his age. In the later sixteenth century, a series of reformist popes sought to address the abuses within the Catholic Church that had provoked the Reformation, and to prevent the further growth of Protestantism. This movement is known to historians as the Counter-Reformation, a designation that is only partly accurate, since reform within the Church was as important as countering heresy. The philosophies and doctrines of this 'Catholic Reformation' were enshrined in the Tridentine Decrees, the ultimate result of the protracted sessions of the Council of Trent (1545–47, 1551–52

The Purification of the Temple
1568–70, National Gallery of Art, Washington
This work was made soon after El Greco's arrival in Venice and shows a young artist trying to establish his own voice whilst wrestling with new styles and approaches to painting that he has just begun to encounter. It shows Christ driving the money-lenders, prostitutes and market traders from the temple with a rare gesture of anger. El Greco compresses the action into the foreground in order to contrast chaos with the more ordered world beyond. He is clearly emphasizing the idea of perspective, as well as a growing interest in Italian architecture; foreshortening the tiles as they recede and creating a temple that looks Roman, set against a distant landscape that is idealized. The figures further suggest how much he is trying to learn from the masters of the Italian Renaissance, not least the muscular forms, which pay homage to the work of Michelangelo.

Colour is slightly garish, not yet harmonized, and the composition itself is slightly disjointed, as if front and back are not quite of one and the same image. The theme of Christ purging the temple appears in Byzantine art but is rare in Western art; however, it seems to have struck a personal chord with El Greco, who was trying to purge his own artistic style of his Byzantine roots and develop a grander, more Italianate manner.

and 1562–63). This church council redefined official interpretation of the Bible and entrenched Catholic doctrine. Art was to play an important part in this process, as the Church insisted that altarpieces and other decorative works should adhere to its strict interpretation. Art therefore assumed the overt role of politico-religious propaganda. Artists were to eschew an elaborate or classicizing style. The primary function of art, the Catholic Church asserted, was to communicate the principles of Christianity; any expression of beauty was secondary. The artist and theorist Francisco de Holanda wrote: 'According the Tridentine Decrees, painting is living scripture and doctrine for the illiterate.' El Greco supported this renewed orthodoxy and became an intelligent and often visionary interpreter of it in his work.

In 1570, after three years in Venice, having absorbed the expressive and colourful style of Venetian art, El Greco travelled to Rome. He was twenty-nine and, like so many artists of his time, he felt his artistic education was not complete without a visit to this seat of classical and religious culture. With the help of Giulio Clovio, El Greco was introduced to an important patron, Cardinal Alessandro Farnese, as 'a young Candiot pupil of Titian', which would have given him both credibility and a certain degree of novelty. It is probable that El Greco lived in the Palazzo Farnese, where he would have mixed with a circle of eminent artists and scholars. El Greco certainly set up his own workshop, taught students and employed apprentices to help him with commissions. He worked for private clients on portraits and a few religious pieces, as well as painting a work inspired by a description in the writings of Pliny the Elder. *Boy Blowing on an Ember* (c.1575, Museo Nazionale di Capodimonte, Naples) was a highly naturalistic work, particularly in its treatment of light. It shows a young boy holding a glowing stick of wood, presumably just pulled from the fire, on which he blows in order to try to light a candle.

MANNERISM

Mannerism is a movement in art and architecture, whose origins can be traced to Rome and Florence around 1520, lasting to about 1600 – a bridge between the High Renaissance and the Baroque.

Giorgio Vasari was among the first to develop it. Mannerism was derived from the Italian word 'maniera', which means 'style' or 'stylishness'. Vasari used the term to describe work that he viewed as graceful and sophisticated. Mannerism discarded the calm balance of the High Renaissance by intentionally opposing its 'rules'. Critics thought that Italian art of this period was artificial, exaggerated, superficial and distorted the work of the masters.

The fundamental characteristics of a piece of Mannerist work would be the dominance of a human figure. The figures are often depicted in an unconventional way – lengthened, or in positions that appear contorted with athletic bending. The work would gain immense worth if it figured a nude in these complicated poses. Colours were often vivid, composition was strained and perspective warped.

The Catholic Church used art to attract people away from other religious denominations,

Both the boy and his illuminated face pre-empt the work of Caravaggio in Rome by nearly three decades. The painting, with its scholarly inspiration, also shows just how immersed in humanist culture El Greco became in the ancient city.

El Greco's period in Rome also brought him into contact with the Mannerism which prevailed in Roman painting. Mannerism was the self-conscious imitation of the style of the masters of the High Renaissance, often leading to either slavishly unoriginal compositions and forms, or their exaggeration in a search for originality. It was an international phenomenon in painting, with regional variants and developments. This art prioritized the virtuosity of individual painters; paintings were displays of painterly skills characterized by inventive and impressive figural poses and actions, and surprising, novel ways of interpreting narrative. Of particular influence, for example, was Michelangelo's *serpentinata* – figures presented in serpentine, corkscrewing, twisting poses, which were compared to living flamelike forms. El Greco was deeply influenced by such ideas and particularly by Michelangelo himself, who had died six years earlier. El Greco is reported to have said that, while Michelangelo was deficient in his use of colour, his ability to depict the human form was 'without comparison'.

By 1576, however, El Greco had failed to secure any important commissions in Rome. He was thirty-five years old, an age by which an artist could expect to be established. It was perhaps this thwarted ambition that led El Greco to leave the city, though Giulio Mancini records a notorious anecdote that 'at a time when there were not many men in Rome with as positive or as fresh a manner as his, he became very presumptuous'. Apparently when Pope Pius V (r.1566–72) ordered the offending nudes in Michelangelo's *Last Judgment* to be painted over, El Greco offered to repaint the whole fresco with 'honesty and decency'

and criticized Vasari and other Mannerist practitioners for their style of work, since it frequently avoided the depiction of religious subject matter.

It would be inaccurate to say that the style was borne out of the troubled political and social conditions which were current in central Italy at that time. These conditions where practically permanent. However, it may be true to say that unsettling circumstances

may have encouraged artists to desert classicism.

Mannerism was best suited to neurotic artists such as Bronzino and da Pontormo. Both produced major works which were highly sophisticated and disturbing. Many less accomplished artists attempted to be neurotically fascinating and failed, producing frenzied and repetitive work. Mannerism came to an end when it was succeeded by the Baroque,

in which artists turned to uncomplicated subject matter and unidealized naturalism.

In the twentieth century, Mannerism was rediscovered and looked upon more sympathetically and accorded a higher value. Work earlier ignored or thought of as dull was suddenly seen as imaginative and innovative.

and equal mastery. The subsequent anger of Rome's painters won him few favours. Like many major artists, El Greco had a self-belief verging on supreme arrogance: 'if once in a while popular taste is right,' he later observed, 'it is usually by accident and is not worth taking into account'. El Greco had alienated himself from the mainstream in a highly competitive city dominated by an artistic as well as a religious orthodoxy. Unsurprisingly, therefore, he left, possibly returning to Venice for a short time before heading west. By 1577, he had arrived in Spain, where he remained for the rest of his life.

The artistic world of Spain contrasted starkly with that of Italy and the Low Countries, especially in terms of patronage. Spain lacked the multiplicity of princely courts and city-republics of Italy, and the urban bourgeoisie of the Low Countries. Spanish art was dominated by two patrons: the Spanish Habsburg court and the Church. Both were effectively controlled by one man, King Philip II (r.1556–98). Philip was the richest and most powerful ruler in Europe, an absolutist monarch in a court that was formal and hieratic even by the standards of the day. As a national concept, 'Spain' was relatively new, and its separate kingdoms still enjoyed many liberties and privileges. In 1561, Philip II decreed that Madrid would be the capital of Spain and permanent residence of the royal court. Madrid's status was thereby promoted over cities which traditionally had stronger links with royalty and were historically more prominent (notably Valladolid, Seville and Toledo). Previously, the royal court had moved from city to city, using the capitals of the various kingdoms into which Spain was divided as temporary residences. After Philip's decree, these cities declined, as the political and cultural focus of the Iberian peninsula shifted towards Madrid.

This austere religious zealot spent his life trying to impose political and religious uniformity on his dominions, which included the New World and the Low Countries. In this single-minded pursuit, Philip

PHILIP II (r.1556-98)
At the start of Philip's reign in 1556, Spain was approaching bankruptcy. And, although he was subsequently to receive generous amounts of silver from the Americas, Philip still, by and large, managed to lose it all. A fortune was spent lining foreign pockets or fuelling costly European wars. As for the rest, it went on palaces, churches and monasteries.

Philip tried to rule without rising from his desk, but never seemed able to surmount the piles of state paperwork. The workload only served to discourage major decisions. His relentless attempt to produce one empire, with one monarch, did achieve some successes – at the sea battle of Lepanto in Greece in 1571, his forces conquered the Ottoman Turks, Spain's Mediterranean rivals.

Elsewhere, he managed to extend his empire overseas. Portugal's king died in 1580 and Philip claimed the country's vast inheritance. But he failed to win a lengthy battle with Holland, which resulted in Dutch independence; he also saw his precocious Spanish Armada fail in its attempt to invade England in 1588.

Philip's obsession with Catholicism and spiritual

offended and provoked rebellion by the Dutch in 1566 and the Aragonese in 1591–92. He aimed to eradicate heresy throughout Europe, imposing the Inquisition on his subjects and expelling the Moriscos, former Muslims who had converted to Christianity (1568–69). His ruthless suppression of the rebellious Dutch, his intervention in the French Wars of Religion and his armadas launched against heretical England combined with widespread plague, agricultural failures and rural depopulation to make his reign both the glory and the ruin of Spain. Having been the richest monarch in Europe, he died bankrupt.

Philip's greatest artistic achievement, was the Escorial, a vast and imposingly severe complex that served as royal palace, monastery, church and royal mausoleum, or even shrine. It was built between 1563 and 1584, and even in Philip's lifetime it acquired renown as an 'eighth wonder of the world'. Philip was a great patron of the arts. Mannerism had far greater impact on Spanish artists than the High Renaissance style. It possessed an emotional response more in accord with the character of the Renaissance in Spain, which was less interested in idealized forms and classicism, and modified by native religious expression. Very few native Spanish artists exhibited an understanding of contemporary developments in Italian painting, the primary exception being the painter and sculptor Alonso Berruguete (1488–1561). As a consequence, Philip II tended to import Italian artists to decorate the Escorial, many of them second rate. It is possible that El Greco approached the court for a commission for the Escorial on his arrival in Spain, but his style initially met with Philip II's disapproval.

As the Church was the other major source of work, El Greco decided to go south to Toledo, the ecclesiastical centre of Spain. Toledo also, of course, had strong associations (if reduced) with the crown. Toledo was now only a provincial capital, but supported a rich cultural and intellectual life, with one of the finest universities in Europe, and

uniformity spelled trouble for many; anyone assumed to be of Jewish or Muslim blood or to have Protestant views had good reasons for fear. He urged the vast network of the Inquisition to persecute them, thus smothering the intellectual life of the country. Book-burning became common and Spaniards were not allowed to study overseas. William the Silent, an adversary, was well founded in his view that Philip was 'a murderer and a liar'.

Philip made the decision in 1561 to turn Madrid into his permanent capital, on the basis that it would help him consolidate his power. Consequently, Madrid attracted European artists in search of commissions: Gaspar Becerra, a Mannerist artist from Rome, was appointed as a royal painter in 1562 and begun an unprecedented programme of decoration of royal palaces over the next four decades.

In 1590, Spain looked to be in crisis again. Plague spread throughout a country already reeling from agricultural failure. Spain faced yet another bankruptcy in 1596, with Philip's death two years later, the Habsburgs were left to try in vain to restore their empire.

attracted many artists and scholars towards the end of the sixteenth century. Miguel Cervantes (1547–1616), the most famous writer in Spain, lived there and described the city as 'O rocky mass, glory of Spain, and light of her cities'. There were significant Jewish and Moorish populations, giving the city a cosmopolitan air. It was a wealthy city, famous for its silks and steel blades, though increasingly an economic backwater with a declining population. In the 1570s, the city council began a large building programme, intended to restore the city's prestige after the departure of the court. During El Greco's time, the Church was the largest patron. The cathedral was a massive institution; it dominated the skyline of the city and employed over six hundred people. There were more than one hundred other religious institutions in and around the city, a remarkable number for a population of 62,000.

In 1577, El Greco's first commission in Toledo was to paint an altarpiece and the side chapels for the convent church of the Dominican Sisters, Santo Domingo el Antiguo. This commission was due, in part, to his friend, the priest Luis de Castilla, whom he had met in Rome. Luis's father, Diego de Castilla, was Dean of the Chapter of Toledo Cathedral, an influential figure in ecclesiastical circles. El Greco produced an elaborate series of paintings, based on the theme of the Resurrrection, over the main altar, flanked by images of St John the Baptist, St John the Evangelist, St Bernard and St Benedict. Already there were signs of El Greco's distinctively expressive style emerging in these works, both in the drama of the large composition and in the less elaborate but more penetrating portraits of individual saints which he produced prodigiously for the rest of his career. But his new patrons had a more prestigious proposal in store for the artist, who, whilst he was still at work at Santo Domingo el Antiguo, found himself with a commission to produce a work for the cathedral, an epic painting for the sacristy, of *El Espolio* or *The Disrobing of Christ* (1577–79, Toledo Cathedral).

The painting depicts the removal of Christ's 'seamless' coat prior to his Crucifixion, as told in the gospels of John and Luke. The subject, which was unusual in Western painting despite Byzantine precedents, is partly explained by the fact that it was to be hung in the newly built vestry, where the priests changed. The rich use of colour focuses attention on Christ's robe and demonstrates El Greco's grasp of Venetian painting. The composition, with its almost vertical-seeming wall of figures, has strong Mannerist overtones, but there are also some more idiosyncratic aspects which are El Greco's own and add to the sense of event in the painting, notably the condensed mêlée of figures forming an almost abstract surge of energy at the heart of the picture, offset by various details which heighten the drama: the soldier in contemporary armour, the figure in the crowd pointing at Christ and the Three Marys in the foreground closest to the viewer who lead one into the scene and seem to be orchestrating the emotional tone of the picture. In the gospels, there are various references to three women present at Christ's Crucifixion: the Virgin Mary, Mary Magdalene and 'the other Mary', 'Mary the mother of James the Less and Joseph', or 'Mary of Cleophas … His [Christ's] mother's sister', depending which gospel you read. Subsequently, the inclusion of the Three Marys became widespread, most notably in Rubens's monumental altarpiece showing *The Descent from the Cross* in Antwerp Cathedral, three decades later. But in this instance it caused problems.

El Greco was accused of impropriety by the warden of the cathedral for his inclusion of the Three Marys, deemed to be only ambiguously present in the gospels, his use of contemporary armour and his failure to make Christ's head the dominant feature of the painting, thereby violating the new visual orthodoxy of the Counter-Reformation. There was, however, a more marked fall-out between El Greco and the Church over the price of the commission. In sixteenth-century Spain, painting was generally still regarded as a craft, not a liberal art. Coming from Italy, this view surprised and dismayed El Greco. In Toledo, he had to accept that patrons and artists used a special system called *tasacion* to value religious works. This entailed the artist and patron nominating appraisers to determine the value of a completed painting. If both parties could not reach an agreed value, an arbitrator would make the final decision. This system meant that artists gambled their time, energy and materials on a project without knowing the value of the finished piece. El Greco was proud of his art and felt strongly that it should be well rewarded, but also that a system of haggling over fees was demeaning. He had seen the lifestyles and status of some of the best painters in Italy and expected to be treated not as a medieval artisan, but as an artist, possessed of creative imagination and intellectual faculty. He often contested appraisers' decisions, occasionally resorting to expensive court proceedings. After a two-and-a-half-year legal battle, El Greco eventually received 317 ducats for the picture – a third of the fee established by his appraisers. More significantly, however, the painting remained unchanged; despite a disappointing fee, El Greco won a moral victory in not bending to Counter-Reformation pedantry.

Despite these problems, or perhaps because of the certain notoriety they brought to El Greco, he was rapidly sought by numerous private clients for commissions in and around Toledo. He also had come to the attention of the most important client in Spain – King Philip II.

In 1580, El Greco was commissioned to paint a work as part of the extensive decoration of the Escorial. Philip gave him the subject of *The*

Martyrdom of St Lawrence (1580–82, El Escorial). The painting was designed for an altarpiece and depicted St Lawrence, the leader of an Egyptian legion of the Roman army, who chose to die for his Christian faith rather than sacrifice to pagan gods. The subject was a strong one in the promotion of Counter-Reformation ideology and El Greco embraced it with gusto, filling the scene with muscular pagans turned Christians and including various contemporary generals clad in sixteenth-century armour. These men, the Duke of Savoy and the Prince of Parma (tucked in between St Lawrence and his standard-bearer in the right foreground of the picture), along with Philip's own bastard son, Don Juan of Austria (visible in the distance on the left, looking at a beheaded corpse), had all been highly successful in recent wars of religion against Protestant forces and their inclusion in the picture gave a clear Catholic message. But, as he'd done in Toledo Cathedral, El Greco took increasing liberties with his subject, showing not one image of St Lawrence but three: debating his fate in the right-hand foreground, wearing a purple-tinted tunic; and overseeing his own execution on the left and in the middle ground, with his beheaded corpse lying before him in the mud. El Greco thus condensed time and space, compressing aspects of the narrative into one image and adding a strange, ethereal touch to the work with his airily painted vision of angels above, which further added to the fantastical effect of the work.

The *Martyrdom of St Lawrence* remains a powerful but quirky picture, a heady mixture of grandeur and dislocated detail rendered in an increasingly expressive manner. Philip II, however, was not impressed

The Disrobing of Christ
1577–79, Toledo Cathedral

Viewed in reproduction, this painting seems highly intimate, an image full of detailed expression as the figures behind Christ crowd both the picture plane and the man who is about to be sacrificed. Viewed high up on the wall of the sacristy in Toledo, it is a grand painting which seems to surge out towards the spectator and make us almost more than bystanders witnessing what is unfolding before us.

Christ stands calmly awaiting His fate, which is brutally brought to life by El Greco in the bottom right-hand corner of the picture, where a young man gouges out the holes in the wooden cross into which the nails will be driven after they have pierced the hands and feet of the Son of God. The vivid red robe anticipates the bloodshed to come and dominates the painting, emerging out of the relative gloom and also reflected in the delicately painted armour of the soldier to the right of Christ. To his left, and clad in a deep green shirt which further enhances the visual impact of the red, a soldier feels the garment with an impressed look on his face. Together with the two figures immediately behind, he will soon draw lots for the robe itself.

The picture is densely composed, to the point of claustrophobia. There is virtually no sense of depth or space. The figures are stacked up vertically, distantly reminiscent of Byzantine art; but the pikes at the very top, set against the brooding sky, create the brief illusion of a world beyond while beating a slow pictorial rhythm across the image as if sounding a death knell. As the crowd bays for blood and surges forward, thrusting Christ out towards us, the distraught but dignified figure of the Virgin, accompanied by Mary Magdelene and Mary of Cleophas, stares at the preparations being made for her son's execution. Just in front of the Cross, as if casually tossed to the ground, is a piece of paper on which El Greco has signed his name and, metaphorically, begins to make his artistic mark.

and, once again, El Greco fell foul of Counter-Reformation theology. The saint appeared to be debating his chosen fate, which was read as moral uncertainty. This ambiguity and the artist's apparent failure to place St Lawrence in the centre of the picture seemed to marginalize the martyrdom. Typically, El Greco also argued over the value set by the appraiser. Philip rejected the finished painting and almost immediately ordered a replacement by another artist – Romulo Cincinnato – although El Greco's work remained *in situ*. However, the affair put an end to any chance that El Greco might have had of becoming a court painter, together with the prestige and regular income that the position would have brought him.

His ambitions severely curtailed, having fallen out with two of the most powerful patrons in Spain over a period of two years, the forty-two-year-old had to accept the life of a contract artist supplying the commissions of individual clients. El Greco was evolving a highly original style and his eccentricities, as well as his religious devotion, seem to have made his work highly prized among wealthy patrons and religious institutions, aside from the cathedral in Toledo. The commissioning process involved detailed discussions, preparatory drawings and a line-

The Burial of Count Orgaz
1586–88, church of Santo Tomé, Toledo

Count Orgaz was a devout fourteenth-century nobleman who had made a substantial donation to the church in which he was buried in Toledo, that of San Tome. At his funeral, a miracle was reputed to have occurred, with St Stephen and St Augustine appearing from on high and assisting in the burial of the Count. Two centuries later, and after a legal dispute involving Orgaz's legacy, the church decided to commission its most celebrated contemporary parishioner – El Greco – to paint a picture commemorating its most celebrated benefactor and this was the result.

The top half of the painting is an ecstatic vision of heaven, with the usual throng of saints surrounding Christ, with the Virgin Mary and John the Baptist seated on swirling clouds between which an angel guides a phantomlike form. This is an unprecedented image of a human soul, that of Count Orgaz, which is being pushed heavenwards through what can only be described as a cosmic birth canal.

Down below, and painted in a contrasting and more graphic style, the funeral of Count Orgaz takes place. Augustine and Stephen hold the body, which is clad in the armour of a sixteenth-century knight. Behind, a gathering of contemporary Toledan dignitaries looks on in solemn awe, with El Greco himself portrayed staring mournfully at the viewer just behind and above the head of St Stephen. On the extreme right of the picture and presiding over the funeral service is Andrés Nuñez, El Greco's parish priest and the man who commissioned the painting. In the foreground, just to the left of the burial, is a young boy who looks out with a piercing gaze and points towards the unfolding drama. This is Jorge Manuel, El Greco's eight-year-old son, whose date of birth is painted into the white handkerchief sticking out of his pocket, along with his father's signature. El Greco is thus immortalizing his son as well as Count Orgaz. Moreover, the boy is drawing our attention to a painted lesson in Counter-Reformation Catholic theology: give generously and live well and your reward will be in heaven, the image seems to be saying, in marked contrast to the Protestant belief that salvation is achieved through faith alone.

There is a final twist to the work, which can only be experienced *in situ*. Directly below the painting is Orgaz's tomb, into which his painted body appears to be descending. The figures are life-size as well as being recognizable to a sixteenth-century parishioner. Then as now, El Greco seems to be suggesting that a miracle is taking place before our very eyes.

by-line contract for the work. The contract itself included not only the subject to be painted, but often also notes about the composition and style. By 1585, his business was big enough to fill three of the rooms he leased in the palace of the Marquis de Villena. There, El Greco organized his studio on the Venetian model, with apprentices and pupils producing copies of his work for sale to less wealthy patrons and institutions in and around Toledo. A large number of studio copies of the paintings he produced in the city therefore exist. This practice, though initially unfamiliar, became well known among potential clients, who would specify in the contract the extent of the master's personal involvement. El Greco also pioneered a new geometrical formula for copying his pictures, according to which a pupil could reproduce an original on a much larger or smaller canvas without distortion of proportions.

The intricacies of the contractual process are most strongly evident in the preparation for El Greco's most elaborate work, *The Burial of Count Orgaz* (1586–88, church of Santo Tomé, Toledo). The painting was commissioned by the parish priest Andrés Nuñez de Madrid for the artist's parish church of Santo Tomé. The priest is represented reading the funeral Mass on the far right. The subject of the painting is the Don Gonzalo Ruiz de Toledo, Señor de la Villa de Orgaz, a Toledan nobleman who had lived in the early fourteenth century and became well known as a donor to religious institutions. When he died in 1323, St Augustine and St Stephen supposedly descended from heaven to attend his funeral. The details of the 1586 contract are specific:

> On the canvas shall be painted a procession of the priest
> and clerics, who were performing the office for the burial
> of Don Gonzalo Ruiz. And St Augustine and St Stephen,
> who descended to bury the body of this knight, one
> holding the head and the other the feet, placing him
> in the tomb. And around are many people who were
> watching and above all of this shall be painted the open
> heaven of Glory.

El Greco painted 'the open heaven of Glory' in an unprecedented way, with the heavenly figures floating on a mass of swirling clouds, their bodies – notably that of St John – elongated and with light flickering down on the multitude below. Once again, El Greco blurs time with the distinguished citizens of Toledo painted in contemporary clothes. Only a few of the figures can be identified with any certainty. The boy in the bottom left corner of the picture is Jorge Manuel, El Greco's son, holding a mortuary candle and pointing to the miracle. There is also a possible self-portrait: the figure looking directly at the viewer on a line between the heads of St Stephen and the Virgin.

Taking their lead from both King Philip II and the Pope, the archbishops of Toledo in the late sixteenth century were keen to establish their credentials as the spiritual leaders of Spain and continued, fervently, to enforce the newly retrenched doctrines of Roman Catholicism. Having previously fallen foul of the new orthodoxy, El Greco's paintings rapidly became important tools for inspiring devotion. He invented an individual style that served as a pictorial language to glorify and dramatize the Catholic faith. The *Burial of Count Orgaz*, in particular, served a didactic purpose. The pointing gesture of the boy indicates that a moral lesson is being taught: that donating good works, as Don Gonzalo did, ensures a place in heaven. The painting thus conveys one of the basic tenets of Roman Catholic theology, a direct challenge to the Protestant belief in salvation by faith alone. Here El Greco reaffirms his own Catholic faith, but he is also thoroughly in tune with the prevailing mood of his place and time. Contemporary Spain certainly seems to have been more concerned with the afterlife than most other countries in Europe. The painting is so completely a reflection of Spanish attitudes and tastes that El Greco has to be counted among the painters of Spain. It is the first major example of a standard characteristic of later Spanish painting: the visionary depicted as the real.

El Greco's private life attained a degree of stability in Toledo. He lived for many years with a Dona Jerónima de las Cuevas, a Spanish woman of distinguished birth, though they do not appear ever to have married. She was the mother of Jorge Manuel (1578–1631), who followed his father's profession. Like his painted visions, El Greco's life in Toledo was one of contrasts. Despite living in a twenty-four-room palace, apart from his modest library, his personal possessions were almost non-existent. Although El Greco's output was consistently large, payment continued to be regularly bogged down in legal wrangles over prices. His extensive debts pursued him to his grave, but, like a prince, he employed musicians to play for him while he ate. He was a solitary person, yet his intellect won him respect in the small group of wealthy intellectual citizens of Toledo. Chief among these was the monk, humanist and poet Fray Hortensio Félix de Paravincino, who wrote of El Greco, 'Greece gave him life and the brush and Toledo a better homeland where he begins to achieve eternities in death.' El Greco's portrait of Paravincino from 1609 is the intimate portrayal of a friend – it seems almost as though they are engaged in conversation. Paravincino appears human and even vulnerable, in clear contrast to the stiff formality then favoured in official portraiture.

By the end of the sixteenth century, Toledo was experiencing an economic slump. The causes were many – a combination of poor harvests, plague, high taxes and the decline of the textile industry, as wars between Spain and her enemies led to a scarcity of raw materials. And after the 1561 *unica corte* decree which sited the royal court solely in Madrid, Toledo's population of 62,000 declined to under 30,000 a few decades later. Between 1606 and 1621, approximately 6,000 people emigrated from Toledo, most of whom were unemployed artisans and cloth workers. These were, in part, the effects of Philip II's policies, and it was this strained and anguished world that El Greco depicted in his later paintings, not the idealized classicism and courtly splendour preferred by the king.

The *View of Toledo* (*c*.1597, Metropolitan Museum, New York) has become an emblematic painting, both of the city itself and of El Greco's art. It is doomladen, with dark black clouds swelling overhead and lightning just about to strike. At the same time, Toledo looks strong in the face of nature's onslaught and the image can certainly be read in terms of a resurgent civic pride which gathered momentum at the end of the sixteenth century. It is an intensely personalized vision, an uncommissioned painting in which El Greco rearranges the architecture of the city to create the most dramatic image possible. By doing this, he continued to break away from one of the central tenets of the Renaissance – art mirroring nature – and asserted the primacy of the artistic imagination over all other art forms. Painting is able to reorder

View of Toledo
c.1597, Metropolitan Museum of Art, New York
El Greco depicted his adopted city in a number of works, but this is the only surviving pure landscape and it has become an emblem of Toledo and its most famous artistic son. Rather than paint a panoramic view, as was customary, El Greco chose to show part of the city from the east, in a vertical format which emphasizes its dominant position on a hilltop visible for miles around. This banking upwards evokes his earlier large-scale religious compositions; this is a rare example of a Mannerist landscape. It is also a good deal more besides.

As if to stress the primacy of the Church in the city, El Greco moves the cathedral centre stage and to the left of the Alcázar, or Royal Palace. From this viewpoint, looking up the valley of the River Tagus, the large spire would not be visible, but here it is set against a sky laden with swollen black clouds, almost like a crucifixion scene. The eye is drawn down over the Alcántara Bridge, built by the Romans, and across to the castle of San Servando. Further down and on the left-hand edge of the picture, the topography is rearranged by El Greco once more, with the depiction of a mysterious group of buildings seemingly set on top of a patch of cloud. These never existed in this location, notwithstanding their ethereal base, but they seem to allude to a monastery on the other side of the city in which St Ildefonso, the patron saint of Toledo, who is buried in the cathedral, once went on retreat. Again, El Greco is stressing the importance and power of the artistic imagination which is able to suggest the presence of heavenly visions here on earth.

The bottom half of the picture suggests a landscape, lush and fertile, fed by the teeming river. The top half is a dramatic contrast, barren, brooding, full of foreboding, where a celebratory vision of the natural world gives way to a threatening one. It is an eerie, haunting image, full of menace, power and paradox. One minute, the viewer is confronted by the sublime forces of nature which threaten to overwhelm the city; the next, Toledo seems to resist the onslaught in a stubborn image of defiance.

the natural world and the architectural one, too. It can also depict the invisible; the divine as well as the human.

As if to assert the primacy of painting still further, as well as to illustrate other aspects of his adopted city, El Greco used Toledo as the backdrop for a more classically inspired work – the *Laocoon* (1610–14, National Gallery, Washington). Laocoon, a Trojan priest, attempted to warn his fellow Trojans about the Wooden Horse being not a gift but a dangerous trap from the Greek forces besieging the city. Apollo sent serpents to kill the priest and his two sons. The myth grew in popularity after a marble sculpture depicting Laocoon and his sons was uncovered in Rome in 1506. El Greco chose to show the Greek myth occurring at the gates of Toledo, a setting that is not as incongruous as it may initially appear, as Toledan history maintained that two descendants of the Trojans, Telemon and Brutus, had founded the city. Historians have also suggested that El Greco was alluding to a conflict between conservative churchmen and those who favoured reform in Toledo. El Greco uses writhing lines, lurid colours and illogically conceived space to convey an unrelieved sense of doom. The artist conveys a haunting, apocalyptic vision. The figures seem unreal, their sinuous outlines and unreal flesh tones enhancing their ghostlike appearance.

This visionary, cataclysmic character in El Greco's late paintings reaches its climax in *The Fifth Seal of the Apocalypse* (1608–14, Metropolitan Museum of Art, New York). The image is inspired by a passage from the Revelation of St John. The Lamb summons St John to come and see the opening of the seven seals:

> And when he had opened the fifth seal, I saw under the altar the souls of them that were slain for the word of God, and for the testimony which they held: And they cried in a loud voice ' How Long, Oh Lord Holy and True, dost thou not judge and avenge our blood on them that dwell on the earth.' And white robes were given to every one of them.
>
> (Revelations 9–11)

On the left is St John in a state of rapture, looking towards heaven and raising his arms in a prophetic gesture. The nude figures represent the martyrs who rise to receive the gift of white robes from Heaven. This work seems startlingly modern; El Greco disregards natural forms and colours. The figures are elongated and contorted, but they are still graceful. There is no clear sense of the environment; the sky and ground are indistinguishable, compressed together in an almost eternal space.

In the last years of his life, El Greco evolved an unprecedented personal style, transcending his Byzantine, Venetian and Mannerist roots. The works were mainly devotional and produced in tall, narrow formats in order to accommodate his increasingly angular, attenuated figures. Works like *The Baptism of Christ* (1597–1600), *The Resurrection* (*c*.1610) and *Pentecost* (1608–10), all commissioned for churches but now in the Prado in Madrid, suggest an atmosphere of ecstatic excitement conveyed through El Greco's vigorous brushstrokes, their spiritual otherworldliness enhanced by the unnatural proportions and dislocated sense of space. In our culture, which pays lip service to individualism (even if it is perhaps more conformist than ever before), the tendency has been to see El Greco's eccentric late style as that of the lonely figure struggling against an uncomprehending world. This was not so, in that he became more popular as he got older, but the relative isolation of Toledo, increasingly cut off from the major developments in European art, perhaps did enable him to develop without the checks and balances of significant competitors.

His last work, *The Adoration of the Shepherds* (1610–14, Prado, Madrid), was created for his own tomb and depicts a darkened scene where the shepherds and Mary and Joseph are irradiated by an intense mystical light emanating from the tiny body of Christ. The figures are impossibly elongated and in the foreground is a white mass barely decipherable as the sacrificial lamb. Here is painting as a leap of faith and a final affirmation of El Greco's belief that the most powerful art is the result of the human imagination as opposed to slavish imitation of nature.

El Greco died on 7 April 1614. He was buried in the crypt of Santo Domingo el Antiguo, the scene of his first Toledan commission and where his last picture was hung before its more recent transfer to the Prado. Within six years, however, his remains were moved to another church (San Torcuato, subsequently destroyed) because his son Jorge could not afford to pay for the rent on the crypt. Just as his mortal remains disappeared, El Greco's reputation sank, if not without trace, then certainly into the margins of mainstream art history. What did remain, however, were his paintings, which struck a powerful chord among a burgeoning avant-garde in Northern Europe three hundred years later. In both France and Germany he was viewed as a pioneering figure in the evolution towards modernism. His status as a mystic and visionary, and as an outsider artist, has been somewhat overplayed in this respect, but he had a strong religious faith, a rich and varied artistic background and a spectacular imagination which helped to create one of the more idiosyncratic styles in Western art.

9.

Rubens
1577–1640

The history of Western art is full of female flesh, but perhaps no artist has quite the reputation for depicting the naked female form as the Flemish painter Peter Paul Rubens. His artistic output, however, was as varied as it was vast. It encompassed altarpieces, mythological and historical scenes, intimate family and formal court portraiture, sophisticated allegories and pioneering landscapes. Yet in all this variety Rubens's style is immediately and internationally recognizable. He was, after Titian, the second great international artist, not merely as a result of his eventful diplomatic career, but because his broad travels, extensive artistic studies, impressive knowledge and keen intellect made him receptive to an eclectic range of influences which, when combined with his acute visual sensibility, created sensual, dynamic, often grandiose works of art. In short, he possessed a very clear understanding of what it was that made a good painting, however restrictive the terms of its commission might be. Rubens's paintings consequently had a very wide appeal, and in the troubled times in which he lived, he enjoyed a fame and success that no artist before him had ever experienced.

Peter Paul Rubens was born on 28 June 1577 in Siegen, in Westphalia, northern Germany. His family had only recently moved to this region from Antwerp to escape religious tensions and political turmoil. In the Dutch Revolt, or Eighty Years' War, (1568–1648), the seventeen provinces of the Low Countries sought to free themselves from the oppressive rule of the Spanish Habsburgs. The region suffered the Inquisition and the atrocities of an occupying army, including the 'Spanish Fury', which raged through Antwerp in the year before the artist's birth. Rubens's father was a Calvinist and in Catholic Antwerp was liable to persecution; thus in 1570 the family became part of an exodus of 100,000 religious refugees from the Spanish Netherlands. For his first ten years, therefore, Rubens was brought up and educated in north Germany. After his father's death in

1587, however, the family returned to Antwerp, having prudently converted to Catholicism. By this time the Low Countries had become irreversibly split. In 1578 the ten southern, largely Catholic provinces had returned to Spanish rule, with guarantees of their provincial liberties; while a year later the seven northern, predominantly Protestant provinces had resolved to fight to the death for complete independence as the 'United Provinces of the Netherlands'. There followed nearly seventy years of periodic warfare in which the Spanish tried to recover these lost provinces, which in turn received the intermittent support of Spain's enemies, England and France. It was in this environment that the adolescent Rubens came of age in a city that struggled to reassert its former dominance in trade whilst coping with the ongoing difficulties of war.

The Rubens family were socially well connected in Antwerp, and when he was thirteen, Rubens became a pageboy for the widow of a local count, giving him his first taste of court life. Sketches of courtiers by the young pageboy survive; they are his first drawings and indicate a growing interest in art. Rubens soon left the court and, like all artists of his day, he served an apprenticeship, although his was a notably elaborate one. For four years he was apprenticed to the landscape artist Tobias Verhaecht (1561–1631) and subsequently studied under Adam van Noort and then the humanist Otto van Veen (1556–1629), from whom he received a thorough classical and literary, as well as artistic, education.

Among his earliest paintings, an image of Adam and Eve (c.1598–1600, Rubenshuis, Antwerp) shows the influence of van Veen, whose figures have the same artificial smoothness and sculptural feel to

THE BAROQUE

The term 'Baroque' has very loose definitions but is commonly regarded as a style evident in painting, sculpture and architecture of the seventeenth and early eighteenth centuries. Following on from the aesthetic perfection of the Renaissance and the eccentric forms characteristic of Mannerism, the Baroque period is characterized by its sense of movement, theatricality, illusion and naturalism.

Rome was the artistic capital of Europe in the seventeenth century and is seen as the birthplace of the Baroque, where Bernini, Borromini and Caravaggio, among others, made their mark in this new style. But it soon spread further afield, to France, Spain and Catholic Flanders, where Rubens fully embraced and developed the ideas.

Its concepts were based on classical principles, particularly in architecture. However, artists and architects no longer felt compelled to abide fully by the 'rules' that dominated Renaissance art and architecture, and found ways to subvert what had gone before, breathing life and movement into antiquity. Jacob Burckhardt described this style in his artistic guide to Italy, Der Cicerone (1855), 'the same tongue as the Renaissance, but in a dialect that has gone wild'. Like the term 'Gothic', the word 'Baroque' was used derogatorily and was coined during the neo-classical period that followed. It appears for the first time with reference to the fine arts in 1755 in a passage written by one of the founding fathers of art history as we know it – Johann

them. It is based on a copy of a work by Raphael, which his teacher would have shown him, but there are signs of a different sensibility trying to emerge. Eve could almost be made of marble and at this stage in his life the twenty-one-year-old painter seems to have had little experience of female flesh. Adam is more alive, with a pronounced musculature far in excess of that depicted by van Veen in his own work. In the background, an idyllic Garden of Eden winds its way into the distance, the beginnings of an interest in landscape which would culminate in the first great topographical works of Northern European art.

About the time that Rubens was working on *Adam and Eve*, he was made a master of the Antwerp Painters' Guild, which enabled him to work independently and to take on pupils. But his own education felt far from complete, not least because he needed to see more major art at first hand. Consequently, two years later, in 1600, he headed south to the region that still dominated the mainstream culture of Europe – the Italian peninsula. His first port of call was Venice, whose sensual artistic tradition struck a chord in the young painter which reverberated throughout his life; but it was the city of Mantua which perhaps shaped Rubens's career most strongly. Within weeks of arriving in Italy, he had been recommended to Vincenzo Gonzaga (1562–1612), the Duke of Mantua, who employed him initially as a court painter, primarily to produce portraits of his numerous mistresses. Rapidly, however, his role expanded and over the next eight years Rubens worked for the Duke in Genoa, Milan, Venice, Padua, Florence and Rome, painting portraits of the noble families in whose houses he often stayed, making copies of works by the major figures of the Italian Renaissance for the Gonzaga

---

Winckelmann, who wrote Barrockgeschmack ('baroque taste'). This composite German word derived from 'pearls and teeth of unequal size'. Much has been made of the meaning and origins of the word 'Baroque', but in terms of explaining the nature of the art produced, it is not particularly useful.

The ideas of Baroque art were firmly entwined with the Catholic Church and, more specifically, the Counter-Reformation. Although much secular art can be classified by this term, the involving and often emotional style of the Baroque movement lent itself to the overt rhetoric and pervasive power of the Catholic Church.

Rubens utilized the stylistic methods of the era for both his religious and secular works. They commonly show figures moving freely in space and in the midst of action. Bodies are captured at their most outstretched, the most dynamic point of movement. Compositions using the device of a strong diagonal line (for example, his celebrated altarpiece in Antwerp Cathedral, *The Raising of the Cross*) can be seen in many of his works enhancing the sense of movement and instability. Like many artists of the Baroque, Rubens used light symbolically to represent enlightenment, reason and truth against its enemy, darkness (as in *Peace and War*). This is carried out with greater subtlety in his portrait of the scholar Caspar Gevaerts in 1627, whose head and book are bathed in soft light, alluding to his enlightened mind and vision.

palaces and advising on the buying of art for one of the great European collections. In addition, the Gonzaga court was a magnet for other major creative figures: Claudio Monteverdi was the court musician at the beginning of the seventeenth century and the great astronomer and physicist Galileo Galilei visited at least twice during Rubens's time there. His experience, therefore, of the most advanced art and culture in Europe was immense and unrivalled among his contemporaries north of the Alps and provided the bedrock of one of the more illustrious artistic careers.

Rubens's own work began to develop more markedly in Rome, where he stayed for over a year from the end of 1601. His first commission was for an altarpiece for a small subterranean chapel in the Church of Santa Croce. The main panel, *St Helena with the True Cross* (1602, now in Notre Dame Cathedral, Grasse), shows the mother of the first Christian emperor, Constantine, on a legendary visit to the Holy Land, where she discovers the Cross on which Christ was crucified. Filled with angels and ornate architectural details, the work is somewhat overcrowded, with the young artist seemingly desperate to show what he has learned. In its playful, exuberant mood, the work shows that Rubens was already beginning to wrestle with Baroque art, a dynamic, sometimes overblown but invariably vigorous style, which became the visual force of the Counter-Reformation. Its greatest practitioners, Annibale Carracci (1560–1609) and Michelangelo Merisi da Caravaggio (1571–1610), currently dominated the contemporary art scene in Rome and their work demonstrated the fundamental differences in artistic theory of the period. Rubens, however, was also coming to terms with the art of a more distant past, notably classical sculpture, which manifested itself in the poses of various figures in the smaller panels of the Santa Croce altarpiece, notably the figure of Christ being mocked, which combines the poses of perhaps the two most celebrated of all antique sculptures: the *Apollo Belvedere* torso and the *Laocoon*. Using classical art in this way had become commonplace, but Rubens was beginning to approach it in a different way. Not only did he study and sketch, but he also reinvigorated both classical and Renaissance forms (particularly the sculpture of Michelangelo) by drawing over reproductions in ink with the point of his brush and then adding yellow and white highlights as if recasting sculpture in his own pictorial language. It also anticipates the Modernist idea of the found object as the basis for artistic transformation by four centuries.

The combination of Rubens's education, his reputed charm and his growing familiarity with court life suggested that he would make an excellent diplomat. Gonzaga must have been impressed with Rubens's conduct, because in 1603, when he was only twenty-five, he was sent to

Spain to present a gift to King Philip III (1598–1621). This was the first
of many diplomatic missions for the artist and it proved to be a highly
successful one. From the copious letters Rubens wrote on this trip and,
indeed, throughout his career, we learn that there were torrential
rainstorms in Spain on his arrival and that many of the paintings that he
was to present to Philip III were badly damaged. Rubens was able to
restore some and replaced others with work he produced there and then.
Subsequently his work was seen by Philip's first minister, the Duke of
Lerma, who duly commissioned the young Flemish artist to paint his
portrait. The resulting image, *The Duke of Lerma on Horseback* (1603,
Prado, Madrid), developed the equestrian tradition revived by Titian in
his portraits of Charles V. Rubens saw this and other major works in the
phenomenal royal collections in Spain and, in turn, was able to set the
tone for a new type of dynamic equestrian portrait, which would
strongly influence his illustrious pupil, Anthony van Dyck (1599–1641).

Back in Mantua, Rubens finally received a big commission from
the Duke, who arranged for him to paint a vast altarpiece in the city's
Jesuit church. Most of the resulting panels were dispersed during the
Napoleonic Wars, but the large fragments of the main picture that
remain in Mantua show a growing boldness. *The Gonzaga Family,
Adoring the Trinity*, (1604–05, Museo del Palazzo Ducale, Mantua) depicts
the lavishly dressed members of the Gonzaga family kneeling beneath
a shimmering vision of God the Father, Son and Holy Ghost set in an
Arcadian, classical world.

Success in Italy bred more of the same and, at the age of twenty-
nine, Rubens received his first high-profile commission in Rome itself.
The project was to paint another altarpiece, this time for the so-called
Chiesa Nuova, the centre of the reforming Catholic Congregation of
Oratorians, described by Rubens in a letter as 'without doubt the most
celebrated and frequented church in Rome today, situated right in the
centre of the city and to be adorned by the combined efforts of all the
most able painters in Italy'. These 'able painters' included Caravaggio,
whose *Entombment of Christ* was already in the church when Rubens
began to work on the high altar.

The commission was a tricky as well as prestigious one which
involved the painting of an intricate scene showing *St Gregory the
Great Surrounded by other Saints* (1606–08, Musée des Beaux-Arts,
Grenoble), but with a fourteenth-century frescoed image of the
Madonna and Child to be contained within it. Rubens's response
was to paint a vast Roman arch, set against a deep, swirling blue
background with the early Christian saints and Gregory himself
looking up at the frescoed image, itself seemingly embedded into

the arch but with angels fluttering around it and one cheeky little cherub leaning against it with its elbow close to the Virgin's face. The work was graceful and exuberant, if slightly melodramatic, a Baroque composition full of movement but verging on the unorthodox. When it was installed above the altar, however, it became invisible, due to light blindingly reflected off its gleaming canvas surface. Unperturbed and keen to impress, Rubens painted a second version on slate which was more elaborate but less radical, with angels clustered, magnet-like, around the icon, but none leaning nonchalantly against it this time, and the saints themselves flanking the main image in separately painted panels. The commission not only showed Rubens's burgeoning talents as an artist, but also his flexibility and an ability to work originally, radically even, within any constraints imposed on him; it demonstrated, too, that he knew when to practise restraint. These were qualities which decisively shaped his future success.

In 1608 Rubens was called home on the death of his mother. He brought his first, rejected altarpiece from the Chiesa Nuova back to Antwerp, and erected it above her grave, describing it self-effacingly as 'the least unsuccessful work by my hand'. Although Italy had become Rubens's spiritual home and he considered living there, his success in Antwerp was to prove so immediate that he stayed there. Despite travelling extensively throughout the rest of his career, Rubens was never to see Italy again. Twenty years after leaving, he was to write: 'I have not given up hope of fulfilling my wish to go to Italy. In fact, this desire grows from day to day, and I declare that if Fortune does not grant it, I shall neither live nor die content.'

THE WORKSHOP

In September 1609, Rubens was appointed court painter by Archduke Albert and Archduchess Isabella but was allowed to stay in Antwerp, could teach whoever he liked and was free from guild regulations which demanded that he declare how many assistants he had (which normally restricted the number of pupils).

As early as May 1611, Rubens wrote that many people wanted to be his pupils and that he had to turn applicants away. He boasted to the agent of James I of England: 'I am, by natural instinct, better fitted to execute very large works than small curiosities. No undertaking, however vast in size . . . has ever surpassed my courage.' He could only make this claim because he had a large studio of assistants. He needed a good deal of this help simply to meet the enormous market demand. Between 1616 and 1621, he could afford to build a new house with a whole wing as his studio. This studio was compared to a Renaissance workshop, where the creative master has his pupils and apprentices helping at different levels (grinding pigment, preparing canvases, actually painting). Studio assistants were employed to copy Rubens's own works: mythological, allegorical, devotional works and portraits exist in multiple copies.

Specialist colleagues painted parts of his paintings (backgrounds and subordinate features, such as landscapes and still-lifes) and he also employed engravers to copy his works and publish them in both the Netherlands and France. A

During the sixteenth century Antwerp had been a flourishing seaport, but had suffered heavily from war. Many of the city's churches had been repeatedly damaged, and the Dutch blocked the Scheldt River, totally closing off the port for a time. The restoration of the city offered Rubens considerable opportunities. In 1599 King Philip II of Spain's daughter, the Archduchess Isabella, and her husband, the Archduke Albert, arrived in Antwerp as Regents, and under their direction the Spanish Netherlands enjoyed several years of comparative peace. In 1609, his reputation bolstered by glowing reports from Italy and Spain, Rubens became painter to the court in Brussels, but negotiated with the Regents to remain in Antwerp; the appointment therefore bestowed a title and honour, but without time-consuming court responsibilities. It also ensured contact with other painters associated with the court, such as Otto van Veen and Jan Bruegel, son of Peter Bruegel the Elder, as well as with the prominent citizens of Antwerp, some of whom became his clients.

In the same year that he cemented his financial and social position in Flanders, Rubens established his artistic reputation with two contrasting commissions: one public, the other private; one devout, the other erotic. The former was for the Statenkamer, or state chamber, of Antwerp's town hall, the first of numerous versions of *The Adoration of the Magi* that Rubens painted for various patrons; a grandiose pageant of presentation by both the depicted wise men and the painter himself. The latter was also a biblical scene, but this time it was an image of lust and betrayal, of sensuality and morality. *Samson and Delilah* (1609, National Gallery, London) was painted for Nicolaas Rockox, a wealthy

---

sketch would be made, then an oil-painting 'modello' for the patron's approval, and then finally the full-scale work.

There is a celebrated account of Rubens, on one occasion, painting while someone read to him from Tacitus, at the same time as he was dictating a letter and conversing with his visitors; while there were 'a good number of young painters occupied in the different work for which Rubens had provided chalk drawings'. Rubens added the final touches 'All this is considered to be Rubens's

work and thus he has gained a large fortune.'

On 28 April 1618, in a letter to an English buyer, Rubens distinguished between works which were 'original, entirely from my hand', works which he had done in collaboration, and studio works which he had only retouched. He tried to persuade the buyer: 'You must not think that the others [i.e. ones which he had not painted alone] are mere copies, for they are so well retouched by my own hand that they are hardly to be distinguished from originals.'

Clearly, there was a marked preference among buyers for paintings entirely by Rubens and some dismay at finding that they were only retouched by him. The importance of the 'name', of the idea of 'individuality', had clearly become firmly entrenched. Rubens was often criticized for selling copies by his pupils under his own name.

Even after 1620, when Rubens was frequently absent abroad, on diplomatic missions, the output of his studio hardly declined.

citizen and Burgomaster of Antwerp, whom Rubens regarded as a 'gentleman of the most blameless reputation' and a 'connoisseur of antiquities'. He subsequently commissioned a raft of works from Rubens, including several significant public pieces, but this one was for his eyes primarily, to hang over the fireplace in his dining room or 'great salon'. The image is a post-coital one. Samson lies slumped across the lap of the woman who has just seduced him and who is in the process of betraying him to the Philistines, who wait at the door whilst a barber cuts off his hair. It is a frozen tableau of quiet drama and of impending doom. Even as his legendary strength drains away, though, Samson is still a monumental figure, like a vast Michelangelo sculpture but made of flesh, muscle and bone. The painting is richly textured and full of contrasts: from the silk of Delilah's dress to the animal fur draped around Samson, all set against some of the most delicately painted flesh that Rubens ever produced. The scene is bathed in a gently glowing light – as if to emphasize the afterglow of sex – with the fatal beauty of Delilah's youthful face illuminated by a flickering candle which also reveals the haggard features of the old maid or procuress. This emphasizes the seventeenth-century view that Delilah was a harlot and Rubens certainly makes clear the point that sexual temptation leads ultimately to tragedy. There is, however, a marked ambiguity in her expression, a mixture of triumph and pity and the way her hand tenderly caresses his back seems to imply that this is a celebration of the sensual pleasures of the flesh as well as a warning.

A similar gesture of tenderness is visible in another painting from 1609 which shows a fresh-faced young woman with her hand resting on that of a clear-eyed, confident man sitting under a bower of honeysuckle. This is Rubens himself and Isabella Brandt – the daughter of a noted Antwerp lawyer and humanist – who had just become the artist's wife. Earlier the same year Rubens's brother Philip had married Isabella's aunt. The painting, *The Artist and his Wife in a Honeysuckle Bower* (c.1609, Alte Pinakothek, Munich), was the first of many family portraits that Rubens made over the course of two marriages which produced nine children. From both letters and paintings, it seems clear that he was a devoted – if frequently absent – husband and father and this early picture shows him happy and at ease, with the arrangement of the two figures symbolic of marital confidence and contentment. It is an intimate and informal portrait, made more interesting by the fact that it is painted in the year he became court painter and therefore had to concern himself primarily with official iconography. It is also suggestive of his enhanced status: Rubens the gentleman rather than Rubens the painter.

In 1610 Rubens began building a large house in Antwerp, which took seven years to complete. Initially, this comprised a traditional Flemish house, but he redesigned it, adding a large Italianate studio and Renaissance garden which eloquently professed his artistic pedigree. As the number and scale of commissions grew, Rubens's workshop became busy with pupils and apprentices. He was also immensely popular with pupils who wanted to join his workshop. In 1611 he wrote, 'I can tell you truly, without exaggeration, that I have to refuse over 1,000, even some of my own relatives or my wife's, and not without causing great displeasure among many of my best friends.' His most famous student was Anthony van Dyck, who would go on to become court painter to Charles I of England and Scotland. Rubens would often start a project by painting a *modello*, a small pen or oil work indicating the basic idea. Then he would draft the design on canvas and indicate with chalk the colours he wanted. His apprentices would do the bulk of the painting and Rubens would finish the piece with his own touches. It has been estimated that of the 3,000 paintings from his workshop, only a fifth, about 600, can be attributed solely to Rubens. There was no sense of misleading or deceiving clients in this practice, which had its origins in the medieval guilds and workshops of Italy and Flanders. The works were collaborative, rather in the manner of latter-day architecture, but their creative vision came primarily from the maestro himself and works were priced according to size and how much time Rubens had put into them. Painting was a business as well as an art form and Rubens was a shrewd operator who also employed graphic artists to make engravings of his paintings; these effectively served as broader advertisements of his talents.

Rubens's reputation as the foremost painter in Northern Europe was established through two monumental commissions between 1610 and 1612. The first was for an altarpiece in the parish church of St Walburga, a triptych showing *The Raising of the Cross* (1610–11); the second an altarpiece for the chapel of the Guild of Arquebusiers (a type of shooting club, of which his friend Rockox was Master) in Antwerp Cathedral, showing the *Descent from the Cross* (1611–14). The two works now exist on either side of the main transept of the cathedral and are among the crowning achievements of religious art. *The Raising of the Cross* suffers a little in comparison, not least because it was taken out of its dark, Gothic setting at St Walburga's into the often dazzling natural light of the cathedral where it seems almost too bright. It shows an heroic image of Christ triumphant even as He is crucified. It is a vigorous image for a vigorous faith; robust, strong, full of taut drama as the eye is taken diagonally from bottom right to top left, charting the ascent of the Cross itself. Move across the main altar and on to the right-hand chapel and you see the consequences of the Crucifixion, a staggering image which reverses the diagonal thrust and pulls the eye from top right to bottom left, as if draining the last drop of life from the limp but still muscular body of Christ. It is a much darker picture, but in death Christ radiates celestial light, even as the sun sets in the background. It has everything the Catholic Church could ask for in a sacred painting and more, from the still-life (the blood-splattered crown of thorns) to moving death, from graphic portraits of saints and soldiers to exquisitely rendered architecture and landscape in the side panels which show the pregnant Mary and the infant Christ being taken to the temple by his mother. It took Baroque painting to another level, that of divinely intimate grandeur, but it also perhaps encouraged lesser painters to try to emulate its achievements and spawned numerous empty, overblown imitations.

Over the next decade, Rubens produced twenty-two altarpieces for Antwerp alone and sixty-three major paintings for churches in the city and further afield. No one matched his scale and technique north of the

Descent from the Cross
1611–14, Antwerp Cathedral
Even though this work has been widely reproduced and it occupies not the main altar in Antwerp Cathedral but that of a side chapel, nothing quite prepares the viewer for Rubens's epic sacred drama in the flesh. Christ's flesh, pallid and with the life drained from it, still seems to illuminate the whole picture ('The Light of the World'). His body is lowered onto a sheet held by two men at the top of the gnarled Cross. The physical sense of descent is made all the more tangible by the fact that one of the men grips the sheet between his teeth, straining to keep a grip on the outstretched arm of Christ. At the base

of the Cross are the three Marys: Mary Cleophas, Mary Magdalene – tenderly holding the foot she has recently washed and dried with her hair – and the Virgin Mary. Her pose is dignified rather than distraught; her expression anguished but not convulsed, emphasizing the strength of Mary encouraged by Counter-Reformation theologians.

The composition is dominated by this diagonal thrust, from top right to bottom left, but look again and you realize that the organization of the figures recreates the form of the Cross itself with John the Evangelist, clad in scarlet, beginning a strong counter-thrust that runs up to the bearded figure of Nicodemus.

The flanking panels are

totally separate scenes – unlike those of *The Raising of the Cross* – but thematically they are very much part of a unified whole. On the left is the young Mary, pregnant and displaying her stomach to her cousin Elizabeth, likewise pregnant with John the Baptist. On the right, the infant Christ is presented at the temple to the high priest behind whom the bearded profile of Nicolaas Rockox, Rubens's friend and the man who commissioned the picture, is clearly visible. The triptych is therefore a depiction of both the relationship between a mother and her son and a condensed life cycle from soon after the Immaculate Conception, via infancy, to death.

On the back of the

left panel is an image of the vast figure of St Christopher carrying the young Christ, visible when the altarpiece was closed at various times during the ecclesiastical year. In Christian legend, Christopher was 'the Christ bearer' and he was also the patron saint of the Arquebusiers, whose chapel the painting adorns. The idea of bearing the body of Christ, of carrying it from birth to death, dominates the entire work. It is a concept that is reinforced every time Communion is given from the altar itself, with bread and wine proffered to the kneeling communicants as 'the body and blood of Christ' set against the backdrop of Rubens's monumental masterpiece.

Alps and his overtly Catholic style was not an impediment to a favourable reception in Protestant countries, even in The Hague, where there were deep sensitivities to idolatry. Now in his forties, Rubens's fame was extensive, and he was the first choice for the most important public commissions in Flanders. In 1620 the Jesuits commissioned him, with the assistance of van Dyck, to paint thirty-nine paintings – parallel cycles of scenes from the Old and New Testaments – for the ceiling of their newly built church in Antwerp, in the design of which Rubens also participated. 'I am the busiest man in the world,' he complained a few years later.

International developments, however, required the famous painter to play the role of diplomat. As part of the general European conflagration known as the Thirty Years War (1618–48), which left few regions unscathed, the twelve-year truce between the Spanish provinces

The Marriage of Maria and Henri IV, Medici Cycle, 1622–25, Louvre, Paris

and the United Provinces came to an end in 1621. War between the Dutch and the Spanish troops broke out sporadically for the next twenty-seven years. Rubens was a close aid to the now widowed Archduchess Isabella, offering her political advice and acting as her intermediary with the Dutch. He travelled under the guise of painter, but was in an excellent position to get close to the dignitaries with whom he negotiated. Art and diplomacy have, perhaps, never had so symbiotic a relationship as they did during this period in Rubens's career.

The largest project, certainly in terms of square footage of painting, came from the French court, and nowhere else did Rubens's double role as painter and diplomat coincide to such a degree. In January 1622 Rubens was called to Paris to discuss the decoration of the new Luxembourg Palace. Marie de' Medici, mother of the French King, Louis XIII (r.1610–43),

The Flight from Blois, Medici Cycle, 1622–25, Louvre, Paris

wanted to celebrate the lives of herself and her late husband, Henri IV (r.1589–1610) in two cycles of paintings. Discussions took six weeks, during which Rubens was careful to suggest non-political subjects. The size of the task was formidable; the Queen's adviser, the Abbé de Saint Ambroise, said in public that 'two painters of Italy would not carry out in ten years what Rubens would do in four and would not even think of undertaking pictures of the necessary size'. Rubens used assistants to help him with the backgrounds and the less significant details, although his contract stated that he was to paint all the figures himself. Marie de' Medici's troublesome past also caused great difficulties for Rubens. He was obliged to paint her as a powerful woman who exuded moral goodness, but there was nothing really to celebrate about her life; indeed, it was besmirched with scandal – she was implicated in her husband's assassination and had later quarrelled with her son. Rubens bolstered the paintings with classical allegorical figures, which allowed him to maintain a degree of ambiguity and avoid delicate issues. When the Abbé de St Ambroise showed the rest of the court around the finished cycle, he introduced the paintings, as Rubens wrote, 'changing or

The Meeting of Marie de' Medici and Henri IV in Lyon
1622–25, Louvre, Paris
Diplomacy, scholarship and artistic imagination are the hallmarks of Rubens's first grand cycle of twenty-four paintings for Marie de' Medici, conceived and created within the space of four years. The entire project was a tricky, if lavish, exercise in flattering the mother of the King of France – Louis XIII – whilst maintaining artistic credibility and not incurring the anger of Louis, whose relationship with his mother was a tempestuous one, leading to two periods of exile for Marie. The series of paintings depicts the life of the Florentine princess from birth and childhood through to her 'reign' as

Regent in France. The high point of her official life and of Rubens's pictorial account was her wedding to Henri IV, and no less than four paintings were dedicated to this subject, of which this is the culmination.

Marie was twenty-seven when she married, mature – to put it mildly – by the standards of the time. Her wedding took place by proxy in Florence Cathedral in October 1600, Henry being too busy to attend what was, in effect, a political union. A few months later, the two finally met in Lyon in circumstances that were far from romantic. Apparently Marie had been kept waiting for the best part of a week and her new husband arrived in the middle of the night. None

of this, naturally enough, is apparent in Rubens's depiction of the event, poetically transformed – with all the licence he can muster – into a classical scene where Jupiter and Juno – alias Henry and Marie – first cast eyes on each other, touch and trigger a star-spangled celebration. Here, the picture tells us, is a marriage made in heavenly splendour. The goddess of marriage – Hymen – joins them together, a lavish union mirrored by two peacocks, the decorative bird associated with Juno herself. Below, riding on a chariot drawn by lions straddled by two putti, is the personification of the city of Lyon (pun doubtless intended), who wears a crown of fortified city walls. The whole image

is topped by a shimmering rainbow signifying peace and harmony.

It is an impeccable allegorical Baroque painting, ludicrous by the standards of historical accuracy but astute by those of diplomatic necessity: Marie was duly flattered; her son took no exception to an image which had a classical twist. Jupiter was a god and a notorious lover of young women; Juno was bitter and sought revenge. The rumours connecting Marie to the assassination of her husband in 1610 were never proven, but the irony wouldn't have been lost on the more knowing courtiers who saw the work in the Luxembourg Palace.

concealing the true meaning with great skill'. The first cycle was finished
in 1625, a grandiloquent set of twenty-four paintings. The second cycle,
depicting the life of Henri IV, was never painted, due to the exile of Marie
de' Medici from France in 1631. Nonetheless, what was produced remains
an extraordinary achievement, an object lesson in the art of imaginative
history painting, a monument to Marie's enlightened if self-serving
patronage, her massive ego and Rubens's theatrical talents. It is both
pictorial masque and art conceived and produced in the grand manner.

In the summer of 1626 Antwerp was hit by the plague and Rubens's
wife, Isabella, died. The griefstricken Rubens responded by throwing
himself even more into his diplomatic duties: 'I should think a journey
would be advisable, to take me away from the many things which
necessarily renew my sorrow,' he wrote soon after. 'The novelties which
present themselves in to the eye in a change of country occupy the
imagination and leave no room for a relapse into grief.' In 1628 he spent
several months at the court of Philip IV of Spain (r.1621–65), a noted art
collector. Here, he copied works by Titian from the vast royal collection,
presumably watched by the inquisitive eye of Velázquez, the young court
painter whom Rubens met and whose distant mentor he became. The
idea that an established artist should spend time simply copying the
work of another had little or no precedent, but Rubens was refuelling
himself creatively and Titian was his great tutor. The lessons he learned
in his second visit to Spain inspired much of the virtuosity of his last
decade. In 1629 he journeyed to England under the official title of
Secretary to Philip's Privy Council of the Netherlands. His mission
was to smooth the way for peace negotiations between England and
Spain. Rubens already enjoyed considerable fame in England and he
was well received by the English court and by Charles I, who conferred
a knighthood upon him.

During his stay in London, Rubens presented a painting to
Charles I as a gift. This was *Peace and War* (1629–30, National Gallery,
London), which illustrated Rubens's hopes for the peace he was trying
to negotiate between England and Spain. The painting is an allegory,
a highly symbolic and complex one which can be intricately decoded
but whose message is abundantly clear: peace brings abundant
reward and prosperity though it is constantly threatened by war. The
central figure represents Pax (Peace), who distributes her bounty to
a group of figures in the foreground, including children, who have
been identified as portraits of the offspring of Rubens's host, Sir
Balthasar Gerbier, another painter–diplomat in the service of Charles
I. To the right of Pax is Minerva, goddess of wisdom and the arts. She
is depicted in the act of driving away the threatening figure of Mars,

the war god, closely followed by Alecto, the fury of war. With this menace averted, a winged cupid and Hymen, the goddess of marriage, lead the children to a cornucopia, or horn of plenty. Two nymphs approach from the left, one bringing riches, the other dancing to a tambourine, while a putto holds an olive wreath, symbol of peace. Rubens's overture to peace and revulsion at war is clear. Diplomacy enriched his art and was served by it too.

London also gave him the opportunity to paint on a grand scale once again and Rubens was commissioned to provide the ceiling decorations for the Banqueting House in Whitehall. Inigo Jones (1573–1652) had designed the building as one of the first in a neo-classical style in the British Isles, completing it in 1622. The ceiling was divided into nine large panels, each glorifying the reign of Charles's father, James I, who had died in 1625. His overriding political legacy was the beginning of the unification of England and Scotland in 1603, a peaceful process which Rubens commemorated with relish. Classical gods and heroes surrounded James, depicted as the new King Solomon, no less. Before he left England, Rubens appears to have sketched designs for the ceiling for approval by Charles I, and after his return to Antwerp he made oil sketches for each of the nine large canvases. The full-scale pictures were then painted in Rubens's studio, completed in 1634, and were in place in the Banqueting House by March 1636. They remain the only significant decorative scheme created by Rubens still *in situ*.

While he was still in the process of completing the Banqueting Hall ceiling, a defining moment occurred in Rubens's diplomatic career. Still passionately convinced that the Netherlands could be reunited, he made a personal, unofficial visit to the Dutch Ambassador to London. Acting on his own initiative, he begged the Ambassador to reopen negotiations, but in vain. His aspirations were worthy but idealized, surprisingly unpragmatic for a diplomat, but then he was first and foremost an artist. After various wrangles over payment for his services and having been snubbed by the England and Flemish court factions who resented his close relationship with the King and Archduchess, he vowed to resign from his official duties, a resolution which became inevitable after the death of Isabella at the end of 1633.

In 1630, at the age of fifty-three, Rubens married again. His second wife, Hélène Fourment, was the sixteen-year-old daughter of a rich silk merchant and the niece of his first wife. In a letter to a friend, he indicated that marriage to an aristocrat was not beyond his reach, but eventually he preferred a wife 'who would not blush to see me take my brushes in my hand'. He was clearly infatuated with her youth and voluptuous beauty and Hélène became Rubens's principal muse. She was painted in

Het Pelsken (The Little Fur) *1635–40, Kunsthistorisches Museum, Vienna*

At the end of 1634, Rubens wrote to a friend that, at the age of fifty-seven, he was 'not yet inclined to live the abstinent life of a celibate', adding, slightly demurely, that 'if we must give the first place to continence, *fruimur licita voluptate cum gratiiarum actione*', which translates as 'we may enjoy licit pleasures with thankfulness'.

Nowhere is the older man's infatuation for the source of his 'licit pleasures' made clearer than in this portrait of his wife, Hélène Fourment, thirty-seven years his junior. She stands before us, modestly attempting to cover herself but with an expression that implies that she has been taken by surprise. Given that she posed for the picture for her husband and that he stipulated in his will that the work was for Hélène and Hélène alone (i.e. not to be sold), there is an artistic as well as erotic conceit at work, but the idea that an intensely private moment has been captured and revealed remains a strong characteristic of the painting. Her gaze is strong and unashamed, a loving look towards her husband that is reciprocated in almost every aspect of Rubens's image.

The work is a labour of love, a homage to the woman who has borne his children and whose body he knows and revels in. Rarely has flesh been painted so sensuously, even if the contours of her body are a little more rotund than contemporary taste now dictates they should be. Even aside from the fact that body fashions change from century to century, Rubens doesn't shy away from Hélène's imperfections; rather, he seems to celebrate every aspect of her physicality: the dimpled knees, the bunions, the folds of flesh under her arms and the lop-sided appearance of her breasts. The fur, previously depicted by Rubens around the body of the dormant Samson, adds texture and an erotic charge, a reference to her covered sex and heightening the contrast with her exquisitely painted hand and wrist. It also refers and pays a less obvious homage to Rubens's artistic hero, Titian, whose image of a *Lady in a Fur Coat* was owned by Charles I and had been copied by Rubens in 1629, during his stay in London.

Hélène appears to be inside, perhaps in her dressing room, with its lush red carpet and a cushion casually tossed on the floor. Look again and you see a fountain with water gushing from the mouth of a lion to the right, a reference to a statue of Venus by the most celebrated of all classical artists, Praxiteles, a Roman copy of which Rubens had seen in the Vatican. In turn, Hélène's pose, with her arm pulled across her breasts, is taken from another celebrated Greek sculpture, the so-called *Medici Venus*.

On one level, it's as if Rubens cannot quite escape his own classical learning and artistic knowledge in order to depict his wife as she really is. On another, Rubens seems to be attempting to give an otherwise explicitly erotic image the respectability of antique art, but the overriding message conveyed is more touchingly sensual and romantic than intellectual: Hélène is Venus for Rubens, his own goddess of love.

numerous poses, seated on a terrace, reading a book, and with her various children. But she also fulfilled another role, that of nude artist's model, still a rarity in Catholic countries and only widespread throughout Europe in the nineteenth century. Hers was the flesh that launched numerous late paintings by Rubens of classical goddesses: she appears as both a supporting nymph and as Venus herself; she is also depicted as simply herself (although there are classical overtones for respectability's sake) in a picture which celebrates erotic desire and unidealized beauty. Like so much of Rubens's later work, *Het Pelsken* (*The Little Fur*, 1635–40, Kunsthistorisches Museum, Vienna) appeals to the senses rather than to the intellect. It shows Hélène naked but for a fur wrap, a mass of soft skin, voluptuous to the point of fat, with folds of flesh visible in an image which paints her as she is, imperfect but a real living, breathing human being whom Rubens loves and desires. There are, of course, complex power relationships evident in the creation and viewing of such a work, but there is also something tangibly real, vulnerable, forbidden and touching about its visual candour.

The year 1635 saw the triumphal entry into Antwerp of Cardinal Archduke Ferdinand of Spain, Archduchess Isabella's successor. Rubens was asked to decorate the city to celebrate the occasion. The surviving designs show ornate and elaborate triumphal arches, floats and chariots, decorated with scenes celebrating Habsburg rule.

Het Steen (or The Castle of Steen)
1635–38, National Gallery, London
Although apparently a topographical study of extraordinary intricacy, this painting is as rigorously composed as any that Rubens made. It was the result of a series of sketches, in chalk and ink and in oil, made outside, and charting both the house – Het Steen – and its surrounding countryside. The finished panel painting is therefore a constructed vision based on acute observation of the natural world. It is also clearly a celebration of Rubens's new estate, title and

liberation from the predominantly urban world which he had previously inhabited.

The scene is bathed in an autumnal light which, given our knowledge that the house faces east, is that of the early morning. The sky orchestrates the mood of the picture and the soft yellow clouds find their echo in the golden-brown hues in the foreground of the picture. On the right, a farmer sits astride one of two horses pulling a cart in which his wife sits. Already, and without overlabouring the point, Rubens creates a narrative of a journey beginning even if it is only to the local market.

Likewise, in the immediate foreground, a hunter carries a gun and together with his dog stalks an unsuspecting flock of plump partridges. It is an Arcadian image, of man in harmonious relationship with the world, but it is also a credible one, where Rubens's manipulation of the landscape from one of dull flatness into an undulating paradise is utterly convincing.

Over towards the house itself, at least three tiny figures are visible, looking out towards the horses and cart and seemingly out towards the viewer. Perhaps it is the Lord of Steen himself, Rubens, and

his Hélène with one of their children, as if re-enacting the process of observation from which the picture was constructed.

In spite of the lowly status of landscape painting, Rubens treats the preparation and creation of this picture with the same meticulous discipline with which he approached his allegorical or portrait commissions. It is an intensely personal painting, never intended for sale, but it is one of the pioneering images in European landscape painting, an inspiration to artists as diverse as Claude, Constable, Turner and beyond.

In the midst of triumph, however, Rubens made pointed references to political reality. His designs for the arches included Mercury, the god of trade, deserting the city – a reference to the Dutch blockade of the Scheldt; another featured Janus breaking out of his temple, a classical symbol of the outbreak of war. Rubens, it seems, was beginning to tire of large public commissions. Although he continued to work for the great rulers of Europe, his letters show him hankering after retirement. His *Self-portrait* (1639, Kunsthistorisches Museum, Vienna) depicts an older, wiser and less self-conscious figure than the one seated under a honeysuckle bush together with his first wife. Just as Hélène was depicted if not with warts and all, then at least with the signs of multiple motherhood visible, so Rubens portrayed himself with a red nose and a lined face, facing up to his ageing self in a way which suggested he felt liberated from the constraints of having to please numerous patrons as he had done for most of his life.

Also in 1635 Rubens and Hélène had bought a country house between Brussels and Malines, the Château de Steen or Het Steen. From 1639 this became a retreat where, in spite of his growing gout, he could begin to focus on landscape. His paintings took on an Arcadian, nostalgic tone, in sharp contrast to the dramatic works of twenty years before. Although he was clearly reducing his prodigious workload and slowing down, there is no sense that Rubens was merely dabbling with nature. His late works have verve and dynamism, but the emphasis shift. Landscape was perceived both as a specialist field and as a minor genre, an adjunct to other forms of painting. Learning, as he so often did, from Titian about the importance of integrating Man and his surroundings, and of the value of landscape as a background to set the tone of the work, Rubens's interest in the natural world slowly developed and moved centre stage in the last five years of his life.

Both of the major oil paintings that Rubens produced at Het Steen were painted for the artist's own interest and pleasure. *Het Steen*, or *The Castle of Steen* (1636, National Gallery, London) and *Landscape with a Rainbow* (1635–38, Wallace Collection, London), bring some of the most monotonous countryside in Europe to life. Rubens, the newly established country gentleman with the title of Lord of Steen, was undoubtedly celebrating his newly acquired estate, but he was also scrutinizing the world around him and developing a technique which would flourish two centuries later, namely observing and sketching directly from nature. Numerous ink and chalk sketches reveal how Rubens charted the landscape around his home and there is evidence to suggest that he also painted some of the small oil sketches outside, focusing on the effect of light at

different times of the day, month and year: the sun is obscured, bursts
through cloud, creates rainbows, illuminates the landscape with a
golden glow or is muted in greyness; sometimes it is moonlight that
Rubens observes and at other times it is the refracted quality of light –
from sun or moon – on water that captures his attention and his
brush. It is this expansive and slightly obsessive approach that gives
the finished works their creative sparkle. Of course, neither of the
large panels was worked on anywhere other than the studio, but the
experience of looking at and being in nature is deftly transferred from
sketch to final painting. Likewise, truth to nature is only an initial
quest and by the time Rubens paints *Het Steen*, his tendency to idealize
and transform all aspects of his painting into a balanced composition
still predominates. The left-hand side of the picture is mainly in
shadow, a tightly constructed image of a farmer and his wife
beginning the journey to market, with a huntsman and his dog
stalking a flock of partridges in the immediate foreground. In the
background, and painted with the care an artist might give a
figurative portrait, is the château itself, illuminated and seemingly
illuminating the world around it. The right-hand side of the picture
is devoid of humankind, bar the faintest glimpse of a town on the
horizon. The flatness of the actual landscape gives way to a gently
undulating terrain created by Rubens through lushly modulated
green and brown hues. In contrast to the left-hand side, it is an
expansive vision. Likewise, in *Landscape with a Rainbow*, the painting
is divided with equal if subtle rigour, though this time more strongly
along horizontal lines, with milkmaid and farmers, cattle and
ducks, haywains and carters all frolicking in the foreground whilst
a magnificent rainbow erupts out of the sky behind. *Het Steen* is
filled with morning light; *Landscape with a Rainbow* shimmers with
the light of the late afternoon, continuing a Flemish tradition of
the depiction of time passing which goes back via Bruegel to
illuminated medieval manuscripts.

There is a tendency to suggest that Rubens loses himself in
landscape towards the end of his life, but nothing could be further
from the truth. He continued to paint allegories wrestling with his
most enduring interest and fear, namely the horrors of war, as well as
producing sensual images of women, and of Hélène in particular. There
is, however, a link throughout his late work, and that is the subtle fusion
of art and life. No longer constrained by positions at court nor worried
by the specific needs of patrons, a more liberated artist emerges who
breaks many of the boundaries he had previously established in terms
of subject matter and technique. His wife steps in and out of her

husband's work; nature begins to break free from human control; and Rubens allows his painterly virtuosity if not to run riot, then certainly to run loose as his brushstrokes become increasingly more personalized and expressive. Sadly, however, the message conveyed so powerfully in his allegorical work, that pleasure will always be shadowed by pain, was borne out in his life as gout made the act of painting increasingly difficult.

Rubens died on 30 May 1640, a month before his sixty-third birthday, paralysed with fever and gout. He was buried in the Fourment family vault in his own parish church of St Jacob's, Antwerp. Subsequently, a funerary chapel was created in his honour, with one of his last paintings above the altar and an inscription on the floor which likened him to the great Roman artist Apelles. He was, without doubt, a formidable classical artist and perhaps the grandest Catholic painter, but he was also a good deal more subversive within the confines of those long traditions than he is often given credit for. The Romantics saw him as one of their own and Delacroix, in particular, claimed that Rubens 'overwhelms you with so much liberty and audacity'. In the twentieth century, almost all the great painters of human flesh, from Soutine and De Kooning to Bacon and Freud have acknowledged a debt to Rubens, whose work, at its best, is intellectually rigorous, extraordinarily ambitious, yet still has a freshness and vitality that transcends the immediate context of the world in which it was created.

10.

Velázquez
1599–1660

The artistic culture of Spain in the early seventeenth century was conservative and restricted by the censures of Counter-Reformation doctrine. This potentially repressive milieu was an unlikely environment to produce one of the most influential figures in the Spanish artistic tradition. Yet Diego Velázquez de Silva became the unrivalled master of the secular portrait and a champion of naturalism in Spanish painting. He transformed the image of the Spanish royal court with a degree of realism that had never been seen before. To the contemporary viewer, his portraits are almost photographic representations, created by methods that appear strikingly modern. In his lifetime, he became unquestionably the foremost Spanish painter, and his paintings subsequently inspired many other great artists, from Goya to Picasso and beyond. The father of French Impressionism and one of the pivotal painters in the evolution of Modernism, Edouard Manet, was stunned when he saw Velázquez's paintings for the first time in 1865: 'He is the painter of painters. He has astonished me, he has ravished me.'

Born in 1599, into a middle-class family in Seville, southern Spain, Diego Velázquez de Silva had a comfortable upbringing. His father was a notary, the son of a Portuguese noble. Velázquez appears to have had an excellent literary education, and in later life his library was considerably more extensive than was normal for a painter. It was seen as unusual for someone of his background to take up the craft of painting in Spain; it was considered a manual rather than intellectual pursuit, and painters were not generally expected to be knowledgeable on any subject other than the application of paint to a canvas. In Velázquez, scholarly learning combined with artistic talent to foster a highly successful career as courtier and painter.

In 1610, when Velázquez was eleven, he was apprenticed to the painter Francisco Pacheco (1564–1644), a cultivated man with a sound knowledge of the Italian Renaissance. For six years, Velázquez learned the skills of painting, living in Pacheco's home in Seville, becoming almost a surrogate son and subsequently cementing his close relationship with the family when he married Pacheco's daughter, Juana Miranda, in 1618. Pacheco later wrote, 'I married him to my daughter, moved by his virtue, integrity, and good parts and by the expectations of his disposition and great talent.' Pacheco was not a particularly outstanding painter himself, but he was well versed in the theory of art and the different techniques available to a painter. Pacheco also developed connections with Seville's intellectual élite, notably humanist scholars and poets who met at an 'academy' overseen by him, and he had access to the library and collections of paintings and antiquities at the palace of the Duque de Alcalá. Velázquez probably learned more from Pacheco's intellect than his master's style of painting, which was formulaic and stilted.

In Seville, Velázquez was surrounded by art that was uninspiring and conventional. The Church engendered a numbing orthodoxy, vetting works of art for their conformity to the rigid doctrinal principles promoted by the Counter-Reformation. Indeed, Pacheco himself was artistic censor for the Seville Inquisition. Sevillian artists were paid little, often pooling their resources in artists' companies so they might share any profits. This further stultified creativity and promoted endlessly unoriginal paintings produced as economically as possible. But beyond the confines of an introspective art world, the city itself – in particular, the daily lives of its citizens – provided Velázquez with a means of escape fuelled by his growing interest in naturalism.

Rather than simply paint figures from life in the studio or produce still-life pictures of inanimate objects as elegant artistic exercises, Velázquez combined the two genres and created a series of pictures which brought the world around him to life: men eating and drinking in taverns, quietly conversing; women preparing food in cookhouses and modest domestic kitchens; an old man selling water. These scenes were known as *bodegones*, a Spanish term which literally means 'chophouse' or 'tavern'. They had parallels in literature, in popular stories of tavern life, but Velázquez was also aware of the work of the influential Italian artist Michelangelo Merisi da Caravaggio (1573–1610), whose work often depicted biblical scenes set in everyday places, populated by ordinary people but painted in a dramatically contrasting combination of dark and light. This graphic realism and unidealized portrayal of individuals formed the basis of Velázquez's *bodegones* and helped to form the artist's own style. In his earliest work, *Three Men at a Table*, produced when he was barely eighteen, Velázquez depicts a simple meal of bread, fruit and fish on a brightly lit yellow tablecloth. Emerging out of the shadows and seated around the table are three male figures, an old man, a young man and a boy. One frowns gently, the next laughs and the third smirks a little. In the background, and barely visible aside from the white collar of her dress, is a waitress who offers a carafe of white wine which just catches the light and so flickers in and out of vision. It is as if the viewer has just wandered into a small bar and stumbled on the scene, perhaps having tripped up slightly, causing the figures to look up and smile. It is painted with a remarkably assured touch and conveys a quiet dignity echoed in all the subsequent *bodegones*. Conventional beauty is nowhere to be found, but these are undeniably beautiful works of art. Velázquez takes the idea of naturalism to another level, even at this early stage in his career . His scrutiny of objects and figures and the effect of light is almost scientific in its exactness and mirrors a growing interest in optical processes which developed throughout his life. Painting becomes not merely an imitation of nature, but a rumination on the nature of transforming what the eye sees into a painted form.

There was allegorical meaning in the work too, notably the transience of life. In both *The Waterseller of Seville* and the *Old Woman Frying Eggs*, his two most accomplished early works, the contrast between youth and old age is writ large and yet there is invariably a touching sense of connectedness between all the figures in these paintings. No artist has ever quite conveyed human dignity in the way that Velázquez does: quietly, calmly, suggesting an intensity of feeling but devoid of all sentimentality or melodrama. If he had died having only completed his *bodegones*, Velázquez would still have been a great artist. But as it transpired, he had only just begun to produce masterpieces.

The *bodegones* were painted in Seville at a time when the city was in decline. Just thirty years or so before, it had been one of the wealthiest ports in Europe and the largest city in Spain. Its wealth was due to the imports of gold and silver from the Americas. But as the River Guadalquivir began to silt up at the beginning of the seventeenth century, economic decline set in. The reduction in imports of silver led to royal bankruptcy, and what money was left was haemorrhaged on perpetual wars – principally renewed attempts to suppress the rebellious Dutch provinces (after 1621), and the broader European conflagration known as the Thirty Years War (1618–48).

Still in his early twenties, but with an impressive body of work already behind him, the increasingly accomplished Velázquez sought to strike out on his own. His father-in-law and former teacher tried to help his young protégé by using his connections to help gain Velázquez a position in Madrid, where he would have a broader experience of art and, indeed, of life. After initial failures, in 1623 both Velázquez and Pacheco were presented to Count-Duke Gaspar Guzman de Olivares (1587–1645), a patron of artists and writers and the most powerful man in Spain. Olivares was the chief minister to the young Spanish King Philip IV (r.1621–65). Olivares aimed chiefly to reverse the recent decline in Spanish fortunes. The previous reign, that of Philip III (r.1598–1621), was regarded as a decadent, corrupt and profligate regime. Olivares required new portraits: a new iconography for a new king. Furthermore, Olivares was himself from Seville, and was therefore keen to establish a Sevillian connection with the court.

Olivares took a close interest in the precocious talents of Velázquez and knew of his ambitions to become a court painter. But it was luck as well as ability that was to shape Velázquez's future. When one of the six court painters died, leaving a vacancy, Olivares permitted the twenty-four-year-old to make the long journey to Madrid to meet the King and paint his portrait. It was a daunting task. Velázquez was a young painter who had little or no experience of life outside Seville. The stakes were high, but Velázquez succeeded in producing an image of the young Habsburg monarch which made such an impression that he was immediately taken on as a court painter. According to Velázquez's biographer, Antonio Palomino, the Count-Duke Olivares

> promised him that he alone would portray His Majesty and that the other portraits [of the King] would be withdrawn. He ordered him to move his household to Madrid and confirmed his title on the last day of October 1623, with a salary of twenty ducats per month and payments [for] his works, as well as medical care and medicines.

The original picture was subsequently lost in the fire at the royal palace in 1734, but Velázquez produced numerous portraits of the King over the next few years which have survived. Philip appears in armour,

THE PRADO

19 November 1819 saw the public opening of Spain's Royal Art Museum – then called the Royal Museum of Painting and Sculpture. The museum had been founded by Ferdinand VII a year earlier, based on the royal collection which had been amassed by earlier Spanish monarchs.

The building is an excellent example of Spanish neo-classical architecture and had initially been intended for a museum of natural science. At the time of opening, the museum displayed 311 paintings, which consisted entirely of the royal collections which had been on view in the palaces of Spanish sovereigns.

The royal collection, which had been amassed over three centuries by the Habsburg and Bourbon kings, is seen as the backbone of the museum. The Prado also boasts works from some of Spain's greatest artists, such as El Greco, Velázquez and Goya (Spain's most celebrated contemporary painter when the Prado opened in 1819).

In 1872 it was renamed the National Museum, when it combined with the contents of the Trinidad collection, which displayed works that had been

on horseback and in shimmering brown-and-silver apparel in works which redefined the royal image as Olivares intended. His pronounced lower lip and slightly sunken doleful eyes give a sense of individual character, but the paintings are essentially images of kingship rather than a particular king. The earliest surviving portrait is perhaps the one which set the tone and became the model for all future royal portraits, the full-length *King Philip IV* (1624), which now hangs in the Prado. Here is a magisterial image for public scrutiny, reminiscent of the way the King received distinguished visitors and depicting a dutiful, austere, immobile and remote figure, rendered in an understated, tightly painted manner. According to Pacheco, this painting was completed in just one day, but this is generous-spirited myth-making. Detailed examination reveals the shadow of Philip's cape and leg under a second layer of paint. This illustrates an important aspect of Velázquez's method of working. It was repainted to portray a more stylish, less bulky pose. He rarely made preparatory drawings, but often reworked figures on the canvas itself.

In many ways, Philip IV and Velázquez came of age together, one as a monarch, the other as a clever propagandist for the monarchy. It was a relationship that would significantly shape the career of a great artist.

The atmosphere among the other court painters rapidly became tense when they realized their work was being overshadowed by the phenomenal talent of the younger man; indeed, Velázquez seemed to get preferential treatment from the start. He was paid more than the previous court painter to join the ranks of the enormous Spanish court, and while payments to other painters were in arrears, Velázquez was receiving not only his salary but also gifts and favours from the King.

Madrid had only been Spain's capital for about sixty years. In that time, its population had increased more than tenfold. The city had much to prove to its European counterparts. Velázquez was given a studio in the royal residence, the Alcazar, sandwiched between the apartments

taken from monasteries and convents. Shortly afterwards, the museum received many religious pieces of work from schools and 'primitives'. It changed its name again in 1873, due to a liberal revolt, and was renamed the Prado.

Throughout the Spanish Civil War of 1936–9, the museum was closed. Many of its works were taken away shortly after the first bombs fell on Madrid in November 1936. By that time, the museum had gained symbolic and political meaning. The Prado's work followed the republican government to Valencia, Catalonia, Perlada and Figueras. The republican government and an international committee led by painter Jose Maria Sert moved the Prado's works across the Pyrénées, where they were given a temporary home in Geneva – in the Palace of the League of Nations – in the summer of 1939. After the war, the collection was returned. The Prado owns 20,000 pieces of work, which include sculptures, decorative arts, drawings and paintings by most of the great names of European art.

of Olivares and the King. His royal patron did not make excessive demands upon his time or impose specific terms on commissions; he did not even require that Velázquez work exclusively for him. 'The liberality and affability with which he is treated by such a great monarch is unbelievable,' wrote Pacheco. 'He has a workshop in his gallery and His Majesty has a key to it and a chair in order to watch him painting at leisure nearly every day.' Envy among his colleagues prompted the slander that Velázquez could only paint heads. When the King wryly mentioned this to Velázquez, he is reputed to have replied: 'My Lord, they flatter me very much, because I do not know of anyone who knows how to paint one.' What followed has become one of the minor legends in art history: a painting competition set up by Philip IV to see who was the most impressive artist at court. The brief was to produce an image in honour of Philip's father, Philip III, showing him expelling the Moors from Spain at the beginning of the century. Three other artists competed with Velázquez in 1627, but with Philip IV choosing the judges – both of whom favoured the more radical, naturalist style that Velázquez had begun to master – there was only ever going to be one winner. Sadly, the successful work was also lost in a fire at the Alcázar, where it hung for more than a century.

Soon after the competition, Velázquez was given his first household appointment, as Usher to the Privy Chamber. It was a minor position, but one that could lead to advancement in the royal household: an

The Waterseller of Seville
1619–20, Wellington Museum, Apsley House, London
Painted when Velázquez was barely twenty, this picture establishes the artist's interest in optical naturalism from the very beginning of his career, as well as his superlative technique. It is a simple scene which shows an old man selling water to a younger man and boy. Velázquez draws on the daily life of his native city and from contemporary literature – from picaresque tales of tavern life which inspired scenes known as *bodegones*.

The three figures emerge from the gloom, in a layered progression into the light. In the foreground stand two flagons and a glass painted to mirror the composition of the figures and offering a visual rhyme which helps to bring the scene a little more to life. It is a painting of subtle contrasts, the most obvious manifestation of which is that between darkness and light. But look a little closer and there is the dusty, parched gown of the waterseller offset both by the crystal-clear glass he offers to the boy and the delicately painted droplets of water on the large

vessel. Like the image of the fig in the goblet, commonly used to refresh water in Seville, the painting seems almost mouth-wateringly real.

Natural as the picture seems, though, it is also carefully contrived. Velázquez staged figures and props in his studio to recreate daily life. Each of the figures is presented in a different pose (fully frontal, side profile and a three-quarter view), and the painting reads as an allegory of the three ages of man. There is also something liturgical about it; a daily ritual which seems to have a grander

significance closer to that of the Catholic Eucharist. None of the figures is idealized, nor are they patronized; instead, Velázquez gives each a quiet, contemplative dignity in an image which seems almost timeless.

It was a painting highly valued by Velázquez, who took it to Madrid three years after its completion as a demonstration work or showpiece. The work was subsequently sold to Juan de Fonseca, chaplain to Philip IV and an early patron of Velázquez.

opportunity that was usually blocked to a mere court painter. The Spanish court was considered the most complex and hierarchical in Europe, and also the most expensive. There was an army of servants, about 1,000 in total, all slotted in to the complicated ranking system. It was a place of discontent, where payments were often late or never materialized, but from the outside, the magnificent Alcázar seemed to be the epitome of power and order.

In 1628, Velázquez met the most important artist in Europe, the great painter and diplomat of the Spanish Netherlands, Peter Paul Rubens (1577–1640). Rubens had been sent by the Governor of the Spanish Netherlands to Madrid on a diplomatic mission, but he found time to study the paintings in the magnificent royal complex outside Madrid, El Escorial. His companion on these trips was Velázquez, who was awestruck by the more experienced artist – not merely by his talents as a painter, but by the manner in which he conducted himself with members of the court. In both respects, Rubens became a role model for Velázquez; as ambitious courtier and successful painter.

The extent of Rubens's direct artistic influence on Velázquez is disputed, but may be discerned as early as 1628 in the *Feast of Bacchus* (1628–29, Prado, Madrid). This was his first mythological scene, which depicted Bacchus, the god of wine. It was possibly because of Rubens's visit that Velázquez started to make more use of classical forms, in particular the nude. It is very different from other Bacchanalian paintings of the time, a more complex piece because the other figures are in contemporary dress. In contrast to the smooth, serene and almost statuesque form of Bacchus, they have weatherbeaten faces, rugged features and ragged clothes. No one before him had approached the subject in this way in a painting: here are marginalized figures – a blind bagpiper, a beggar and a soldier – whose lives are made bearable by the pleasures of drinking. It is a dignified celebration of low-life, with Velázquez drawing on his experience in the *bodegones* to grapple with a classical subject and empathize with the common man.

Undoubtedly motivated more directly by Rubens, Velázquez requested leave from the court to visit Italy in order broaden his artistic knowledge beyond the horizons of the royal collection. Philip signalled his approval by providing Velázquez with all the documentation he required to smooth his path from one court to another. In 1629, he sailed to Genoa, travelled to Milan and then moved on to Venice, where he could admire the paintings of Titian, Tintoretto and Veronese. These were to have an important effect on his artistic development, but he spent most of his time abroad in Rome, to where many artists gravitated not only as a centre of antiquities, but also as a place where artists and scholars discussed and assessed the most recent artistic developments and which had now emerged as the dominant city in Italian art. Velázquez stayed at the Villa de' Medici, where he studied ancient sculpture, and was a welcome guest at the Vatican.

The lessons Velázquez learned in Italy are evident in a work painted in Rome in 1630. *The Forge of Vulcan* (Prado, Madrid) is a mythological scene in which Apollo appears before Vulcan, the blacksmith of the gods, to warn him of his wife's infidelity with Mars, the god of war. It is a wonderfuly painted frozen moment, with the workers stopped dead in their tracks as they listen with disbelief. Colour, notably in Vulcan's robe, is heightened and suffused with light and seems to have been inspired by Titian and Venetian art in general. The bodies are pure classical creations, which stemmed from Italian painting and his studies of antique sculpture, but the faces and expressions are exercises in Velázquez's developing brand of naturalism. Their reactions range from a flicker of surprise to incredulity, but are depicted in a restrained way; all the emotion is shown on the face, in the eyes, the subtle tilt of a head or a wrinkled brow. By studying directly from nature and not simply by rehashing ideas and techniques from other artists, Velázquez (Vulcan-like himself in this respect) forged his own style and came closer to realizing what many others had singularly failed to do: breathing life and feeling into the painted figure.

On his return to Madrid in 1631, Velázquez embarked on the most productive period of his career. Count-Duke Olivares had just presented a new palace, the Buen Retiro, to Philip IV, and Velázquez was commissioned to decorate part of the interior, principally the Hall of Realms. For this room, he designed a large cycle of portraits and produced the most prestigeous of twelve planned battle scenes, *The Surrender of Breda* or *Las Lanzas* (1635, Prado, Madrid). This shows the victory of the Spanish after the year-long siege at the Dutch city of Breda in 1625. The painting is thus a documentary of the event, albeit not an entirely faithful one. The Spanish general Ambrogio de Spínola is shown graciously accepting the key to the fortress of Breda from the Dutch commander, Justin of Nassau. This 'event' never happened; it is rather a symbolic summary of the outcome of the siege. It is thought that Velázquez was inspired by a play of Pedro Calderón (1600–81), which was performed at court in 1625 to commemorate the victory. In reality, the Dutch were allowed to withdraw quietly three days after the surrender, but Velázquez turns it into an iconic image charged with resonance and political meaning.

Spinola has dismounted, to be on the same level as Nassau, and touches him on his shoulder to console him and prevent him kneeling

235

before him. This is an unusual approach to take; traditionally, in such paintings, the victor is shown on horseback, receiving the keys from a prostrate enemy. It is clear from the contrasting armies who has won. The ordered ranks of Spanish soldiers, elegantly attired and with their pikes standing menacingly to attention and punctuating the entire right-hand side of the painting like the beat of a military drum stand in marked contrast to the Dutch on the left, bedraggled and tired as they face up to their defeat. Likewise, the wretched Dutch horse which froths at the mouth seems ready for the knackers' yard, unlike the frisky stallion opposite, which is game for more action. But this is not a triumphalist picture which trumpets victory. There are no dead or wounded bodies in the foreground, no melodramatic movements and no commotion. This was what the Spanish court wanted: simplicity and modesty. By underplaying Spanish military and political superiority, the moral force of the Spanish cause is emphasized. Here, the true soldiers of Christ chivalrously vanquish the misguided forces of Protestantism.

Once again, Velázquez realizes a monumental subject through his empathy with the common man and his ability to create searingly naturalistic portraits. Each of the soldiers seems true to life, contemplating what is happening with expressions similar in range and intensity to the viewers who stand looking at the picture itself in the Prado in Madrid. Some seem to be questioning the nature of war; others celebrate the apparent generosity of the human spirit. On the extreme right-hand edge of the piainting, clad in a fetching grey-green jacket and hat, topped with a feather to emphasize his growing stature, is Velázquez himself, looking out at us as we look at his work and signalling his total involvement with the pictorial world he has created.

Velázquez's career at court was certainly on the rise. In 1636 he was made Assistant in the Wardrobe and 1643 Assistant in the Privy Chamber. During the 1630s, the chief part of his artistic work comprised portraits of the royal family, but also of the *hombre de placer*, the dwarfs and buffoons of the court. These entertainers were the only court members able to avoid the strict laws of etiquette, amusing the King with magic tricks, jokes and general tomfoolery. By the standards of the twentieth century, their treatment as toys and figures of ridicule seems inhumane, but, without wanting to see Velázquez as a man of our times, his paintings of these figures of fun has something of the same quiet dignity that had been present in his work from the *bodegones* onwards. In works like *The Buffoon Calabazas* (1639, Prado, Madrid) and *The Dwarf Francisco Lezcano* (1643–45, Prado, Madrid), Velázquez once again identifies with the marginalized figure but also experiments with composition and technique. In these closely cropped pictures there is a feeling of being pushed up against the surface, of making the viewer a little uncomfortable. The faces stare back with a wry condescension, accentuated by the looser brushstrokes with which Velázquez has painted the clothes and surrounding space.

The 1640s was a bitter and turbulent time for the court. Olivares's aggressive centralizing policy within Spain led to an uprising in Catalonia (1640–48) and to the catastrophic secession of Portugal in 1640. Resorting to oppressive measures to obtain funds, Olivares's unpopularity led to his downfall in 1643. It was also a time of great personal tragedy for the King, when in 1644 his wife, Queen Isabella, died, followed two years later by their seventeen-year-old son, Balthasar-Carlos. During this period, Velázquez's chief task was to design and redecorate some of the rooms of the enormous Alcázar. It was a mammoth task, and some rooms even had to be demolished and rebuilt. As part of the project, King Philip ordered Velázquez to visit Italy once again. His mission was to acquire new works for the royal collection, specifically from Venice and Naples, and to hunt out young, talented artists to paint frescoes for the palace. He was also to collect sculptures for the Alcázar and to have casts made of antiquities: no royal court with serious aspirations to high culture could afford to be without a collection of classical masterpieces. Philip IV was becoming a great art collector – he added perhaps as many as 2,500 substantial pictures to the royal collection – while Velázquez became highly regarded for his connoisseurship.

Velázquez's second visit to Italy lasted for nearly two years, from 1649. As before, his main destination turned out to be Rome, where he set about the business of expanding the royal collection with considerable zeal. He also continued to expand his own artistic repertoire and produced two of the most accomplished portraits of his career.

Juan de Pareja (1649–50, Metropolitan Museum, New York) is a phenomenal painting by any standards, but it seems all the more remarkable given that Velázquez used it as a preparation for a much bigger commission produced soon after. It shows his studio assistant, a forty-four-year-old Sevillian of Moorish extraction, staring nobly out of the canvas like a latter-day Othello. In fact, Juan de Pareja was effectively an artist's slave, not uncommon in seventeenth-century Spain, but Velázquez conveys a man of airy disdain. Pareja was also a painter himself, frustrated by his limited opportunity, but he seems to have been given his freedom by Velázquez soon after the work was finished and did indeed pursue a career as a minor artist. Pareja's portrait is rich in texture, from the lace collar to the velvet sleeve and coarser woollen cloak. Colour is restricted to brown and grey in addition to black and white tones, but

what ought to be a muted picture comes alive through the subtle play of light across the body and face of Pareja, culminating in the steely glint in his dark, expressive eyes.

The portrait was briefly shown in an exhibition in the Pantheon in Rome in March 1650 and the response was very strong. One critic who saw it reputedly dismissed the rest of the work on show as 'mere art', while describing Velázquez's work as 'truth'. More important, however, was the admiration of the most powerful figure in Rome, Pope Innocent X, who also wanted his portrait painted by the Spanish maestro.

Velázquez had met Innocent when he was still Cardinal Giovanni Battista Pamphili and a papal nuncio (or ambassador) before his elevation to the papacy in 1644. Velázquez's reputation and status as court painter to Philip IV made him an almost inevitable choice to paint the Pope once he arrived in Rome. Innocent was widely known to be mistrustful and impatient, a seventy-six-year-old man of waning strength who has become one of the best-known popes through the likeness that Velázquez produced of him on canvas. The *Portrait of Pope Innocent X*, (1650, Galeria Doria Pamphili, Rome) is both an image of papal majesty and a symphony in red. Like the portrait of Juan de Pareja,

Portrait of Pope Innocent X
1650, Galeria Doria Pamphili, Rome
In some respects, this is a conventional formal state portrait. It depicts one of the most powerful men in Velázquez's world, Pope Innocent X, who is turned away from both the painter and the viewer in order to emphasize his remoteness from the mortal world. But it is so much more than an image of papal power. It has an aura of its own. Francis Bacon, one of the great painters of the twentieth century, who used the image as a springboard for a series of works in which the Pope is depicted racked in an agonized scream, described it as 'one of the greatest portraits that has ever been made'. Bacon

added that he had become 'obsessed' by the painting: it 'haunts me and opens up all sorts of feelings and areas of imagination, even, in me'. The Pope sits with an air of irritation about him, as if he's been coerced into a lush velvet box and is on the verge of breaking free. The self-conscious look in his eyes and the appearance of a frown on his face make him seem more human. Innocent was described in various accounts as an ugly man, but that has been softened, along with signs of his age. He was seventy-six when he sat for Velázquez, but that is not evident in the portrait. Without therefore being a penetrating psychological study, which would have been inconceivable for an artist

who barely knew his sitter and who would have been compelled to maintain a respectful distance, Velázquez's portrait captures something of the sitter's character – his vanity, pomposity, impatience and vulnerability.

Velázquez follows in the tradition of papal portraiture established by Raphael in his *Portrait of Julius II* in 1512, but, technically, the work is highly original. As in so many of his portraits, Velázquez uses a limited palette, but he turns the picture into a highly charged symphony in red. Scumbled brushstrokes of black and a flicker of white turn the background into one of thick velvet; smoother strokes of white

render the hat (or biretta) and cape a shimmering mass of satin, and then, using thick, impastoed white paint dragged across a thinner grey/white ground, Velázquez creates the cascading lace and cotton drama of the Pope's alb. Close up, the details blur. Move away, though, and the picture comes into focus, sharper here, less so there, mirroring the way the eye perceives and bringing a potentially stiff image fluidly to life. No one, not even Velázquez's artistic heroes Rubens and Titian, had been so bold with a formal portrait, whose spontaneity and vitality remain, for many, a minor miracle even today.

it seems almost to breathe, full as it is of luxurious painterly textures. By turning Innocent slightly away from the viewer, Velázquez creates a respectful distance between us mere mortals and the head of the Catholic Church; but the slight frown on his face and a hint of self-consciousness in his eyes reaffirm the fact that he was human after all, and frail and vulnerable, too. When Innocent saw the work, he declared it to be 'troppo vero' – 'too true' – but accepted it nonetheless and the work has remained in the Pamphili family ever since.

Velázquez, now fifty years old, appears to have settled comfortably into the artistic life of Rome. He was admitted to the city's prestigious Academy and seems to have been in no rush to return to Spain. He fathered a child whom he called Antonio, by an unnamed woman, and was perhaps contemplating a long stay in the Eternal City when Philip IV summoned him back to Madrid. In spite of his subsequent efforts to return, this was to be his last visit to Italy.

On his return home to Spain, he discovered that much had changed. He found the King remarried to his niece, Mariana, who was to bear him four children. Philip IV was eager to push forward with the decoration of the Alcázar, but Velázquez was again forced to balance the roles of court painter and court functionary. The combination of roles, however, was

The Toilet of Venus (or The Rokeby Venus)
c.1644–48, National Gallery, London
The date of this work remains something of a mystery, with some scholars dating it between 1644 and 1648 and others arguing that it was produced just before or even during Velázquez's second visit to Italy, from 1649 to 1651. What we do know is that it was painted for Gaspar de Haro, a notorious libertine and the son of the Spanish Prime Minister, who later became the Marquis of Carpio. Nudes were rare in seventeenth-century Spanish art and this picture indicates just how much creative freedom and status Velázquez had.

It shows a woman lying naked on her bed, contemplating herself in the mirror. Her hair is tied up in a style which identifies her as a modern woman. The veneer of classical respectability is achieved through the presence of Cupid, who holds the mirror and transforms the woman into a goddess. Venus reclining or studying her own beauty was a recurring theme in Venetian painting, notably that of Titian, whom Velázquez admired deeply, but here he plays a more seductive game of hide and seek than in previous images of the subject. Venus stares at herself in the mirror, which in turn reflects her gaze out towards the viewer who contemplates the picture. It

is a cyclical process, compounded by the fact that her mirror is pointed not towards her face but at her genitals, which transforms the viewer into an uneasy voyeur, unwittingly (or perhaps in some cases desperately) trying to devour her body through the act of looking.

It is a highly sensual work, not least because of the long, languid brushstrokes applied by Velázquez down the length of her body to differentiate her flesh from the black satin on which she reclines. The erotic charge of the painting has been both celebrated and attacked, most notoriously by Mary Richardson, an English suffragette who took an axe to the painting

in 1914 at the National Gallery in London. Vilified in the press as if she had murdered someone, Richardson subsequently explained that she had wanted 'to destroy the picture of the most beautiful woman in mythological history as a protest against the Government destroying Mrs Pankhurst, the most beautiful character in modern history'. She added later that she 'didn't like the way men visitors to the gallery gaped at it all day'. Ironically, though, the painting depicts a woman whose image remains elusive and who appears to be in control, revealing only a part of her nakedness, however intensely she is scrutinized.

a determining factor in the subjects and character of his paintings. Velázquez's relationship with the King set him apart from other painters. In a country dominated by the Church, Velázquez was the only painter of the time who was exempt from carrying out religious commissions. Furthermore, he had the freedom to paint nudes, and historical and mythological subjects – vividly illustrated in his painting of *The Toilet of Venus*, otherwise known as *The Rokeby Venus*, after a future owner. In this, one of the most celebrated of all depictions of a nude woman as goddess, both mythological and sexual, Velázquez demonstrated that he was effectively beyond the control of the usual agents of artistic censure in seventeenth-century Spain.

Aside from restrictions in their artistic subject matter, other court painters had to carry out relatively menial tasks, such as gilding woodwork or repairing paintings. Velázquez, however, was exempt from such activities. In 1652 an election was held for the office of Palace Chamberlain, for which Velázquez was one of six contenders. The King chose him for the post, even though the court voted otherwise. His chief responsibility was the maintenance of the King's quarters, which involved a host of mundane tasks: ordering an army of servants to clean, make fires and change bed-linen. He was also in charge of planning royal itineraries and arrangements at large ceremonies. The position was well rewarded, both in salary and additional perks. When Velázquez first started at the court, his salary was 20 ducats plus individual payments for each painting, which varied, but by the end of 1648 his annual income was 3,300 ducats, which was occasionally supplemented by massive grants of up to 2,000 ducats. He moved his family to the 'Treasure House', valued at 500 ducats a year, adjoining the palace. Equally important to him was the prestige which accompanied such appointments and through which he hoped to shed the image of the artist as mere artisan or craftsman and to acquire, as Rubens had, the status of a gentleman of the court.

As his role in the functioning of the court became more extensive, the number of his paintings appears to have dwindled. The quality of his output, however, seemed to improve. Painting is an art whose most illustrious practitioners tend to take time to mature, but few artists produce their very best work at the end of their lives. Velázquez did, in a painting which remains both a great enigma and, in the words of E. H. Gombrich – not an art historian prone to hyperbole – 'artistically the most perfect'.

Las Meninas (1656, Prado, Madrid) is rather oddly named after the maids of honour who attend the young Infanta Margarita, the King's daughter, but the painting was originally called *The Royal Family*. It is

Las Meninas

1656, Prado, Madrid

Less than half a century after this work was completed, the Italian painter Luca Giordano proclaimed it to be 'the theology of painting'. It has always been revered by artists. Goya, Degas, Manet, Picasso, Dalí and, more recently, Richard Hamilton are just some of the illustrious names who have made work in homage to and been inspired by Velázquez's undisputed masterpiece. It seems both of its time and of a future when art fell under the spell of those who sought to produce a seemingly immediate impression of what the eye sees in painted form.

It is an extraordinarily sophisticated spatial construction, made up of visual, as well as intellectual, layers which give the work a feeling of immense depth. There is a line of continuity running from left to right, starting with Velázquez's canvas and the painter himself, and moving through Maria Augustina Sarmiento, the youngest maid of honour (or *menina*) to the angelic Infanta Margarita Maria, and then onwards via Isabel de Velasco (*menina* number two) to the two court dwarves, one of whom playfully kicks a docile dog in the foreground. Visually interspersed between the children, but further back in the room, are the Infanta's chaperone and bodyguard, while beyond them, silhouetted in an open doorway which adds yet more depth, is the Palace Chamberlain. Around the walls, as if to suggest other worlds which mirror this one, are paintings and then on the far wall comes the crux of the work: the image of Philip IV and Mariana of Austria reflected in a mirror.

The debate about what has happened to make the figures stop and stare out of the canvas so graphically, as if caught in a freeze-frame or photograph, is irresolvable, but the visual evidence which makes for such endless speculation is compelling. Whether or not Velázquez is painting the King and Queen or their daughter; whether or not the royal reflection is from the entry of Philip and Mariana into the room from where the viewer now stands; or even, as some have tried to assert, the mirror is no such thing but rather a painting, the experience of looking at the work is one of endless visual toing and froing, where the viewer's gaze is absorbed and repelled, first this way and then that. And just when you think you've grasped the picture, it eludes you.

Artists are drawn to the work because it wrestles with the fundamental problems and process of painting itself, of how an image is reproduced and perceived. Others, though, are endlessly attracted to the work because, aside from the charming nature of the children themselves and its quirky approach to a royal portrait, in reversing the traditional relationship between painter and sitter and showing us the back of Velázquez's canvas on the left, it ultimately puts the viewer at the heart of the picture.

indeed a royal portrait, but composed in a way that has no precedent in European painting. Velázquez captures a frozen moment with an almost photographic precision. The seven figures in the foreground and middle ground of the picture (maids, chaperones, bodyguards and court dwarfs, forming an entourage around the angelic young Infanta) seem startled, as if someone has just walked into the large room in the Alcázar where Velázquez has set up his vast easel and is in the process of painting. What exactly he is painting and what it is that has startled the Infanta and her attendants is not totally clear, but the key to this pictorial riddle seems to lie at the back of the room. On the far wall, and clearly visible, the figures of Philip and Mariana, the King and Queen, are framed – either reproduced in a painting, as some scholars would have it, or, as seems almost certain to be the case, reflected in a mirror.

The image of Velázquez and the royal couple in the same painting both acknowledges the painter's close and privileged relationship with Philip and is a wry play on the nature of painting as an art which mirrors nature – something which Philip would have clearly understood. It also focuses the viewer's attention on the nature of looking and being looked at, cleverly skewing the traditional relationship between painter, sitter and viewer. Ultimately, it is a rumination on the process of painting itself, a summary of Velázquez's life's work, from the intense observation of the *bodegones* to his inventiveness as a court painter. It is a work of optical precision and immensely complex composition, with delicately handled passages of paint, dramatic lighting and an elusiveness which makes the work endlessly compelling.

Las Meninas is also a statement of social intent on Velázquez's part. Here is an artist not content to paint in a small studio, but instead in a grand room in the royal palace festooned with works by Rubens, whose stature as both an artist and a courtier Velázquez so admired. Emblazoned on his chest and completing the picture in more ways than one is the cross of the Order of Santiago, the highest honour in Spain and one which he spent the last decade of his life trying desperately to achieve. He was knighted four years after the completion of the painting and the cross was either painted long after the completion of *Las Meninas* by Velázquez or perhaps even posthumously. One unlikely legend has it that Philip IV added it himself after news reached him of the painter's death.

It seems churlish to overstate Velázquez's social aspirations, particularly as they underpinned a good deal of his creative drive and were also inspired by an almost missionary zeal to upgrade the status of his profession in a world which seemed to value art more for the possibilities it offered for political or religious propaganda than for intellectual enlightenment. However, his biographer, Palomino, did lament the fact that court duty impeded Velázquez's supreme talent as an artist: 'Although we professors of painting are very proud of Velázquez's elevation to such honourable positions,' he wrote, 'at the same time we are very sorry to have missed so many proofs of his rare ability, that would have multiplied his gifts to posterity.' At the age of sixty-one the strain of his court responsibilities was taking its toll. Two months after he travelled north to the French border to attend the wedding ceremony of Louis XIV and the Infanta Maria-Teresa, on 7 June 1660, he fell ill. Whether or not he harboured hopes of painting the young *Roi de Soleil* we'll never know, but the thought is mind-boggling nonetheless. On 6 August 1660, Velázquez died in the Alcázar and was buried in the church of San Juan Bautista in Madrid. Neither palace nor church, nor even Velázquez's grave, remains today, but his ongoing power and impact as an artist has never seriously been threatened.

11.

Rembrandt
1606–69

The eyes always meet our gaze, even when they peer out of the gloom cast by the shadow of a ruffled mop of hair. They are quizzical, sometimes searing, occasionally contemptuous but always unflinching. The nose is even more distinctive; a bulbous great schnozzle, magnificent in its way but, sometimes hidden in the shadows or presented as if from some hopefully ennobling angle, until finally, in old age, it is fully lit, red-veined and shining like a beacon. It is the most familiar face in Western art, painted over and over again, and demonstrates the deepest knowledge: that of the self. Rembrandt was the most prolific self-portraitist ever to have wielded a brush and he remains unsurpassed in the art of self-expression. His legacy of well over a hundred drawn, etched and painted images of himself is, as his most recent biographer Simon Schama put it, an 'exhaustive archive of his face' which serves as both a pictorial biography and a profound rumination on the passing of time. Had Rembrandt been merely a portraitist, his achievement would have been immense; but his self-awareness and his technical mastery, particularly the expressive play of light, fuelled a more expansive artist who produced landscapes, biblical and historical subjects – not to mention the occasional vast composition of contemporary militiamen or surgeons at work – variously produced on canvas, paper and etching plate. His work, perhaps more comprehensively than that of any other artist, makes us aware of our mortality and of our individuality, striking a humane chord that seems universal.

Rembrandt Harmenszoon van Rijn was born on 15 July 1606 in Leiden, then the second city of Holland. He was the eighth of the nine children of Harman Gerritszoon van Rijn, a miller, and Neeltje van Suijttbroeck, the daughter of a baker. He was brought up and educated in Leiden. At the age of seven, his parents – having had all of Rembrandt's brothers apprenticed as craftsmen – sent him to the Latin School in

Leiden, to prepare for a learned profession. Rembrandt studied religion, languages and the liberal arts, and formulated a Latin version of his name, 'Rembrandus Harmensis Leidensis'. During this period, he adopted the monogram 'RHL' which he subsequently used to sign his early works of art. Seven years later, he matriculated into the Philosophical Faculty at the University of Leiden, the oldest in Holland, to study classics, but there is no record that he ever attended classes. Instead, he left to become an artist's apprentice, fuelled – we can only guess – by a strong creative desire but none the worse for having had a strong literary education. The notion, expressed by some historians, that his parents would have been dismayed seems overstated. Painting was a more than respectable profession in the Dutch republic and Rembrandt opted to learn the rudiments of his chosen vocation with a popular local painter from a prominent family – Jacob Isaakszoon van Swanenburgh. Isaakszoon was a decent enough draughtsman, but a mediocre artist who painted images of classical hellfire and damnation in the (by then) quaint manner of Hieronymous Bosch. Nonetheless, he seems to have been a competent teacher who taught Rembrandt the first principles of technique and preparation.

In 1624, Rembrandt finished his apprenticeship in Leiden and went to Amsterdam for six months to study under Pieter Lastman (1583–1633), a famous and highly esteemed artist of historical, religious and mythological subjects. Lastman had been to Italy – specifically to Rome – and so served as a channel through which Rembrandt experienced contemporary developments in Italian painting; Rembrandt subsequently never felt the need to visit Italy himself. Most significantly, Lastman was familiar with the works of Michelangelo da Caravaggio (1571–1610), whose dramatic and powerful style was characterized by unidealized naturalism, and a depth and space created by sophisticated use of light and shadow, or chiaroscuro. These influences had a profound and enduring impact on Rembrandt's art, and his early work owes much to Lastman, notably in colour, dramatic lighting and the construction of pictorial narrative. After studying with Lastman for six months, Rembrandt, aged nineteen, returned to Leiden in 1625 and set up a studio with a fellow artist, Jan Lievens (1607–74), whose reputation at this period was more established.

His first signed and dated painting, produced back in his home town, owes a good deal to his former teacher. It shows *The Stoning of St Stephen* (Musée des Beaux-Arts, Lyon), a subject that Lastman himself had painted. Space is tight, colour is bright, as is the light, and the death of the earliest Christian martyr is vigorously portrayed. Just above the defiant head of Stephen, peering between the arms of two men who prepare to pummel the saint with rocks, is a familiar young face – Rembrandt's – making an early appearance in his own work. Here, he seems to be a horrified but implicated witness; a year later, in a classically inspired but largely inpenetrable painting now called *History Piece* (Stedelijk Museum de Lakenhal, Leiden), Rembrandt depicted himself again, this time as a more detached observer of a solemn ceremony.

The source for these images – and indeed for the faces of many of the other figures who populated his larger paintings – was a series of physiognomical studies he produced occasionally in ink and gouache but mainly on an etching plate. He made some remarkable and moving studies of elderly individuals which formed the basis of a number of oil paintings which was rare if not unprecedented, certainly among younger artists. It was as if he was confronting mortality for the first time as a young man barely in his twenties, and he applied the same intense scrutiny to his own face in a series of etched images which show him laughing, scowling, howling, smirking and simply staring. These etchings were a kind of laboratory of enquiry into how the human face worked and how best to capture its range of expression and emotion. They helped form historical and biblical characters for other work; they were pieces in their own right, which were subsequently sold; and in turn, they encouraged Rembrandt to think about painting his self-image in oil, which he did with a vengeance.

His first fully fledged self-portrait is probably the one which hangs in the Rijksmuseum in Amsterdam, dated around 1628. Along with the similarly titled *Self-portrait as a Young Man* which hangs in the Alte Pinakothek in Munich, which is signed and dated 1629, these are the earliest of a series which placed his own face at the centre of his art. Both depict a tousle-haired young man lit from the left, with half his face in shadow, including his eyes. In some respects, it is as if he is playing a cerebral game of hide and seek with the viewer – and perhaps with himself: now you see me, now you don't. Conventional portraiture held to the belief that the eyes were windows into the soul; Rembrandt flaunts this convention and hints, perhaps, at melancholy in his expression – the self-absorbed angst of a young man. But, in these two pictures, he is using his face as a site on which to experiment with the effects of light and shade, of chiaroscuro. Furthermore, he is not painting a simple portrait but a version of what was called a *tronie*, a Dutch term for a picture somewhere between a portrait and a historical character. In *tronies*, the sitter is often portrayed dressed in the appropriate clothes of his would-be character, and both Rembrandt and Lievens painted numerous such pictures using local models, both young and old. Here, though, Rembrandt began to look in the mirror and use himself as a model.

In the same year, 1629, he painted himself variously in armour, with a plumed hat, a high hat and a beret. The last of these, which became the traditional garb of the bohemian painter in the nineteenth century, thanks to Rembrandt, was an outmoded, sixteenth-century fashion. Consequently, when Rembrandt donned his beret at various jaunty angles, he was rooting himself in history, playing the dandy or the fool and framing his face in specific ways. Over the course of his career, he painted about seventy-five self-portraits in oil, about ten per cent of his output. They are a combination of both fact and fiction, document and created image, as he wants to be and as he is. Dürer had painted the first fully fledged self-portrait back in the 1490s, and after the Reformation, with the emphasis more on the individual and his direct relationship to God, cultural interest in the self grew. With the growth of scientific and philosophical rationalism based on empirical observation, the context in which Rembrandt was beginning to work became clear in a world where intellectuals were trying to define the relationship between human beings, their world and its creator. The French

The Painter in His Studio
c.1629, Museum of Fine Arts, Boston

The subject of the artist in his studio was both a widespread phenomenon and often a vehicle through which some of the most powerful statements were made by painters about what they did and why they did it. From Velázquez to Vermeer and on to Courbet, Picasso and beyond, the theme has been profoundly explored, yet no one has ever painted anything quite like this picture.

It shows a painter at work but not at his easel; instead, he stands as far back as possible and contemplates what he has done or is about to do. There is little or no extraneous detail in the picture save that which focuses our attention on the process of painting. On the table to his left are jars and bottles of varnish and oil; to his right is a whetstone perched on part of an old tree stump, used for the grinding of pigment. On the wall, two palettes – one large, the other small – hang on a nail. The room is sparse, shabby even, and the cracks in the wall and the flaking plaster serve to remind us that the simplest of spaces is all that is needed in which to create. They also give Rembrandt a chance to show us the range of his talents. The painter in the picture holds a number of brushes: broader ones for the expressive strokes; smaller ones for detail, together with a maulstick to steady his hand on the most intricate of painterly passages; just like those cracks, which would need the steadiest of hands and the tiniest of brushes. Finally, the cracks illustrate Rembrandt's early interest in mortality and decay – in what one historian called 'the poetry of imperfection'. In his later work, the attention to detail required in these studio blemishes shifted to Rembrandt's own face: wrinkled, red-veined, blotchy and beautiful.

The light is pronounced. It rakes across the room, having entered through what must be a high window because of the shadows cast by the easel. Lurking in the furthest shadows is the painter himself. He is small, compared with his easel, which has led some to suggest it might be the figure of Gerard Dou, Rembrandt's young pupil. But the face is too familiar; the bulbous nose and the searing eyes, even though they are black rather than blue-grey, even though they are socket-like in the darkness; this is Rembrandt himself, scrutinizing his work, a young man of twenty-three contemplating the essence of what he does and what he will do for the rest of his life.

Like so much major painting, the work leaves a great deal to the imagination. We can't see the front of the canvas, so we have no idea whether he is about to begin, is in the middle, stepping back to take a look at what else he must do, or whether he has just put the finishing touches and stares at what he has achieved. But that, perhaps, is the point: an evocation of the ongoing process of painting that requires not just action and dexterity, but distance and detachment, thought and imagination.

philosopher René Descartes (1596–1650) had just produced his *Discours de la Méthode*, published in Leiden in 1637, and who later condensed the nature of human existence and the self into the dictum 'I think, therefore I am'. Rembrandt wrestled with similar concerns, perhaps not quite as rigorously, but he came up with an answer in the self-portraits in general and in one painting specifically, *The Painter in His Studio* (c.1629, Museum of Fine Arts, Boston), which seems to proclaim: 'I paint, therefore I am'.

The picture shows a young painter, rather elaborately dressed in his work clothes, together with a large, brimmed hat, standing in the shadows of his shabby studio. He is staring out of the gloom at his canvas, which is tilted away from the viewer to face the slanting light from the left, as we look at it. The scene is stripped to bare essentials: the grinding stone, a couple of palettes hanging on the wall, a bottle of oil and some varnish on the table are all part and parcel of the process of painting and serve only to sharpen the focus of the painter and his easel. Oddly, though, the figure is as far away from the easel as is possible in the room; he is looking and thinking rather than painting, although he holds brushes and a palette which emphasize that he is indeed poised to paint. There were plenty of examples of paintings of artists in their studio, but none like this. It makes clear that painting requires distance and detachment as well as preparation; that it requires thought, both imaginative and intellectual. There is a certain ambiguity about the figure, not least the diminutive size of the painter, that has led some to speculate that it might be one of Rembrandt's younger pupils, but the eyes give it away: it is Rembrandt himself, studying himself studying the ritual and the reason behind what he does.

In Leiden, Rembrandt was making a name for himself. He had taken on a number of pupils, the most illustrious of whom was Gerard Dou (1613–75), who both assisted his young master on various religious commissions and painted his own work, heavily under the influence of Rembrandt, including an image of an old painter sitting behind his easel writing notes.

In 1628, Constantijn Huygens, the cultivated secretary to Prince Frederik Hendrik, came to Leiden and 'discovered' Rembrandt, buying his work and introducing him to various potential patrons. But the word was already out and collectors from Antwerp and Utrecht had begun to buy his work, too. In 1631, after the death of his father, Rembrandt finally left Leiden and moved his studio to Amsterdam, exchanging his provincial home town for a booming international metropolis.

Amsterdam was the largest and richest city in Holland, itself the wealthiest province of the United Provinces of the Netherlands or the Dutch republic. This was a loose federation of the seven predominantly

Protestant provinces that had seceded permanently from the rule of the Spanish Habsburgs during the on going Dutch Revolt or Eighty Years' War (1568–1648). The United Provinces were a phenomenon distinct from the rest of seventeenth-century Europe. First, they had been created in part with the intention of achieving religious liberty for Protestants. A peculiarly far-reaching spirit of religious tolerance therefore pervaded the country, which equally accommodated Catholic worship, a variety of Protestant denominations and Jews. Second, at a time when other European monarchies were tending towards absolutism, the seven provinces, jealous of their provincial liberties and privileges, had rejected monarchy altogether and constituted a republic. In each province, the dominant oligarchy of wealthy merchants elected a stadholder, or governor, as the chief provincial officer, whose primary function was to ensure provincial autonomy. In time, however, the pressures of continued war against Spain demanded a stronger executive, and the stadholderates of each of the seven provinces became exclusively associated with the House of Orange-Nassau. Frederik Hendrik, Prince of Orange (1584–1647), the third hereditary stadholder (r.1625–47) of the United Provinces, effectively assumed semi-monarchical powers in foreign and domestic affairs.

The United Provinces prospered in the early seventeenth century, becoming a great sea power with extensive colonial possessions in the East and West Indies, which brought considerable material wealth to the Dutch nation. This 'Golden Age' is attested in the outstanding architectural and artistic production of the period. Much of the art of the United Provinces was characterized by a sober restraint. This was to some extent a reflection of the prevailing Calvinism, which placed great emphasis on moral rectitude, purity of lifestyle, frugality and hard work. But this historical character can become a caricature. The mercantile class and the urban bourgeoisie enjoyed privileged lives of conspicuous consumption; they possessed lavishly furnished houses and indulged in such luxuries as art collecting, including the apparent vanity of commissioning portraiture. Seventeenth-century Dutch society thus presented Rembrandt with a number of sources of potential patronage. In The Hague, the Stadholder, Prince Frederik Hendrik, sought to enhance the prestige of his office both within the United Provinces and on an international level. The mercantile bourgeoisie of Amsterdam – the economic and cultural heart of Holland and the centre of Dutch international trade – promised a lucrative market for artistic commissions. This sophisticated and cosmopolitan city, open to exotic commodities and influences from the East and West Indies, was to be Rembrandt's home for the rest of his life.

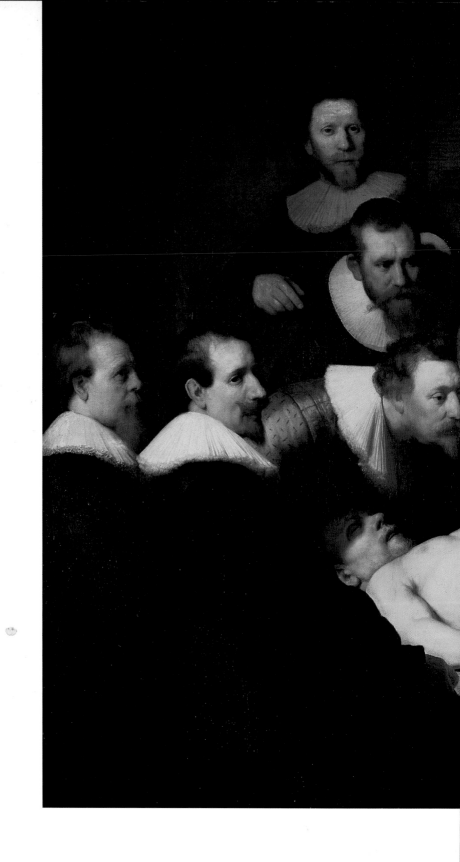

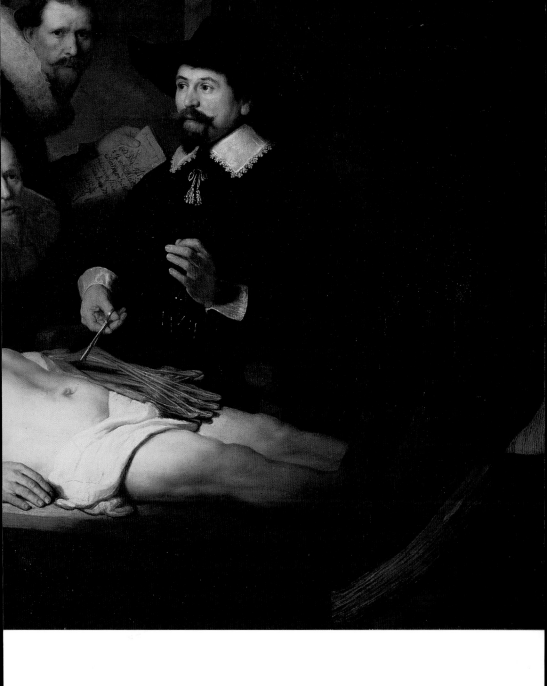

At first, Rembrandt moved into the house of Hendrik van Uylenburgh, an art dealer, with whom he negotiated an arrangement which placed him outside the established artistic guild system and accorded him a freedom that is evident in the range and variety of his subsequent work. Rembrandt rapidly began to make a name for himself through his portraits of the wealthy bourgeoisie of Amsterdam, beginning with a life-size portrait of Nicolaes Ruts, a Calvinist merchant whose swaggering image now hangs in the Frick Collection in New York. Subsequently, as the word began to spread, Rembrandt received commissions from a variety of different professions: a preacher called Johannes Wtenbogaert; a shipbuilder called Jan Rijcksen and his wife, Griet Jans; and – the most celebrated – a surgeon, a man born Claes Peieterszoon who boasted a signboard outside his house with a tulip on it and so became known as Dr Tulp.

In 1622, Tulp began his political career when he was elected to the city council; in 1628, he reached the pinnacle of his medical profession, becoming Praelector of the Guild of Surgeons. Among his duties was the annual public anatomy lesson, which involved the dissection of the freshly killed corpse of a criminal in the guild's anatomical amphitheatre. In January 1632, he conducted his second public dissection, and among the eminent citizens of Amsterdam in

The Anatomy Lesson of Doctor Nicolaes Tulp
1632, Mauritshuis, The Hague
This painting is both a radical group portrait and a radical depiction of the dissection of a human body. Surrounding the illustrious Dr Tulp (but clearly apart from him) are seven eminent citizens of the city of Amsterdam, who have paid to be included in a portrait which would hang on the walls of the guild chamber. Their names are writ large on the wall behind and their faces loom large in an image which involves them in the very latest developments of science and the pursuit of knowledge.

Compositionally, the picture is immensely sophisticated. The men form an arrow-head which draws the eye towards Tulp, but is also a two-pronged formation. From the top down, the heads direct the viewer's gaze towards the dissected arm of the corpse; while the line of figures from left to right draws our attention to Tulp's own hand, which demonstrates the same mechanical process that he has revealed with scalpel and forceps. The figure immediately behind Tulp holds a piece of paper, perhaps an anatomical text, the implication being that written theory is one matter, but seeing it

demonstrated in the flesh – both living and dead – is what really matters in order fully to understand the workings of the human body and, by extension, the world at large.

The painting is a tribute to the power of empirical observation. It is also a celebratory demonstration of manual dexterity by Tulp, with his deft surgical skills which reveal how the human body operates, and by Rembrandt, whose artistic talents bring human flesh to life in paint. He also conveys the waxy, grey, pallid nature of dead flesh. The corpse was that of a fellow Leidener, Adriaen Adriaenszoon, a thief and mugger

nicknamed 'Aris Kindt' (or 'The Kid') who had been hanged for his crimes. Public dissection was a way of inflicting posthumous punishment, but it also furthered human understanding. By revealing his face, as no other painter of anatomies had done, Rembrandt illustrates the individual life that has been lost as well as the more dispassionate view of a body dissected. The picture therefore becomes a more pronounced rumination on human mortality and attempts to adhere to the principles of the growing Enlightenment: 'Know thyself' – both physically and spiritually.

attendance, together with the paying public, was Rembrandt.

The commission to paint *The Anatomy Lesson of Doctor Nicolaes Tulp*, (Mauritshuis, The Hague) was one of personal aggrandizement and the demonstration of skill and learning – and this applied to Tulp himself, Rembrandt and the seven men depicted watching the dissection unfold. These were all wealthy and influential members of Amsterdam's social and political élite. They paid to be in the picture – in effect, a group portrait – which showed their interest in current scientific developments, establishing them as men of culture for posterity.

Like group portraits, the subject of anatomies had become a familiar theme in paintings of this period, but Rembrandt's treatment of both was radical. The composition, while bringing each of the figures to life and affirming their individuality, was also bound together in a dynamic whole, unlike the static nature of most such portraits. The men form an arrow-head which leads the viewer's eye both down to the corpse and on to the dissection of the arm being performed by Dr Tulp. Significantly, Tulp shows the workings of the human hand by pulling at the muscles of the corpse while brandishing his own fingers in demonstration. Rembrandt pays homage both to the manual dexterity of the surgeon and of himself, the artist: one skilfully revealing the mechanisms of the human body; the other bringing it to life in paint. But death, naturally, looms large in the image, and with a neat twist Rembrandt paints a bigger picture: the body in question was that of a thief known as 'Aris Kindt' (or 'The Kid'), but Rembrandt gives us more information than had ever been shown before in such pictures by painting his face; no longer is it just a corpse in the service of science, but the body of an individual human being who lived and died and is paying his debt to the society against which he sinned; likewise, as the living breathing figures of those burghers in attendance stare at the anatomy lesson itself, Tulp gazes off into space as if aware of the larger implications of what is occurring. This, after all – certainly in seventeenth-century Amsterdam – is God's creation explored. Once again, powerfully and profoundly, Rembrandt ruminates on the nature of mortality.

It was *The Anatomy Lesson of Doctor Nicolaes Tulp* – in particular its representational realism, high quality of finish and compositional finesse – that really made Rembrandt's name in Amsterdam. He had, after all, managed to paint immensely flattering portraits of seven high-ranking citizens in one picture and also produced a tribute to the ability and knowledge of a leading surgeon who went on to become Burgomaster of the city. Whom you knew, as well as what you knew and how you conveyed it, counted for a good deal in mercantile Amsterdam; and from this point on, commissions flooded in. In the same year, 1632 alone, he received over thirty, mainly from the city's élite – international traders, soldiers and civic dignitaries who wanted to follow in the footsteps of Tulp and his acolytes.

In addition, through the enthusiastic recommendations of Constantijn Huygens, a small-scale but highly prestigious project came from the Stadholder himself. Prince Frederik Hendrik commissioned two cabinet-sized paintings of *Christ's Passion*, *Christ Raised on the Cross* and *The Descent from the Cross* in 1633. On the basis of these, the Stadholder went on to commission a further three pictures from Rembrandt, depicting scenes from the life of Christ. These paintings were ostensibly intended for prayer and devotion in the Stadholder's private apartments. It seems clear, however, that in the first two works Rembrandt sought to make highly personalized statements and compete with his only serious rival in the Low Countries.

The entire series now hangs in the Alte Pinakothek in Munich, but the spirit of the paintings began in Antwerp with the work of Peter Paul Rubens, who painted both *The Raising of the Cross* and *The Descent from the Cross* two decades earlier, the former for the Church of St Walburga and the latter for the cathedral. Rembrandt had not seen the Rubens pictures in the flesh, but knew them from etchings by Lucas Vosterman. Like his reputation, Rubens's works were vast; a dramatic and monumental vision of the death of Christ. Rembrandt used the Flemish master as a starting-point, but he intensified everything, made the pictures smaller and tauter; he paid homage to Rubens but proclaimed his own vision.

In *The Descent from the Cross*, X-rays have shown that Rembrandt originally painted a figure of the Virgin Mary, as in the Rubens painting, behind Joseph of Arimathea, grasping Christ's arm and reaching for His leg. In the end, Rembrandt removed her and relocated her at some distance from the Cross – she is seen swooning in the left foreground. The composition is close to that of Rubens, but the mood is not; there is a mysterious light and a contrasting darkness which is closer to the work of Caravaggio. It is a brutal image, where Christ's body not only looks drained of life, but like that of a frail human being, a sharp contrast to the muscularity of Rubens's depiction. There, the emphasis is on action and reaction; in Rembrandt's, it is on contemplation and witness – the proper Calvinist response. In Rubens's version, all the figures are in direct contact with the Saviour, physically experiencing the martyrdom of Christ – a Catholic message reinforced in the Eucharist when the bread and wine are believed to become the body and blood of Christ. In Rembrandt's work, however, the doers are replaced by watchers. Calvinism proposed the notion of collective responsibility for Christ's sacrifice, a heavy burden of shared guilt. Each figure watching is responsible, the paintings seem to say, not least the painter himself. In *The Descent*, clad in blue, Rembrandt helps to lower the body; in *Christ Raised*, dressed in a blue doublet and beret, he helps to raise the Cross itself, a shocking image of the artist-turned-executioner immersed in the horrifying scenario he is depicting.

In 1634, Rembrandt married Saskia Uylenburgh, the niece of Hendrik, his art dealer, who had a large inheritance and was socially well connected. Rembrandt also became a member of the Guild of St Luke, which allowed him to take on pupils and apprentices as an independent master, and subsequently he established a workshop. Saskia's dowry gave Rembrandt access to levels of funds he had never previously enjoyed. He produced *Self-portrait with Saskia on His Lap* (*c.*1635, Gemäldegalerie, Dresden), in which he depicted himself as the Prodigal Son, a debauched libertine, with Saskia portrayed as a prostitute. He raises a glass to the viewer, a celebration of the good life he has attained and almost an invitation to share in his abandon. Interpretations vary, ranging from Rembrandt cocking a snook at his new in-laws and wallowing in love, lust and money to the idea that he shares in the sinful nature of all humanity but that God forgives all who repent. Biographically, this painting does indeed depict Rembrandt at the height of his material prosperity, when he was reported to be spending his own and his wife's money rapidly, principally on works of art and curiosities. In 1636, Rembrandt moved into a new house in Nieuwe Doelenstraat, which he began to fill with artistic treasures and exotica. Saskia's relations grew worried about his extravagance and openly accused him of squandering his wife's finances; Rembrandt responded with legal proceedings.

In 1639, Rembrandt bought a house in Breestraat (now Jodenbreestraat). He wanted an address which was worthy of his enhanced reputation and a place large enough to accommodate his family, assistants and collection. The Rembrandthuis is now open to the public as a museum. Aside from paintings (long since sold) by those artists he admired and sought to surpass – Raphael, Bruegel, Rubens and van Dyck – the house still contains numerous objects that fed his imagination and often became props in his paintings – sculptures, scientific instruments, costumes, feathers, swords, a lion's skin, plants and animals. Such encyclopedic collections or *kunstkamer*, microcosms of the wonders and curiosities of divinely created nature, were originally established by the aristocracy, but were mimicked by the middle classes as a means of promoting their cultural credentials. Rembrandt's studio was upstairs, and on the top floor were more studios used by his pupils. Here, they prepared his materials or made copies of the master's paintings, which he himself altered or reworked. It was, in effect, an industry and a highly successful one, too. At the beginning of the twentieth century, over a thousand oil paintings were considered to be by Rembrandt; now, thanks mainly to the work of the Rembrandt Research Project, established in 1968, around two hundred and fifty have been authenticated.

Despite his increasing success and recognition, by 1640 events in Rembrandt's private life were deeply distressing. He and Saskia had lost three of their children when they were only weeks old, and Rembrandt also lost his mother and sister-in-law. In 1641 their fourth child, Titus, was born. He survived, but less than a year later Saskia herself died, aged thirty, a victim of tuberculosis. Her last days are poignantly captured in various drawings and etchings, mournful images of life turning to death in black ink.

While he suffered in his personal life, Rembrandt's professional life continued to blossom. In the year that Saskia died, he painted what has become his most legendary work. The commission was part of the most prestigious project of the decade in Amsterdam: a series of group portraits to adorn the banqueting hall of the Kloveniersdoelen, the recently built headquarters of the *kloveniers* or Guild of Harquebusiers, part of the city's civic guard. Other leading painters were invited to produce portraits of the militia, but the eye-catching commission came from a Captain Frans Banning Cocq and his Company of the Second Precinct, a district in the north-east part of the city.

Now known as *The Night Watch*, Rembrandt's epic painting is correctly entitled *The Officers and Men of the Company of Captain Frans Banning Cocq and Lieutenant Willem van Ruytenburgh*. It was misinterpreted in the nineteenth century because of its dirty condition and believed to be a nocturnal scene. In 1946, it was cleaned and renamed *The Day Watch*, but the name never received wide usage. *The Night Watch* was originally nearly four by nearly five metres but has since been trimmed; nonetheless, it remains Rembrandt's largest work and probably his most ambitious.

The painting depicts the captain and his lieutenant together with their company of civic guard, the militiamen who served as a police force, conducted ceremonial duties and defended the city in time of war. Since each guardsman had to provide his own weapons and equipment, the civic guard tended to be the preserve of a narrow wealthy class, and companies doubled as gentlemen's dining clubs. A large cartouche bears the names of eighteen members of the guard, a later addition to the painting required by those seeking to enhance their position in posterity. Like *The Anatomy Lesson of Dr Tulp*, each of the figures paid to be included (Rembrandt's fee totalled sixteen hundred guilders) and, as in his earlier masterpiece, Rembrandt sought to reinvent the staid nature of the group portrait. The painting now hangs in the Rijksmuseum in Amsterdam, surrounded by other militia portraits of the period, some from the same commission. Accomplished as they are in many respects, they look leaden in comparison, static lines of men as if coerced by a domineering photographer at a family wedding. In 1678, one of Rembrandt's former pupils, Samuel van Hoogstraten, acknowledged this in praising *The Night Watch*, when he wrote that 'it will outlive its competitors, being so painterly in conception, so daring in invention, and so powerful that, as some people feel, all the other pieces stand beside it like decks of playing cards'.

Captain Cocq and Lieutenant Ruytenburgh appear to be striding out of the picture, a common element in Rembrandt's portraits. It is dynamic and dramatic, but without losing the psychological penetration of each individual. Portraiture and narrative painting are brilliantly combined. Cocq is shown giving Ruytenburgh the order to march out, which he will convey to the men behind them. It is a theatrically staged, frozen moment, the point just before this ragbag of individuals moves off into action out of the darkness and into the light; a microcosm not just of the militia but of the city itself, teeming with life and verging on chaos, but somehow held together.

Cocq and his company seemed to like the painting, which was hung on the walls of the Kloveniersdoelen in a prime position, opposite the windows overlooking the River Amstel and bathed in glorious daylight. Critics and other artists, however, were divided. Bernhardt Keil, another pupil of Rembrandt, discussed the work with an Italian writer called Filippo Baldinucci, who subsequently wrote that the painting was 'so jumbled and confused that the figures were barely distinguished from each other, although', he added, 'they were made with great study from nature'. In many respects, however, the picture's apparent confusion is its strength. It never allows the eye to remain still; it pulsates with life from both the contrast of light and shadow and from its composition and yet it is bound together in a vast, unified whole in a format which seems to squeeze the figures in from left and right and out through the front of the picture. It also shows Rembrandt trying, in his own terms, to out do Rubens. The monumentality of scale, the complex interplay between the figures and the sheer theatricality all evoke the Flemish master, but the image is altogether more humane. Rubens was undoubtedly the master of religious Baroque painting; here, Rembrandt lays claim to dominate the secular version.

Rembrandt may have fathered a new conception of secular painting

and group portraiture, but he was also the sole parent of an infant son with whom he shared Saskia's inheritance. In 1642, Geertje Dircx joined Rembrandt's household as a nursemaid to Titus, but subsequently became Rembrandt's mistress. Geertje appeared in various paintings, most alluringly in *Woman in Bed* (c.1645, National Gallery of Scotland, Edinburgh), but also perhaps in the guise of Mary holding the infant Jesus (Titus) in *The Holy Family with a Curtain* (1646, Staatlich Museum, Kassel). Some historians have argued that Rembrandt's earlier painting of *Christ and the Woman Taken in Adultery* was an image of the painter's own feelings of guilt over his liaison with Geertje, but any trace of guilt seems to have evaporated by 1647 when a much younger woman called Hendrickje Stoffels (c.1625–63) joined Rembrandt's household as a maidservant and the painter quickly became infatuated. Consequently, and unsurprisingly, a dispute arose between Rembrandt and Geertje, in which she claimed an unfulfilled promise of marriage. This culminated

The Night Watch (The Officers and Men of the Company of Captain Frans Banning Cocq and Lieutenant Willem van Ruytenburgh)
1642, Rijksmuseum, Amsterdam
Almost everything about this picture is slightly larger than life, from the figures who threaten to march out of the canvas, to the monumental conception of what a group portrait was and could be. It shows Captain Frans Banning Cocq and his band of militiamen in a dramatic if slightly chaotic formation. They are preparing to move off into action. The captain gives the order; his lieutenant prepares to pass it on to the company, who gather their weapons and assemble behind.

It is a frozen moment and a theatrical staging, where a cast of disparate characters emerges from out of the darkness and into the light. Each of the sixteen men, together with their two leading officers, paid to be included in the picture and Rembrandt depicts each as a striking individual as well as part of a broader whole. The most eye-catching figure, at least initially, is Lieutenant Ruytenburgh, a swaggering dandy dressed in an outlandish yellow ensemble with fancy boots, stockings and plumed hat. Conventionally, bright colours emerge and dark ones recede but look how Rembrandt turns this idea inside out. Captain Cocq is clad mainly in black and yet he is clearly the dominant figure, ahead of Ruytenburgh and stronger. This is partly through his orange-red sash and the light on his face, but also because of his pose and the gesture of his outstretched hand, which points the way forward and reaches out towards the viewer, thereby engaging us, and which casts a shadow across the front of his deputy, holding him back and making sure he doesn't get ideas above his station. In short, and in every sense, Cocq overshadows him and is the focal point of the picture, a visual pivot effectively binding every component together.

In spite of the potentially pompous nature of the subject, it is a playful image in parts. In the right-hand foreground a dog turns and barks, balanced by a powder-monkey on the other side. To the left of Cocq are two small girls, caught up in the action and excited by it all, one bizarrely carrying a chicken on her belt – a gentle subversion of the harquebusiers' guild (of which this company was a part) whose heraldic emblem was a raptor's talon, here replaced by a hen's foot. Framing the scene on the extreme left and right are two contrasting figures: on the right, one Rombout Kemp, a Calvinist deacon and pillar of the community clad in appropriately austere clothes; on the left, Reijnier Engelen, a shadier character whose rakish past is perfectly suggested by the antique warrior's helmet he wears jauntily and with some pride. As if to complete the picture, or make his mark all the more emphatic, directly above Cocq a black hat is a face that has already featured prominently in Dutch painting, by this time with one eye visible. Looking sideways and upwards at the same time – as if to reinforce that his was increasingly an offbeat and original vision – is Rembrandt.

in a court battle and, although she was awarded alimony, Rembrandt ultimately had her confined to the Spinhuis (or house of correction) in Gouda when he discovered that she had pawned some of Saskia's jewellery. Hendrickje Stoffels testified against Geertje Dircx in these proceedings and became Rembrandt's lover. Twenty years his junior, she lived in his household until she died, but they never married, probably because Saskia's will specified that her entire legacy should pass to Titus should Rembrandt remarry. Hendrickje bore Rembrandt two children; their first died in infancy, but the second Rembrandt named Cornelia, in memory of the two daughters with Saskia who had not survived. When Hendrickje was pregnant with Cornelia in 1654, she was summoned before the Dutch Reformed Church to answer the charge that she had 'committed the acts of a whore with Rembrandt, the painter'. She acknowledged the charge and was banned from Communion. Rembrandt was not admonished, presumably because he was not a member of the church.

The complexities of Rembrandt's emotional and sexual life had little or no direct impact on the number of commissions he received in the 1640s and 1650s, except, perhaps, from the circle of his former dealer Hendrik Uylenburgh, who was strictly religious and his late wife's uncle, too. However, there is no doubt that Rembrandt began to look inwards at both himself and his subjects and this psychological scrutiny began to draw some criticism. He was accused of painting too much to please himself as an artist rather than painting the requirements of the sitters. His clients wanted a realistic likeness at a good price in few sittings; Rembrandt wanted to paint more penetrative portraits. In turn, artistic fashion was changing and a new generation of portraitists was emerging in Amsterdam, including Govaert Flinck and Bartolomeus van der Helst, who favoured a grander, more elegant style, lighter in tone, more colourful and painted in thin, fluent brushstrokes – all of which flattered their sitters and ensured a flourishing business among Amsterdam's patrician class. Subsequently, many of Rembrandt's former pupils and imitators followed this new artistic path with success.

While Rembrandt himself was perfectly capable of exploiting these new artistic values, he refused to be bound by an exclusive commitment to them. From the mid-1640s onwards, his work appeared to invert popular artistic trends. His brushstrokes became thicker and more uneven; some of his contemporaries ridiculed his style and dismissed it as mere smearing, but it heralded the onset of a new and radical late style. In *Woman Bathing* (National Gallery, London), painted in 1654, Rembrandt produced a small, beautiful, intimate image which seems to be so informally painted, so spontaneous that it might be a sketch.

But Rembrandt is not known to have used oil sketches as preparation for his larger works and the idea that he simply left the work unfinished is countered by the fact that he signed it. It shows a woman crossing a stream, her white shift held up to reveal her thighs, a sensual and erotic image but above all a tender one of a woman who is widely thought to be Hendrickje, his mistress – painted in the same year she was publicly humiliated for sexual immorality by her own church. On the bank behind her is a sumptuous robe, a sign that this can also be read as a history painting; a mythological or biblical scene, with Hendrickje perhaps in the guise of an Old Testament figure such as Susannah or Bathsheba, or possibly Diana the Roman goddess of the hunt, all of whom were subject to the prying eyes of men while bathing and, in Susannah's case, innocently aroused the desire of old men who falsely accused her. Rembrandt seems to be apologizing and proclaiming his love and support for the woman with whom he lives and has had a child. Like Rubens's intimate portrait of his own young mistress, Hélène Fourment, painted in the 1630s, it is a private image, but it is also an experimental one where Rembrandt lets himself go, away from the prying eyes of both patrons and moralizers. In parts of the picture, the ground is left

Self-portrait with Two Circles
c.1665–69, Kenwood House, London
There has been endless speculation about the mysterious background of this painting, whereby the circles have been interpreted as everything from hemispheres and mapping devices to kabbalistic signs or Aristotelian references to the idea of unifying the body with the soul. Perhaps more plausibly, they might refer to one of the enduring stories in art history – that of 'Giotto's O', wherein the Italian master was reputed to have drawn a perfect circle in a single fluid movement in demonstration of his artistic dexterity. Rembrandt certainly didn't produce either part of his two circles in a single motion – they are made up of numerous brushstrokes – but the idea that the work was a further example of his own talent seems reasonable enough. Better still, the work seems to re-explore the ideas so profoundly depicted in his early painting of *The Painter in His Studio*, those of artistic process. Here, perhaps, is an image which suggests a life and career that have turned full circle.

Rembrandt holds the tools of his trade in his hand: two or three sketchily painted brushes, a maulstick and a rectangular palette, with a painting rag underneath. In the background is a blank canvas on which, by implication, he will soon start to paint. His own face and clothes are depicted with the deftest and most economical of means; a few streaks of white create his hat; some smears produce his fur-edged robe or *tabard*. His hair is a mixture of brushstrokes and scratches which are even more pronounced on his white smocking below his neck. The face is mere paint, but it seems so much more; it has the tone and the pallor of ageing human flesh, blotched and wrinkled and with a shining red patch or pimple on the end of Rembrandt's gloriously bulbous nose.

His expression is one of melancholy, defiance and serenity; it is filled with the knowing resignation of a man who understands his life will soon end but it is also, as the American painter Chuck Close recently commented, 'a road-map of human experience'. It is both pictorial alchemy – the magical transformation of base material or paint into something rich and precious – and the result of a lifetime of hard work, study and developed skill. It strikes a universal chord about what it is to be a human being but it seems to have special resonance for artists in particular. Lucian Freud, the celebrated portraitist and figure painter and not a man known for his effusive pronouncements, said recently that it is 'one of the most beautiful pictures ever painted; it's just so perfect; so right'.

uncovered, as if to suggest shadow, but also emphasizing speed and process itself. Likewise, the white shift is painted with such directness that not only is every visceral brushstroke visible to the naked eye but colours are applied unmixed from the palette on to still-wet paint and the process of mixing often takes place on the surface of the canvas itself and occasionally remains unresolved. Painting, Rembrandt seems to be showing us, is like alchemy, where base material is transformed into something precious. From out of simple pigment, the most wonderful things can emerge, but only through the magic of the painter himself.

During the next ten years of his life, Rembrandt incurred increasingly heavy debts, despite constant commissions, pupils' fees and sales of etchings. Although much has been made of Rembrandt's poor business sense and his loss of popularity, the broader economic and social factors of a competitive and changing world also affected the lives of artists. Rembrandt's ostentatious living eventually led him to financial ruin, but his insatiable acquisitiveness and poor financial management were compounded by an economic slump in the United Provinces in the early 1650s. In 1656, his creditors triumphed and forced him to declare bankruptcy. His assets were liquidated and his paintings and curiosities auctioned off in 1657–58, though the price raised was insufficient to cover his debts. Fortunately, Rembrandt's copper etching plates were not included in the inventory of his possessions sold at auction. Subsequently, a long court case led to the return of Titus's part of his inheritance from his father's bankrupt estate, which was held in trust until he came of age. Rembrandt, however, was forced to move from his spacious townhouse to a much smaller one in the Rozengracht in the Jordaan, a poorer district inhabited mainly by artisans.

To enable Rembrandt to keep working while bankrupt, Hendrickje and Titus went into business together as art dealers in 1658 and formally employed the painter. He was still very much in demand, but seemed even more intent on pursuing his own interests. There is a subtle knowingness verging on world-weariness about his later work, and an altogether more sombre mood. In a group portrait *The Syndics of the Drapers' Guild*, a prestigious commission from 1662, he simplifies the composition and lines up six serious-looking guildsmen in an oak-panelled room. One holds his gloves, as if about to get up, another is in the act of rising from the chair. All look directly at the viewer, pillars of the establishment, depicted from a lower than usual vantage point and thus looking down on all they survey. The technique is loose but not over-expressive and wonderfully differentiates the various textures of flesh, wood and the rich fabric on the table in the foreground – a nice touch, given that 'syndics' were the official samplers of the cloth trade.

In 1663 Hendrickje Stoffels died of the plague that constantly seemed to surface in Western Europe at the time and Rembrandt's retreat into an inner world of contemplation became more pronounced. In a painting begun soon after Hendrickje's death called *The Jewish Bride* (c.1663–66, Rijksmuseum, Amsterdam), he depicts a recently married couple in the biblical guise of Isaac and Rebecca. It could, perhaps, be a lament for the woman he never married, but the most striking aspect of the work is the image of two people gently holding each other, utterly lost in reverie. The flickering brushwork emphasizes the transient nature of the moment, but also helps to convey a sense of transcendence. It is an image of intense self-awareness: from the couple to Rembrandt himself and to the viewer, too, contemplating the nature of the subject depicted.

Inevitably, though, the final and most profound paintings were self-portraits, a handful of which were painted in Rembrandt's last year after the devastating loss of his son Titus to the plague in 1668. Here, the craggy face is revealed, warts and all, sombre, resigned, to whatever lies ahead by facing up to his own ageing flesh and rendering it in the most breath-taking manner, as if paint were the stuff from which human beings were made. X-rays show that he made constant adjustments to the last self-portraits, still searching, wrestling for some kind of truth about the human condition. He died on 4 October 1669 and was buried in an unknown rented grave in the Westerkerk.

12.

Vermeer
1632–75

Although his work is now among the most instantly recognizable of all the great masters, Jan Vermeer remains an enigma. He was barely known as an artist in his lifetime. Little is known of his life and all that remains of his work is a legacy of about thirty-five paintings. He is therefore an inspiration for all who struggle to make art in obscurity, a shining light to all painters who feel the threat of an historical darkness. Light, of course, was Vermeer's artistic passion. Perhaps with the exception of Turner – and to very different effect – no one has ever quite matched his mastery of illumination. Vermeer's paintings create a serene and intimate world, largely a domestic one where women go about their daily tasks or dream or read letters, but there is always mystery and the picture itself remains partly elusive. They are absorbing images in every respect, but they also seem to radiate light themselves as well as depicting it. Consequently, they are among the most mesmerizing images in European art.

Vermeer was born in 1632 in Delft, a small but thriving town in Holland. He was one of two children born to Reynier Jansz, a man of many trades. Like many other people in Delft at the time, Reynier worked in the cloth industry. He was a weaver, producing fine silks and satins, but he also owned a fashionable inn, The Flying Fox, just off the market square. When Jan Vermeer was nine, his father bought another inn right on the market place, The Mechelen, which was a meeting place for many painters and art dealers. Reynier himself became a dealer of contemporary Dutch paintings and this was how Vermeer came into contact with several Delft artists. Reynier died when Vermeer was twenty years old, and the art dealership and the inn both passed to him as the only son, although his mother and sister Gertruy seem to have undertaken most of the day-to-day running of the place.

By 1650, the United Provinces of the Netherlands was the most important commercial and maritime power in Europe, with Amsterdam as its financial and mercantile centre. Consequently, living standards were high for many Dutch citizens and Vermeer's serene, well-furnished interiors bear witness to this prosperity. So, too, does the fact that Vermeer spent a great deal of time composing and painting each work, producing only two or three per year. He was, therefore, distinct from other artists whose livelihoods were reliant on commissions. Delft at the beginning of the seventeenth century was not a notable artistic centre like Amsterdam or Utrecht. An influx of Italian or Italianate works of art into the town offered Delft's artists experience of the great masters of the Renaissance, but Vermeer's sources of inspiration appear to have been more local. The Delft that Vermeer knew was a prosperous town, its wealth based on trade from tapestry weaving, breweries and Delftware, the characteristic blue-and-white ceramic used for kitchenware and tiles. In several of his interiors, Vermeer depicts Delftware tiles on the skirting of the walls. It is perhaps significant that Vermeer's predominant palette is blue and white. Furthermore, the artists and intellectuals working in Delft showed a particular interest in perspective and optics, and Vermeer's paintings clearly demonstrate an awareness of these studies.

The contemporary artists of Delft who would have been familiar to Vermeer were Pieter de Hooch (1629–c.1684), who favoured scenes of domestic life, so-called 'genre' paintings, and Carel Fabritius (1622–54), the most talented of Rembrandt's pupils, who arrived in Delft in 1650 and whose use of unusual perspective and light effects made him the central figure of the town's artistic scene. On the basis of certain similarities in technique, some critics believe that Vermeer was taught by Fabritius; he was certainly Vermeer's most talented and original predecessor in Delft. Many who knew of Fabritius's talent were devastated by his early death in 1654, killed by the 'Delft Thunderclap', an horrendous explosion of a gunpowder magazine in the town centre which killed over a hundred people, as well as destroying a large number of buildings and, indeed, many of Fabritius's paintings . A poem to commemorate Fabritius's death compares Vermeer with the mythical phoenix that rose from the ashes – 'But happily there rose from his fire Vermeer, who, masterlike, trod his path'. It is evident that even by the age of twenty-two Vermeer had made a favourable creative impression on some of the citizens of Delft.

There is no documentation of Vermeer's artistic training, but a year earlier, in 1653, he had become a master of the Guild of St Luke, the traditional institution that regulated the training of artists and the marketing of their work in a particular city. Becoming a master painter in the guild usually involved having completed three years' apprenticeship in the technique of oil painting, resulting in the production of a 'masterpiece'. There is no record of Vermeer having been registered as an apprentice in Delft, but guild regulations were not always adhered to. Soon after becoming a master, he painted a mythological scene of *Diana and her Companions* (*c.*1653, Mauritshuis, The Hague), a competent, traditional image of the goddess of hunting and her entourage viewed close up, with Diana having her feet washed by an attendant. At first glance, it seems to have little or no relationship to his later, more celebrated work, but the quality of light flooding in from the left-hand side and the sense of an intimate moment gently unfolding hint at what was to come.

Three years later, Vermeer painted *The Procuress* (1656, Gemäldegalerie, Dresden), his earliest – and one of only three – dated work. The painting depicts a woman in black, a procuress or prostitute's maid, together with the prostitute herself in bright yellow. A cavalry officer gropes the latter, fondling her breast whilst offering money for her services. The procuress herself looks on with a mixture of greed and expectation whilst to the right a young man, theatrically clothed, raises his glass and toasts the transaction. He stares out towards the viewer and implicates us all as uneasy voyeurs. The prostitute has been drinking. She clutches a glass of wine and closes her eyes as if not quite wanting to take in everything. Her cheeks are flushed by alcohol and although she holds out her hand for the coin, there is little doubt that she is being exploited. Technically, *The Procuress* does not display all the characteristics of Vermeer's later, more successful paintings. It lacks the simplicity of his later compositions; it is crowded and slightly unbalanced and, unlike his later works, space is not yet the dominating factor in the basic composition. It does, however, show an awareness of the work of Caravaggio in its detail and darkness of background, contrasting with the light in the foreground. It also introduces the idea of modern life into Vermeer's art and heralds his intention to observe and depict intimate aspects of the world around him rather than focus on biblical, classical or historical subject matter. Most interestingly, the faces of the figures reveal animated psychological details which the artist was later to abandon in his work, but it shows the beginnings of his painterly talent, especially in the handling of the young woman and her clothes, the delicate textures and rich colours of which contrast with those of her client.

It has been suggested that the man smiling on the far left is possibly a self-portrait. If so, this is particularly important as there are no surviving images of the artist. The identification is at best speculative, however, being based on the direction of the figure's gaze towards the viewer (a device employed in self-portraiture but widely used in all forms of portrait painting) and on his wearing the same outfit as the figure painting in a studio in a later work, *The Art of Painting*, which is also thought to be a rear view of Vermeer himself. By extension it has also been suggested that the courtesan is a portrait of Vermeer's twenty-six-year-old wife and the procuress his mother-in-law.

The strong moral content of such scenes of virtue and vice was popular in the Dutch republic at this time, and the procuress was common in contemporary iconography. Women were often depicted centrally in pictures where the choice between a moral and an immoral course was to be made. Exploitation aside, and it is not to be dismissed lightly, Vermeer invites the viewer to question the fate of the young girl, but ultimately there is no contest. Lying on the table is a piece of lacework, abandoned and symbolic of the domestic virtue she has cast aside. What could have been a painting of her lace-making has turned into a scene of corrupted chastity and vice.

At twenty-one, Vermeer had married Catharina Bolnes, a Catholic girl from Delft. In order, perhaps, to maintain good relations with her family, Vermeer converted from Protestantism to Catholicism, a minority religion in Holland, and moved to a Catholic quarter to live with his wife in his mother-in-law's house. His embracing of Catholicism can also be seen in his image of *St Praxedes*, produced around this time as a devotional painting which celebrates the cult of saints, something that

Christ in the House of Martha and Mary

c.1655, National Gallery of Scotland, Edinburgh

Although Vermeer was born and brought up as a Protestant, he married a Catholic woman in 1653 – Catharina Bolnes – having duly converted to Catholicism. This work was painted soon after and can be seen as a proclamation of new faith, love and ambition. Its scale and monumentality are those of an altarpiece, perhaps painted for Vermeer's small adopted religious community. It shows a scene from St Luke's gospel where Christ is travelling with his disciples, healing the sick, helping the poor

and preaching the new Word. Needing food and rest, He is welcomed into the house of two sisters – Martha and Mary. Martha prepares food and brings it to the table whilst Mary sits at the feet of Christ, listening with rapt attention to what He has to say. Martha gets angry and demands that her sister comes and lends a hand; Christ replies: 'Martha, Martha, thou art careful and troubled about many things: But one thing is needful; and Mary has chosen that good part, which shall not be taken away from her.'

Vermeer paints the moment when Christ speaks, looking at Martha

whilst gesturing towards Mary. Like the story, the painting is vivid but far from clear cut. It offers the choice between the active and the contemplative life, pointing the way to the latter but still acknowledging the importance of the former. The composition is triangular and harmonious, with Christ linking the two sisters and, by implication, the two paths. The bread on the table is just above Christ's hand, symbolic of the Catholic Eucharist, where bread becomes the body of Christ.

Interestingly, in the context of post-Reformation Europe, this particular biblical episode

is fraught with ambiguity: Protestantism affirmed the idea of justification by faith alone whilst Catholicism stipulated the necessity of good deeds in order to gain eternal life; Vermeer seems to be wrestling with this duality and, like Christ in his painting, suggests ultimately that there is room for both doctrines.

More broadly, although the image initially seems far removed from Vermeer's later work, it anticipates a number of central elements: domestic virtue; internalized emotion and thought; and a household scene illuminated by light from the left-hand side.

the Protestant faith had abolished, but which was re-established during the Counter-Reformation as a characteristic feature of renewed and reinvigorated Catholicism. The house was large enough to accommodate his fast-growing family – Catharina was in a state of near-constant pregnancy, giving birth to fifteen children over the next two decades, four of whom died in infancy. It was an unusually large number at a time when families in Holland averaged only two children, the lowest in Europe. Children are rare and undeveloped in Vermeer's work; perhaps an indication that his paintings are a separate, artificial world rather than a direct reflection of his lived experience.

His income from the inn and the art dealership was enough to keep the family; had he wanted solely to dedicate his life to painting, it would not have been a sufficient means to support them all. As with many other areas of Vermeer's life and works, mystery surrounds his less than prolific output. Some believe that his meticulous manner of painting was the main limiting factor. He was thus caught in a vicious circle; his slow output meant that he required income from other sources – the inn or

A View of Delft
c.1660–01, Mauritshuis, The Hague

As Delft flourished as an art centre in the seventeenth century, numerous images of the city were painted, but none were as accomplished or arresting as this. Vermeer's panorama of his birthplace became an emblem of the city, an image which helped to promote and define the evolving character of Delft.

The view shows the southern gateway into the third oldest city in the Netherlands, after Dordrecht and Haarlem, at the point where the River Schie flows into the Kolk (literally, 'pond'), creating a triangular harbour which was usually a hive of activity. Instead, Vermeer depicts the city on a lazy Sunday afternoon, with strollers out taking the air and enjoying the tranquillity. Immediately across the water is the Schiedam Gate with a small turret on top and a clock which seems to suggest the time is about twenty to three. To the right is the Rotterdam Gate with its distinctive entrance which resembles a castle and its phantom-like shadow looming out over the harbour back towards the viewer. The buildings and their shadows create a continuous band across the canvas and seem to beat a gentle visual rhythm as the eye is taken from left to right. Towering above the horizon in the distance is the Nieuwe Kerk (or New Church) built in the fifteenth century and subject to religious turmoil and iconoclasm in the following one.

Delft's prosperity was based on trade and its connection to other Dutch cities and to the sea itself via an intricate network of waterways, which is subtly evoked by Vermeer with a view of river and canal running to the left, right and straight up the centre of the scene. Dominating the picture, however, is the sky; two-thirds of the painting is devoted to billowing clouds through which the sun breaks, revealing patches of deep blue and illuminating the roofs of the city on the right-hand side of the scene. The view faces north and therefore has the consistent quality of light favoured by artists. It is as if Vermeer is paying homage to that which will bring his painting to life – daylight; not controlled and depicted streaming in through a window, but here, in one of only two exterior scenes he ever painted, unfettered, expansive and quietly magnificent.

Vermeer's technique is in transition in this painting, with evidence of both the broad impasto of his very early work and the smooth, transparent touch of his later pictures. On the darkest areas of the painting, particularly the boats, he puts tiny flecks of white to articulate form in a way that led one critic to describe it as 'optical carpentry'. Equally deft is the way that he spreads thicker areas of white across the water, both to create the shadows and to suggest the illusion of glittering light.

art dealership – which in turn decreased the time available for painting. His contemporaries certainly effected a much higher turnover – Jan Steen (1625–79) and Pieter de Hooch painted faster, even though their compositions often contained many figures and much detail, though it is worth noting that Steen also kept an inn to support himself commercially. Vermeer was clearly less interested in working to commercial demands. Much time was invested in achieving the perfect balance in each composition and in every painting the play of light on surfaces could only be accomplished with considerable patience.

A *Street in Delft* (1658–60, Rijksmuseum, Amsterdam) is one of only two exterior scenes Vermeer is known to have painted. He was about twenty-five at this time, but the handling of the different textures shows a maturity that marked him out from his contemporaries. Other Dutch artists would have painted each brick with great precision; the ground would have shown every stone. But Vermeer only *suggests* these forms; he does not *describe* them. He paints details in a way the viewer can easily digest, so as to appreciate the whole scene, not just its separate parts. He has also started to work out his compositions rigorously, a vital element to their overall harmony. There is a great sense of order here; the buildings are parallel to the picture surface, and the calming geometry of the window frames and doorways is a device he used in almost every subsequent painting. Here, he uses these doorways as framing devices for two women, one a maid at a water butt, the other the lady of the house busy making lace. The only view of the interior is through the front door, where we can see the lacemaker herself. The two women involved

Maid Pouring Milk
1657–58, Rijksmuseum, Amsterdam

If you attempted to describe to someone who had never seen this picture what was happening, it would seem prosaic in the extreme, but Vermeer's image of a strapping maid delicately pouring milk into a bowl still reverberates around Western art. For some, it is the light, streaming in from the window and illuminating the cracked paint and plaster of the wall behind the figure in such a quietly dramatic way as to seem

almost enough in itself to satisfy the viewer; for others, it is the woman herself, caught in a moment of quiet reverie as she goes about her daily work, an image of virtue in a country where hard work and a sense of domestic duty were highly valued.

Although it is a wonderfully balanced and harmonious image, where colour and form merge neatly and seamlessly together, it is also one of strong contrast. At the physical heart of the painting is the act of pouring; a frozen moment,

indeed a split second held eternally in what seems a timeless setting. The tension between motion and stillness is surpassed, though, by that between darkness and light. Out of the blackness of the jug, a stream of luminous liquid emerges. It's a kind of simple creation myth: 'And God said, "Let there be light", and there was light; and God saw that the light was good and he separated it from the darkness' (Genesis 1). On every conceivable surface, from wicker to silver to terracotta to bread, flecks

of white paint create the illusion of flickering, pulsating, life-giving light.

There is a feeling that the viewer has stumbled on a mundane but intensely private scene; one that has a much broader resonance. It is a simple domestic ritual in one respect, but it has strong spiritual overtones which once again evoke the Christian Eucharist and the notion of redemptive sacrifice. But its wholesomeness and life-affirming imagery – the bread of life itself, perhaps – have more universal overtones.

in their work are anonymous. The face of the woman at the water barrel is turned away to obscure her features, while the seated woman's face is little more than a blob of paint. Two children – as has been discussed, rare in his work, though not in that of other Delft artists, notably Pieter de Hooch – have their backs turned to us and it is unclear what they are doing, although some kind of game-playing seems likely. There is no communication between the figures in this picture; they are all absorbed in their own quiet activities. Silence in activity is a common thread in Vermeer's work. A certain amount of tension is created by the placing of these figures at the boundary between the home and the outside world. In seventeenth-century Holland, the place for virtuous women was firmly in the home; to stray beyond these limits meant exposure to vice and danger. As if to underline that these particular women have not transgressed the physical and, by implication, moral boundaries and that they remain paragons of virtue, Vermeer also included a vine growing over the building to the left, symbolic of love, fidelity and marriage.

The supreme example of the virtuous woman appears in another of Vermeer's paintings produced around the same time, *Maid Pouring Milk* (1657–58, Rijksmuseum, Amsterdam). This is probably Vermeer's most celebrated picture, painted when he was about twenty-six. From early on, it was considered a valuable work – at auction in 1696, after the painter's death, it fetched 175 guilders. It was a high price to pay for a small painting showing just one anonymous figure. His popular contemporary Jan Steen would perhaps receive that much for three paintings.

Once again Vermeer portrays female virtue and with deftness and subtlety. One has also to remember that Vermeer is painting for a largely male audience and there is undoubtedly an air of voyeurism, of intrusion into a private, domestic and mainly female world. It is less unnerving and less complicit than the sense of voyeurism experienced when looking at *The Procuress*, but it is still there nonetheless. Dutch moral concerns loom large in the picture; many believed that whether the country stood or fell depended on the virtue of their women. Integral to these moral concerns was practical housekeeping; visitors to the United Provinces at this time commented on its particular cleanliness. To neglect the household was tantamount to abandoning civic duty; it was a collective responsibility to protect the country from disease and vermin and engendered a certain patriotic pride in elevating the Dutch above other, apparently less clean nations.

The figure of the Dutch maid in this painting is a personification of the Netherlands, itself the promised land of milk and honey. She is the embodiment of hard work in the house. It is a wholesome image; she is robust and healthy, while the meal of bread and milk is modest yet inviting. The natural light falling on her and the white wall behind gives a sense of purity. Originally Vermeer had included a painting on the wall, but painted over it, as it did not suit this humble scene. The concentration on her face as she pours the milk elevates this action to something monumental, almost religious. It is a humble yet opulent scene where bountifulness, cleanliness and godliness seem to merge together. The pouring of liquid from a jug might also have been recognized as an allusion to an allegorical figure, perhaps Prudence.

In this, as in all his subsequent paintings, Vermeer used the best-quality pigments available, often chosen specifically for their luminous qualities. He probably visited an apothecary for the more precious pigments that were not available from the usual artists' suppliers. An indication that he was fairly affluent was his fondness for natural ultramarine blue, a rare and expensive colour used here to depict the lowly maid's dress. In other work, he not only used it on the surface of the work, but even as a rich underlayer on top of which less expensive pigments were applied. These were all prepared in the attic above his studio, mixed together with linseed oil on a stone table.

His composition and painting technique is now more established. The maid takes centre stage in a kitchen. The white wall makes her body stand out as a very strong image, almost in silhouette. The arms, face, food and vessels on the table catch the light in a remarkable and lifelike way. At this time there was no one who could rival this study of natural light and replicate it so convincingly. Vermeer places the table with dark cloth in the foreground to give distance and depth between the viewer and the maid – this occurs in almost all of his interior scenes, creating a barrier and heightening the sense of intrusion on what is clearly a private moment.

Another important feature in this work is Vermeer's use of scientific devices. His treatment of the bread, with the highlighted spots, has been related to the artist's use of a camera obscura, which helped capture the subtle effects of daylight suffusing a room and playing across different surfaces. A camera obscura, literally 'dark room', was an early forerunner to the modern-day camera, but without film, and the device became widespread largely through its use by Leonardo da Vinci in the early sixteenth century. It was created by piercing a tiny hole in one wall of a darkened room or box. An inverted image of the scene outside was projected on to the opposite wall. The image produced created certain effects. Most obvious was that certain parts of the image were out of focus, just as when the naked eye regards an object. This effect can be observed in most of Vermeer's paintings. Even if he did not directly copy images created by a camera obscura, he used it as a compositional aid and employed some of the effects, such as the blurring of foreground objects, to give the illusion of spatial depth. If the lens was not perfectly ground, it would cause distortions in the image, making objects nearer to the lens seem disproportionately larger than other objects in the room. It would also concentrate the colours of the scene and in Vermeer's work there does seem to be a saturation of colour, a jewel-like quality. It has been deduced from aspects of the *Maid Pouring Milk*, such as the viewpoint, the differential focus and the planes of saturated colour, that Vermeer used the camera obscura for this picture and for numerous others, not least the *Girl with a Red Hat* painted around 1665–7 and hanging in the National Gallery of Art in Washington, which presents a close-up image of a young woman where almost all detail bar her face and hat is out of focus. It is not known, however, whether he transferred the image to the canvas by some unknown method, or simply observed the scene in a camera obscura before painting it.

The relationship between science and art was of increasing importance in the cultural climate of seventeenth-century Holland, where the avid pursuit of scientific knowledge both served to keep the country abreast of international learning and helped to proclaim intellectual independence as an element in national identity. The growth in printing and publication made new discoveries in geography, physics, astronomy and mathematics more broadly available, while the manufacture of precision instruments such as microscopes and lenses in Delft played a significant part in the local economy. Vermeer would have been aware of this scientific exploration, particularly the properties of lenses, from the Delft-based scientist Antony van Leeuwenhoek

PERSPECTIVE AND OPTICAL AIDS

There is good reason to believe that Vermeer made use of the camera obscura, a forerunner of the modern-day camera. Meaning literally 'dark room', the camera obscura has a long history dating back to ancient times. In the fifth century BC, the Chinese apparently discovered that if a tiny hole was made in the wall of a darkened room and light from outside allowed to enter through the hole, the exterior image could be projected on to the far wall of the room. The image would be inverted, but during the sixteenth century advances in lens technology meant that the image passing through the hole could be manipulated, re-inverted, enlarged or reduced.

Vermeer would have been aware of these technological developments and seems to have been acquainted with Antony van Leeuwenhoek, a cloth merchant by trade but better known for his discoveries using optical lenses.

These allowed the principles of the camera obscura to be used on a smaller scale and instead of rooms, portable boxes were used to capture the images. The projection would show an image similar to that which the eye sees. Some of the objects would be in sharp focus, leaving the foreground slightly blurred. This is

(1632–1723), who was born in the same year as the painter. He was an extremely skilled lens-grinder who developed the earliest microscope and was the first to observe bacteria and blood cells. The implications for art were profound; both the new painting and the new science involved meticulous, empirical observation. Armed with the new technology, the artist, like the scientist, could attempt a perfect description of natural appearances, a quest which was only diminished – if not terminated – by the development of photography.

Vermeer's admiration for intelligence, exploration and those who devoted their lives to the pursuit of knowledge is clearly demonstrated in two memorable pictures he painted in 1668 and 1669. *The Geographer* (Stadelsches Kunstinstitut, Frankfurt) and *The Astronomer* (Louvre, Paris) share a similar format, with light flooding in from the left, illuminating the desk at which each man sits. The astronomer studies his celestial globe, his mind on the star-spangled firmament; the geographer seems to be gazing out of the window at the world around him, his hand poised with measuring compass ready to chart new territories. Above his head is a terrestrial globe; above the astronomer's is a picture of the discovery of Moses in the bullrushes, an image of an infant sailor in his basket who was sometimes described as 'the oldest geographer'. Set side by side, the two men look so similar at first glance and then you realize they are one and the same person, sharing the same quest: to discover the governing principles of the world and universe in which they exist. Vermeer details everything with intense scrutiny, including maps and charts in pictures which themselves chart the powerful combination of ancient wisdom and contemporary curiosity whilst celebrating the dignified work of the gentleman scholar. There is an almost perfect balance struck in these images between the small spaces in which people live and work and

a feature of many of Vermeer's works, where he imitates this quality by painting 'circles of confusion', small dots of paint resembling the blurring of detail.

In addition to his use of the camera obscura, Vermeer practiced what is called the chalk-line method. Evidence of this method can still be seen in thirteen of his works under certain conditions. It was a tried and tested method used by many artists wishing to depict the illusion of depth and recession. A pin would be placed in the grounded canvas at the vanishing point, the point where all lines of perspective converge. From this position, he would attach long lengths of string which could reach all edges of the canvas. These carefully positioned lines would form the orthogonals, the guidelines of perspective. To translate the lines to the canvas, chalk dust would be applied to the string and, holding the free end down on to the canvas with the thumb of one hand, the other could snap the string against the surface, leaving a faint white mark. To make this more permanent, it could be drawn over with either pencil or brush. The tell-tale pin marks can still be seen when the paintings are examined by X-ray.

their desire to experience a wider world, itself a metaphor for the Dutch nation with its seafaring prowess and colonial aspirations.

Vermeer is thought to have sold his works privately to a small number of discerning clients. Some might have been commissioned; he is, after all, unlikely to have invested so much time in painting with only a vague hope of reward. Most of his paintings were sold to one wealthy citizen of Delft called Pieter Claesz van Ruijven, although he also is known to have sold one picture to a local baker; both men paid high prices for the works. Years after van Ruijven had died, his collection was auctioned in Amsterdam. Twenty-one of Vermeer's works were sold, well over half of the painter's total output. But what had attracted van Ruijven to Vermeer's work and what compelled him to buy so many? Van Ruijven would certainly have been captivated by the incredible painterly qualities and serenity, and fascinated by the subtle layers of meaning. He may also have been drawn to Vermeer's very particular subject matter and style. His collection of Vermeer's paintings were dominated by similar formats; the same generic characters, clothes and props appear from one work to the next. Wealthy young women predominate: they play lutes or virginals; they read or write letters or weigh pearls – their faces lit up with expectation, concentration and, more prosaically but still crucially, by the rays of daylight which come flooding in from the window usually on the left-hand side. There is an erotic charge to many of these works, understated but no less powerful, a sense of sexual yearning, flirtation and occasionally of frustration. Ultimately, however, they are ambiguous. Just when their true nature seems about to crystallize before one's eyes, just as their narrative suggestion seems to move into a sharper focus, things suddenly blur again and the essence of the painting seems to have evaporated into thin air. Perhaps no one ever painted such visually clear but emotionally elusive pictures as Vermeer did.

One of Vermeer's simplest compositions is also one of his most spellbinding and open-ended. *The Girl with the Pearl Earring* (1665, Mauritshuis, The Hague) shows a young woman close up; only her head and shoulders are visible. Her face is seen in three-quarter profile, as if she is in the process of turning towards the viewer, but she is also pushed up against the picture plane, into the viewer's face almost, by the black background which emphasizes the glimmer of light reflected in her eye and which sparkles off the pearl earring hanging from her left ear. Pearls were often seen as symbols of vanity, but here many think they appear to signify chastity or purity. The composition of this painting is different from his earlier work, giving full weight to the portrait rather than to the broader scene of a woman in a domestic context. Indeed, it is possible that this piece is a marriage portrait, where the representation of chastity would be a particular concern. But here is Vermeer at his ambiguous best; there is no sense that the viewer is being told what to think, but the seemingly simple iconography produces an openness of meaning that places the onus of interpretation on the viewer. Her gaze is both innocent and seductive; her mouth parts as if to speak, perhaps to express surprise, but the wetness of her lips is sensually alluring. Her blue and gold turban is exotic, her brown robe a little staid; every element is distinctly visible, but each seems to merge into an harmonious whole, partly through Vermeer's development of the technique of *sfumato*, where contours are diffused and edges are softened, notably the side of her face where the flesh tone has been extended over part of the dark background. This was a technique pioneered by Leonardo, but it is probably more the image's elusiveness and the arresting but slightly haunted stare of the girl that have led to the work often being described as the '*Mona Lisa* of the north'.

In 1908, a Dutch artist and critic called Jan Veth saw *The Girl with the Pearl Earring* and was inspired memorably to exclaim: 'More than with any other Vermeer one could say that it looks as if it were blended from the dust of crushed pearls.' But so many of Vermeer's works have what might more prosaically be described as lustre. Even in a late work from around 1670, *The Lady Writing a Letter with Her Maid* (National Gallery of Ireland, Dublin), where the women are older and the mood is more sombre, the surface still shimmers. It is a complex composition and one in which Vermeer shows his range of pictorial talents: his mastery of perspective, the way the chequered floor recedes so convincingly, the way the table and chair seem like real, almost tangible objects in discernible space. But Vermeer's interest in perspective goes beyond merely creating a deft illusion. He uses it as a device to draw attention to certain features, to move the eye around the canvas. The maid in this painting is placed right in the middle of the canvas, but at the back of the room. Her face is turned slightly towards the window, opening up the image, but her torso is turned towards her mistress, who sits writing in the foreground. Finally, the maid's folded arms form a line which leads from window ledge to the head of the seated woman and so the figures are linked and a potentially disparate image is brought serenely together, but in a way that is unforced and barely discernible.

It is easy to imagine the tranquillity of Vermeer's paintings reflecting a peaceful period in the history of the United Provinces, but this was far from the truth. During much of Vermeer's life, the Low Countries were the scene of political and religious turmoil and, in this context, his pictures read as images of refuge, of provincial and private worlds which were precious and needed to be preserved. In 1650 the Stadholder,

William II of Orange, died without an adult heir, which resulted in the fall of the House of Orange from supreme political power in the United Provinces, and a period of twenty-two years without a figurehead overseeing government. The celebrated William I ('the Silent') had first led the national movement against Spanish oppression in the Dutch Revolt (1568–1648), and many ordinary Dutch citizens possessed a great attachment to his family. The wealthy oligarchies of the seven provinces, however, resented the semi-monarchical status of the princes of Orange as a severe limitation to their own political authority, but the dynasty had provided a strong central executive for the factious and loosely organized United Provinces. Having finally gained recognition from Spain in 1648, the United Netherlands were now endangered by the imperial ambitions of Louis XIV of France. In 1672 an advancing French army threatened to swallow up the Spanish Netherlands and to reduce the Dutch nation to client status. Under these circumstances, the House of Orange returned to the stadholderate in the person of William III (later King of England, r.1688–1702) in the hope that he might provide the leadership necessary to defeat the French.

This political background is thought by many to be important for

The Art of Painting
c.1666-73,
Kunsthistorisches Museum, Vienna
This was one of only two full-blown allegories painted by Vermeer, the other being the more Baroque *Allegory of Faith, c.1670–72,* which now hangs in the Metropolitan Museum of Art in New York. It is the largest and most ambitious of all his mature works and one which fundamentally wrestles with the process of its own creation.

It shows a painter clad in clothes from a bygone era, as if to emphasize the relationship of art to its own past. He has just begun to paint a beautiful young woman, lit from the window and wearing a rich blue gown balanced by a golden tome which she clutches in her hands. Everything thus far implies that the painter is Vermeer himself. Unlike any of the women he painted previously, however, this one is wearing a laurel crown and brandishing a trumpet, the attributes – together with the history book – of Clio, the muse of history. In a world where history painting was valued above all other subjects, Vermeer is almost attempting to paint the ultimate image.

He gives us both a front-row seat in the unfolding process of depiction and what is effectively the painter's-eye view. On the floor, the receding tiles suggest a carefully calculated perspectival space and from the chair to the table and its contents, the focus is blurred to remind us how we see and that Vermeer has used a camera obscura to realize his painting. Science is thereby utilized in the service of art. Likewise, the engraved map, the plaster or marble sculptural head and the intricate chandelier are props in the painter's private world. In the foreground on the left-hand side, a tapestry is pulled to one side, its rich pattern a continuation of the ornate rhythms running through the rest of the picture. Like all other visual art forms visible in the image, it is subservient to painting, a mere theatrical curtain whose purpose is to stage the drama of painting itself, which effectively sounds its own trumpet and hails its own fame and prestige.

The work was never sold by Vermeer and there has been much speculation about its purpose. It seems odd, to put it mildly, that he would paint such an ambitious work without a commission or that he painted it mainly for his own pleasure. Delft had begun to attract numerous visitors, diplomats, connoisseurs and collectors, who came to survey its growing art scene. Vermeer, it seems, produced the painting as a demonstration piece, as a means of showcasing his extraordinary talents, as well as proclaiming more broadly the power of painting itself.

an understanding of Vermeer's most ambitious and elaborate work, *The Art of Painting* (sometimes called *The Allegory of Painting* or *The Artist in his Studio*), which now resides at the Kunsthistorisches Museum in Vienna. It was widely believed to have been painted between 1666 and 1668, but certain symbolic elements within the work suggest that Vermeer probably painted it in 1673, after the start of the French invasion. A starting-point for interpretation is the map in the background, an ornate, expensive item that alludes to the wealth of the sitter and also suggests a high level of education. It depicts the Netherlands, but it is an old map, showing the seventeen provinces of the Low Countries before the seven northern provinces achieved independence from Spanish rule. Down the sides of the map are tiny images of different Dutch cities. It is believed that the city next to the young woman's head is The Hague, the home of the House of Orange. Some critics feel that here Vermeer is showing his allegiance to the House of Orange through the juxtaposition of the trumpet of fame and the laurel-clad beauty, who is thought to be Clio, the muse of history.

This reading is a complex one and credible in many respects, but the painting is proclaiming something more powerful and perhaps closer to Vermeer's heart. In what can now be seen as a developing tradition in the Netherlands, Vermeer shows – first and foremost – an image of the artist in his studio at work. Tantalizingly, the painter's back is facing the viewer but it is tempting to see this as a self-portrait, particularly when the subject painted is a woman in a room illuminated from a window on the left. Her attributes do indeed identify her as the muse of history, but just as she clutches the tome in which all will be recorded for posterity, so the artist begins to paint history itself and will potentially be ensuring his own place in it. Significantly, he begins with the laurel crown, both versions of which frame the map on the wall. Art, Vermeer seems to be saying, brings fame and glory to countries and to cities. In addition to the intricately engraved map, there's a sculpture and a vast book on the table and a tapestry in the foreground to the left, pulled open to reveal the unfolding studio scene. But there is no doubt which of all these art forms dominates, which is blowing its own trumpet. For here, Vermeer proclaims in his largest mature work his total belief in the pivotal importance of painting.

The almost perfect, painted worlds of peace and beauty that Vermeer created for himself and others were shattered by the harsh reality of the Franco-Dutch War (1672–78), which marked a turning point in Vermeer's life. As a last resort, William III opened the sluices in the dykes around Amsterdam, flooding the land before the French invaders arrived. It was an effective manoeuvre but it had disastrous effects on all the citizens of the United Provinces, where agriculture lay in ruins and economic collapse followed. Vermeer no longer received rent from the inn. Nor did he sell a single painting of his own or from his art dealership. These years were characterized by financial strain. Vermeer's wife Catharina recalled, 'because of the large sums of money we had to spend on the children, sums he was no longer able to pay, he fell into such a depression and lethargy that he lost his health in the space of one and a half days, and died'. Vermeer's death was recorded in the winter of 1675. He was just forty-three. Catharina was declared bankrupt and was forced to sell the two paintings remaining in her possession; one of them was *The Art of Painting*. Vermeer's own fame and place in history dwindled to the point of obscurity over the next two centuries, but the idea so strongly implied in his grand allegory, that Vermeer's painting would live on in posterity, has since blossomed to the point where he is now one of the most cherished of all the great artists by the gallery-going public, even if, with his back turned away from us, he remains essentially a man of mystery.

13.

Turner
1775–1851

One much mythologized Varnishing Day at the Royal Academy, when painters were permitted to add final touches to their work once it had been hung on the walls, John Constable arrived and noticed a recently amended oil painting by his great rival J. M. W. Turner. 'He has been here,' exclaimed the only artist to rival Turner's genius in the history of British art, 'and he has fired a gun.'

Turner's impact, not just on British art but on European painting too, was explosive. His work ranged from topographical studies of painstaking exactitude to explorations of light and colour which many view as forerunners of Impressionist and even Abstract Expressionist painting. Landscape was the means through which he was able to ruminate, pictorially, on the broader issues of his time: the development and threat of vast empires; political and moral corruption; and man's place in an increasingly industrialized world. His creative imagination was vast and his poetic sensibilities were enough for *The Times*'s obituarist to call him 'The Shelley of English painting', but he had a keen intellect too. 'He is beyond all doubt', wrote the most influential English critic and writer on art, John Ruskin, on first meeting Turner, 'the greatest man of the age: greatest in every faculty of the imagination, in every branch of scenic knowledge; at once the painter and poet of the day ... shrewd ... highly intellectual, the powers of his mind not brought out with any delight in their manifestation ... but flashing out occasionally in a word or a look'. But there was something else, more mundane but no less crucial in establishing his importance in nineteenth-century culture, and that was his prolificacy. Turner was once asked to what he owed his artistic achievements. 'The only secret I have', he replied, 'is damned hard work', a comment supported by the evidence: over 510 oil paintings; some 1,600 finished watercolours and nearly 20,000 sketches in a career spanning just over sixty years.

Joseph Mallord William Turner was born on 23 April 1775, above his father's barbershop in Maiden Lane, near London's bustling Covent Garden, then a noisy and crowded market place. His father William was a barber and wig-maker, uneducated but close to his son, eventually abandoning his own profession to help the artist's career. Turner's mother, Mary, was a troubled woman – violent and unstable, she eventually suffered a nervous breakdown. Little is known about her save for the tragic fact that she was admitted to Bethlem Hospital in 1801 and died there in 1804 when Turner was nearly thirty. It is difficult to assess the direct impact of his mother's mental health on the young boy, but it seems to have encouraged him to be self-contained; perhaps his early and intense interest in art was partly connected with this. Certainly Turner had a precocious and self-taught talent for drawing and indeed for marketing his art from an early age. Some of his work was shown in the window of his father's shop when he was nine or ten; at the age of eleven he made copies of antiquarian engravings at his uncle's house in Brentford, where he went to school. His formal education as an artist began in 1788 when he was apprenticed to Thomas Malton (1748–1804), a watercolourist specializing in topographical and architectural scenes. Here, the adolescent Turner would have developed the skills he had shown as a boy, but his most important professional training came from a new and illustrious institution which had begun to change the face of art in Britain.

The Royal Academy of Arts was founded just seven years before Turner was born. In 1768, led by Joshua Reynolds, thirty-six artists, sculptors and architects established what was tantamount to an exclusive club to promote British art, enhancing its status and profile through a prestigious programme of annual exhibitions. Like the academies that already existed across Europe, it aimed to provide

THE GRAND TOUR

By the eighteenth century, a tour of Italy came to be regarded as an essential part of the education of young gentlemen from northern Europe, and Britain in particular. This 'Grand Tour' often required a stay of over a year in the Italian peninsula. Its route passed over the Alps, usually via the St Bernard Pass, to Turin, then down the west coast successively to Florence, Rome and Naples. The return journey normally traversed the Appennines to the Adriatic coast and Venice. The purpose of the tour was ostensibly educational, with the 'Tourists' studying Italian art and Roman antiquities, through which they hoped to acquire a continental cultural polish prior to entering English society. Many of the young 'milordi' who undertook the Grand Tour, however, were more intent on enjoying themselves in the south, where a warm climate and looser moral restrictions permitted a physical and psychological escape from England. The Grand Tour also became an important expression of status and wealth; by undertaking the Tour and by collecting its 'souvenirs', 'Tourists' were buying in to the idea of an international cultural heritage and a life of excitement and elegance previously open only

a training school for promising artists. From the age of fourteen Turner began what turned out to be a lifelong involvement with the institution when he was admitted as a student at the Academy Schools. Tuition was free and classes were held in the evenings, enabling Turner and his fellow students to continue their technical studies by day. Not surprisingly for an institution whose name originated from Plato's celebrated 'Academy' in Athens, the educational emphasis was intellectual. Painting and sculpture were learned through the craft-based 'guilds' or via apprenticeships; drawing (or *disegno*, to give it its Italian, classically inspired name, which summarized the aspirations of Joshua Reynolds and his followers) was taught in the academies – with particular emphasis on the life class – along with scholarly subjects which would help students to master the art of visual appearance (such as perspective and anatomy), as well as history and literature to help elevate the understanding of subject matter. The Academy had a strict hierarchy of picture types, with 'history' and 'allegory' at the top, followed by portraiture, with 'low-life' or 'genre' paintings, together with still-life, further down the order; and at the bottom came landscape. It was a model established from the High Renaissance onwards, but it could be subtly challenged. Indeed, following the example of the two great seventeenth-century French painters Claude Lorrain and Nicholas Poussin, as well as the eighteenth-century British artist Richard Wilson, who produced classically idealized landscapes with strong moral overtones about order and harmony, Turner spent a good deal of his future career challenging the idea that landscape was the lowest form of art.

Turner's interest in landscape began through the medium of watercolour, at which he began to excel to the extent that in 1790, at the age of just fifteen, he was selected to exhibit at the Royal Academy

to the aristocracy. Such souvenirs included ancient sculptures and other antiquities, the trade in which flourished, especially in Rome. More significantly, wealthy travellers commissioned paintings, usually watercolours, as both mementoes and advertisements of the travels that their status had enabled them to undertake. The wealthiest travellers often employed a watercolourist to accompany them, to maintain a pictorial record of their journeys. The most famous collection of watercolour travel sketches was that of the romantic painter John Robert Cozens (1752–99), whose imaginative and interpretive landscapes undoubtedly promoted Turner's keener interest in the genre. By Turner's day, extensive touring through Alpine and Italian scenery had become a standard element in an artist's development, offering broader horizons and new sources of 'picturesque' landscape, but also, at a more prosaic level, effectively serving as commercial trips for the production of topographical drawings as the basis for saleable paintings and prints.

annual exhibition in Somerset House. A watercolour of *The Archbishop's Palace in Lambeth* (1790, Indianapolis Museum of Art) may not have been high on the selection committee's priority list, but it was still an astonishing achievement for an adolescent. It shows the red-brick, fortress-like building on the south bank of the River Thames with figures strolling along the cobbled streets and a horse and carriage moving into view from the right. But it is the light that makes the viewer look again, a bright, confident image full of luminous promise. In turn, the success of this early work gave Turner the opportunity to learn more about the techniques of watercolour painting and to earn some money.

Dr Thomas Monro (1759–1833) was a specialist in brain disorders who may have treated Turner's mother in Bethlem Hospital. He was also a keen collector of watercolours and drawings, and an amateur watercolourist himself. At his house in the Adelphi, just down the road from the Academy, Monro paid young artists to spend their evenings copying or adapting pieces from his collection, which Monro could then sell. This effectively served as an informal training school for a number of artists, including Turner – from 1794 – and his talented but short-lived contemporary Thomas Girton (1775–1802), of whom Turner remarked, 'had he lived, I should have starved'. Dr Monro asked them to produce watercolour copies of the travel sketches of the Romantic painter John Robert Cozens (1752–99), and these imaginative and interpretive landscapes certainly enhanced Turner's interest in the genre. From the mid-eighteenth century, artists of the so-called Picturesque movement had initiated the taste for touring the country in order to discover and immerse themselves in dramatic scenery, sites of natural beauty and crumbling ruins. They sought to glorify the irregularities and roughness of landscape in drawings and watercolours, which often served as models for engravings, which were sold as prints or published in the new guidebooks. Such works were also very popular with the wealthy, either as representations of their estates or records of their personal travels. Turner was one of the many artists who profited from this growing cultural phenomenon.

Turner's own yearning to experience the Picturesque landscape at first hand grew, as did his reputation as a talented watercolourist and topographical illustrator. In 1794 he received the first reviews of his career – reasonable ones, too – and decided to expand his creative horizons. Not yet wealthy enough to travel to Europe, where the upheavals of the French Revolution made matters difficult if not quite impossible for travellers, Turner remained on British soil and embarked on a series of journeys that would make him probably the best-travelled English artist until the arrival of air travel. The young artist made two short trips to the West Country and South Wales in 1791 and 1792, and in 1794 he spent the entire summer travelling around the Midlands, plus trips to the cathedral cities of Lincoln, Peterborough and Ely and a brief incursion to North Wales, filling the earliest of 250 sketchbooks with drawings and detailed notes describing the weather, light and colour of the landscape and sky. These trips were both to gather visual data and to fuel his creative imagination, a process he adhered to all his life. Later he began to make watercolour sketches on his travels too, but the process of producing finished works of art, both watercolours and oil paintings, and the technical experimentation he began to pursue, all took place back in the studio.

He spent the following summer from June to October in Wales and then the Isle of Wight, which resulted in increasingly visionary topographical studies but also provided Turner with the inspiration for his first major oil painting, *Fishermen at Sea* (1796, Tate, London).

The painting was exhibited at the Royal Academy in 1796, when Turner had just turned twenty-one, and shows a night scene of fishermen off the Needles of the Isle of Wight. Given that he had started

Fishermen at Sea

1796, Tate, London

This picture was Turner's first exhibited oil painting, shown at the Royal Academy in London in 1796 and confirming the emergence of the most precocious talent in British art. It is an iridescent image, so much so that it appears to be back lit as if through the canvas. The moon illuminates an ominously cloudy sky casting a pool of light in a trough in the sea into which a small fishing boat slowly slides. Over the crest of a wave which threatens to smash into, if not quite obliterate, the vessel, another boat is just visible in the murky night. The fishermen struggle against the elements, lit by the orange glow of an oil lamp; heroic figures going about their nightly task with the threat of nature itself constantly looming large. In the distance are the dramatic but perilous Needles, a sharp regiment of rocks just off the Isle of Wight which had claimed many lives in their time.

The mood of the painting is one of quiet but growing menace. The viewer is slowly sucked into the vortex-like structure of Turner's composition, a feature that would become more pronounced and dramatic over the years. The darkness envelops and the light reflects off the surface of sea and canvas, gently but insistently spiraling around the small boat at the centre of the scene. It is an image which both celebrates the beauty of the natural world and conveys the potential terror of its immensity and power. The idea that human beings experience a perceptual fear when confronted by vast and mysterious natural forces had been eloquently expressed by the writer and philosopher Edmund Burke in a treatise in 1757, *An Enquiry into the Origin of our Ideas of the Sublime and Beautiful*, which remained an influential work for artists and poets well into the nineteenth century. Turner conveyed the notion of the sublime more powerfully than any other painter and it effectively began in this work.

It is an image of contrast between light and darkness; between Man and the world around him; between the small time-scale of human life and the longer, grander time-span of an evolving land- or seascape. It continues a tradition of moonlight scenes established in European art by Claude Joseph Vernet, Philip James de Loutherbourg and more recently Joseph Wright of Derby, whose *Moonlight with a Lighthouse, Coast of Tuscany* was exhibited at the Academy in 1789, the year before the fifteen-year-old Turner made his début there with a watercolour. In this respect, it sets the tone for Turner's artistic achievement: working from an earlier model, but already hinting at a radical reworking of landscape and indeed the process of painting itself.

using oils just three years before, it is a remarkably accomplished painting. The technique is unlike that used in his watercolours of the period, however; it is very carefully executed and borrows heavily from other moonlight scenes of the time, notably by Joseph Wright of Derby (1734–97). But it also shows elements that were to become more pronounced in his later works. First, the subject matter is fishermen struggling with the elements and the swell of the sea. Turner maintained a lifelong fascination with the frailty of man subject to the power and immensity of nature. Second, there is an acute attention to the qualities of light; the white brilliance of the full moon overshadows the orange light of the fishermen's lamp. The portrayal of light becomes almost an obsession in his later works. Third, the composition seeks to heighten the sense of drama. Turner encapsulates the scene in an oval patch of light, a forerunner of the swirling vortex compositions he used later to draw the viewer's eye into a painting and create a strong sense of physical immersion.

The painting marked a significant moment for Turner, making it abundantly clear that he was not just a watercolourist, perceived as a lesser medium by the Academy. Over the next fifty-five years, he exhibited oil paintings in fifty of the annual exhibitions. His work was increasingly sought by patrons, but he was already able to pick and choose, declining Lord Elgin's offer to accompany him on the now legendary trip to Athens to make drawings of the Parthenon and other classical ruins on the grounds that he would be in danger of being pigeon-holed as a topographical artist. In 1799 Turner produced his only known self-portrait, which shows the twenty-three-year-old fashionably dressed with an arresting gaze and a confident pose. In the same year he was made an associate of the Royal Academy and three years later, on 12 February 1802, he became the youngest Royal Academician, two months before his twenty-seventh birthday.

The same year, Turner undertook his first tour of Europe. In 1801 the Peace of Amiens provided a brief lull in the wars with the French

---

UNUSUAL PRACTICES

Turner was an eccentric who not only broke rules of painting but invented many himself. In the media of oils and watercolours Turner explored many unique and sometimes strange methods of producing brilliant effects.

The watercolours he created throughout his life can be read as an inventory of technical virtuosity and experimentation. It is known that Turner cultivated a long thumbnail that he used to scratch at the surface of the paintings to reveal the white paper underneath. When painting outdoors, he used pieces of stale bread to blot out areas of wet colour. His paintbrush was used in the conventional sense, but he also made use of its sharp wooden end, again to vary the quality of scratch marks in the paint. To help create texture, he used his fingers or stippled the paint using a stiff, dry brush.

republic, which had effectively barred continental travel to English artists. It was the first of many European tours and a pivotal experience for the Londoner. On a mundane level, these were 'business trips', in which he made topographical drawings from which he could produce saleable paintings. But they also served as a form of cultural and artistic education. The previous decade had seen continuous warfare, in which revolutionary France had eventually defeated the various European powers trying to extinguish the fledgling republic. Ironically, the plundering of French republican armies, especially by General Bonaparte in Italy, had greatly enlarged the collection of art housed in the Louvre. As a consequence, Turner was able to see a vast array of European masterpieces in Paris. To an artist from England, still without a national gallery, the impact of viewing such a collection cannot be overestimated. Of particular inspiration were the landscapes of Claude Lorrain (1600–82), which were to inspire his work throughout his life. He also visited the studio of the illustrious neo-classical painter Jacques Louis David (1748–1825), whose grandiose style and vision bolstered Turner's own ambitions, if not his specific approach to painting. Equally significant to Turner's work were the improvements to communications throughout the Alpine region, instigated in large part by Bonaparte's campaigns in northern Italy. Turner's response to the magnificent Alpine scenery is attested in over 400 drawings collected in six sketchbooks. These served as a personal reference library for Turner, one constantly refreshed with extensive touring. Many of the sketches were later worked up into watercolours for his patron Walter Fawkes, the most spectacular of which was *The Passage of Mount St Gothard, Taken from the Centre of the Teufels Bruch, Switzerland* (1804, Abbot Hall Art Gallery, Kendal). It is an image which would give vertigo to the faint-hearted, painted by Turner on the rickety bridge across a rocky chasm. The format is vertical, which emphasizes the plunging sensation of looking down almost into a void. Furthermore, the size of the image, over three feet by two, both amplifies the physical presence of the work

---

Some areas he 'stopped out' by using glue size to prevent the paint from reaching either the white paper or an area of dry paint. These blocked-out areas could be rubbed off later; this was a useful technique for painting the turbulent action of the sea or highlighting areas in his landscapes. He also built upon the layers of the painting with opaque watercolour, otherwise known as gouache. In this way, his watercolours often show the characteristics of his oil paintings, with areas of saturated colour.

In the 1830s and 1840s, he became even more experimental, using wide, expansive washes. It was never Turner's intention to exhibit these works and for many years after his death they were dismissed and kept in storage. Now they are considered a major part of his output.

and signals Turner's intention to challenge the dominant status of oil painting through the ambitious use of watercolour. It is as if he is conducting a private battle between his two favoured media, as well as making an emphatic public statement about the ludicrous constraints of received opinion.

The dramatic image of the St Gothard Pass was shown in the inaugural exhibition of Turner's own gallery in 1804. In 1799 he had taken rooms in a house in Harley Street, where he proceeded to build both a studio and a space in which he could display between twenty and thirty pictures at any given time. From the middle of the eighteenth century, it was not uncommon for artists to set aside a room or 'shop' to display their work to customers. Later, successful artists like Turner, who could afford more space, were able to turn the 'shop' into a gallery in a city where the opportunities to show work publicly were still very limited.

If his new gallery was a barometer of success, then receiving an important appointment at the Royal Academy elevated his position in an expanding British art world still further. In 1807 he was appointed Professor of Perspective, a post which required him to give six lectures

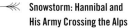

Snowstorm: Hannibal and His Army Crossing the Alps
1812, Tate, London
This is, perhaps, Turner's most eloquent expression of the status of landscape in painting. History is certainly writ large. Hannibal's epic and legendary journey through Spain and over the Alps to Italy is brought to life even as the Alpine tribesmen pick off the hapless stragglers in a valley ambush. On the horizon, silhouetted against the sunlight which bursts through the clouds and shows glimpses of their destination, Italy, are an elephant and rider, perhaps the great Carthaginian general himself (although this is more poetic yearning than historical fact), a symbol of perseverence and heroism. But humanity accounts for the bottom quarter of the painting. The rest is nature in full, majestic force. The title reinforces Turner's intention: the snowstorm gets top billing, then Hannibal and his cohorts. Man's inhumanity to man, the butchery visible in the left-hand foreground, is as nothing compared with the swollen clouds that gather above. The vision of hope, of reaching the end of the journey, is revealed by the sun but threatened by its temporary obliteration. In short, the natural world renders mankind powerless.

The picture was partly inspired by Turner's interest in classical history and his brief travel experience in Napoleonic Europe. There is certainly a contemporary resonance in the depiction of the clash of empires, Carthaginian and Roman, and in the difficulties of armies covering vast distances, as Napoleon planned in his advance on Moscow. But the power of the picture stems from Turner's trip to the Alps a few years before and his direct experience of a storm in North Yorkshire. Visiting his early patron Walter Fawkes at Farnley Hall in 1810, Turner was deluged by a thunderstorm, which he sketched, and made colour notes on the back of a letter. Calling Fawkes's son out to admire the storm, he finished his jottings and told the young man that 'in two years you will see this again and call it Hannibal crossing the Alps'.

When the painting was hung high in the Academy exhibition in 1812, Turner objected strongly; he wanted it placed lower so that the viewer could fully appreciate the pull of the vortex and the centrality of the sun. Seen from this perspective, there is an immense physical presence to the work, drawing the viewers into the image and threatening to overwhelm us. Here, then, is an image not just depicting the sublime but attempting to create it too, and, in many respects, succeeding. One contemporary critic saw it in London and remarked,' the moral and physical elements are here in powerful unison blended by a most masterly hand, awakening emotions of awe and grandeur'.

a year, although over the next three decades he only managed a fraction of this total. What set him apart from other lecturers was the quality of his visual aids, notably his graphic diagrams; one observer who was deaf went only to see these 'works of art'. Unfortunately for the rest of his audience, these events were a source of frustration, as he addressed much of his lecture to his assistant, who stood behind him, holding up these pictures, so much of what he said was inaudible. Furthermore, he was an appalling public speaker: 'Turner's conversation, his lectures, and his advice were at all times enigmatical not from want of knowledge, but from want of verbal power,' commented a contemporary observer. 'Rare advice it was, if you could unriddle it,' he continued, 'but so mysteriously given or expressed that it was hard to comprehend – conveyed sometimes in a few indistinct words, in a wave of the hand, a poke in the side, pointing at the same time to some part of a student's drawing, but saying nothing more than a 'Humph!' or 'What's that for?' In 1816, another contemporary critic gave his particular perspective on the Professor: 'Excellent as are Mr Turner's lectures, in other respects there is an embarrassment in his manner approaching almost to unintelligibility, and a vulgarity of pronunciation astonishing in an artist of his rank and respectability.' Perhaps what is most telling in these remarks is the inherent snobbery of the Academy and indeed of the broader art scene. Artistic vision, even perhaps that overused word 'genius', was one thing, but a Cockney who couldn't speak clearly was almost, if not quite, beyond the pale. Ruskin's later observation that Turner was both 'good humoured and bad tempered, hating humbug of all sorts' and that he was 'shrewd and perhaps a little selfish' seems understandable if not restrained, given the social sniping he seems to have faced.

Verbal clarity aside, the lucidity of Turner's thoughts become apparent in his lecture notes, many of which survive. At the end of his first series of talks, Turner confronted the issue of scenery and background in painting and proposed what, in effect, became a manifesto proclaiming the importance of landscape:

> To select, combine and concentrate that which is beautiful
> in nature and admirable in art is as much the business of
> the landscape painter ... as in other departments of art.
> And from the earliest dawn of colouring, of combinations
> from nature, there can be traced ... the value of attending
> to a method of introducing objects as auxiliaries by which
> each master endeavoured to establish for himself a
> different mode of arrangement by selecting what
> appeared most desirable in nature and combining it with
> the highest qualities of the Historic school as part of the

subject, or even at times allowed it to be equal in power to
the Historic department.

A year later, in 1812, he put his words into visual practice when he
produced his first mature masterpiece, *Snowstorm: Hannibal and His
Army Crossing the Alps* (Tate, London).

Ostensibly, the painting depicts the famous Carthaginian general
Hannibal crossing the Alps into Italy in 218BC. Turner shows the hopeful
moment when the fertile plains of Italy are revealed by the sun breaking
through the storm clouds. Many believe that Turner might have been
alluding to contemporary events, likening Napoleon to the great
Carthaginian leader, a comment on the fate of the French Emperor
who had recently embarked on his (subsequently disastrous) march on
Moscow. Both subjects, ancient and modern, suited Turner's romantic
view of history. In both, the great events and movements of mankind
could be rendered diminutive and temporary in comparison with the
immensity and potential violence of nature. Thus, the passage of the
Carthaginian army is almost insignificant against the dramatic backdrop
of the snowstorm, the dark clouds and the brilliance of the light in
the distance. In Turner's painting, a mighty army is dwarfed by the
overwhelming power of the natural elements. To highlight this, Turner
built a dynamic vortex into the composition, the swirling black cloud
drawing the viewer into the heart of the painting and giving prominence
to the sun, the object of hope for Hannibal and his army. Landscape
and history seem to vie for attention, their relationship a symbiotic one
where the genre of history painting enhances the seriousness of that
of landscape, which in turn adds to the drama of an epic journey.
Ultimately, however, the forces of nature threaten to obliterate all
which stand before them.

The Carthaginian Empire was of considerable interest to Turner and
featured in several of his other paintings. In contrast to the apocalyptic
scene of Hannibal's army, however, Turner deployed this subject in
imitation of Claude Lorrain, the great seventeenth-century master
of idealized classical landscape, whose works he had studied in Paris.
Claude, who worked for most of his life in Rome, created calm and
majestic antique landscapes, peopled by toga-clad figures and studded
with classical follies. He was also interested in perspective, with objects
and buildings dissolving into the light towards the horizon. Claude's
images of pastoral serenity, of a perfect classical 'Golden Age', greatly
influenced Turner, along with other English artists of the time. In *Dido
Building Carthage* or *The Rise of the Carthaginian Empire* (National
Gallery, London), painted only three years after *Snowstorm*, Turner
borrowed heavily from Claude's style and paid homage to a particular

painting by the Frenchman, *Seaport with the Embarkation of the Queen of Sheba* (1648), which, as stipulated in Turner's will, hangs next to it in the National Gallery in London. Again, the painting is essentially a landscape, yet the allusion to classical history and literature elevated the piece to a history painting. The building of the ancient city of Carthage appealed both to audiences' imaginations and their knowledge – the scene from Virgil's *Aeneid* would have been broadly familiar among educated people and permitted them to show their learning when viewing the painting. There is considerable architectural detail, carefully composed like a stage set, with buildings receding into the distance on either side and the sun rising up and over the horizon in the very centre of the image. It is a product of the imagination, but Turner's background as a topographical artist clearly helped him attain a sense of almost having been there. Furthermore, his poetic interest in the sublime gave the work a dazzling serenity that, in some respects, seemed to surpass Claude's achievement. The composition of Turner's painting has more movement than the French artist's work; the buildings and scenery are more monumental. The painting as a whole is greater than the sum of its parts. Turner saw this painting as one of his finest, but it did not sell after it was exhibited in 1815. This clearly affected Turner, who, when approached many years later, in the 1840s, by a group of gentlemen eager to buy it for the new National Gallery, declined the offer of ten times the original asking price. He told them that he would 'leave the picture in the gallery', referring to his subsequent bequest to the nation. He seemed to have been placated by their offer, however, being heard to mutter repeatedly, 'That makes amends, that makes amends.'

After the final defeat of Napoleon in 1815, Turner had much greater opportunity for European travel. In 1817, he visited the Low Countries,

THE INDUSTRIAL REVOLUTION

The 'Industrial Revolution' is a convenient historical label applied to a wide range of interrelated technological and economic changes from the early eighteenth century. These developments are now viewed as one phase of the broader historical concept of 'modernization', a complex process by which an agrarian, peasant-based society is transformed through urbanization and industrialization, with all the associated benefits and problems. The most conspicuous of the many aspects of the Industrial Revolution were developments in steam power and machinery, factory production and mass markets, expanded mining and improvements in metallurgical production, urban expansion and improved commercial communications, greatly enlarged food production and population growth. The complex interaction of these and other factors initially produced the most rapid and successful results in Britain, aided by the existing advantages of productive farming, a relatively skilled workforce, mineral wealth, long traditions of trade and commercial expertise, financial reserves and an entrepreneurial ethos, and relative political stability. These developments made Britain the

including Waterloo itself, and then the Rhineland which inspired a series of fifty-one gouache and watercolour drawings, until recently believed to have been painted in Germany but now known to have been finished in his studio. Their appearance was looser and more sketch-like than before and certainly the gap between study and finished work was shrinking as his technique grew quicker and his interests became more experimental. Two years later, in 1819, he visited Italy for the first time, at the age of forty-four. Like so many artists before him, he went in search of classical history and the Italian masters, and in Florence and Rome he certainly spent time studying what he increasingly felt were his predecessors rather than remote figures from the mists of art history. One resulting picture, *Rome from the Vatican. Raffaelle, Accompanied by La Fornarina, Preparing his Pictures for the Decoration of the Loggia*, produced back in London in 1820, shows the celebrated master of the High Renaissance and his mistress doing just what the title suggests, with a view of the city opening out from under the great arch and balcony in the Vatican. More telling than even this fusion of classical and art history together with landscape, however, is a detail in the foreground. The pictures which Raphael prepares to hang are mainly identifiable as portraits and images of the Madonna and Child painted by the Italian artist. But tilted at an angle away from the light, though still luminous enough, is a landscape by Turner. The message could not be clearer: Turner emphasizes his difference from but deep connection with the art of the past and affirms that he views himself as part of the great pantheon of Western artists.

If Rome affirmed his illustrious relationship to the past, another city further north had a more profound effect on his work of the present and future. In Venice, he observed the magical buildings, the reflections of the sky in the water and the distinctive clarity of light, which enhanced

most prosperous and powerful country in the world, before other countries, notably Germany and the United States, began to reap the benefits of similar socio-economic transformations. The response of artists and writers to the Industrial Revolution was generally negative, tending to emphasize its harmful effects upon both the natural world and an earlier, and increasingly idealized, pattern of human existence. An awareness of the social, environmental and spiritual price of rapid industrialization was one of the main stimuli of the Romantic movement. Turner was certainly aware of these anxieties, but was at the same time conscious of the artistic potential offered by this new and powerful future. The forces of the Industrial Revolution that rapidly transformed Britain even within Turner's own lifetime offered new inspiration for his landscapes and seascapes. For Turner the new machines of his age were merely aspects of Man's continuing attempt to master the turbulent and transcendent power of Nature. His images of steam trains and steamboats thus paid tribute to Man's technological achievements, but – with the notable exception of Rain, Steam and Speed – simultaneously expressed his view that in this struggle nature would inevitably triumph.

his optical studies. This purity of light gave a new momentum to his painting. His palette became more vibrant; his sketchbooks are crammed with densely annotated sketches that would be used as references for oil paintings in subsequent years. He made three more trips to Italy, in 1828, 1833 and 1840, during which time he spent no more than a total of six weeks in Venice itself. Yet he has become one of the most celebrated painters of the city. Gradually, after his first visit, his visual interest in the architecture diminished, metaphorically sinking down into the lagoon as the idea of ambience took over. He almost always painted as if from the water itself, unifying every element in a luminous whole.

If Italy became a constant source of inspiration for Turner throughout the rest of his life, Britain remained closest to his heart. Through his widely circulated engravings as well as his watercolours and oils, he helped construct a sense of national identity that ranged from the picturesque to the industrial; from one kind of sublime to another. Viewers remain drawn to his breath-taking images of the Lake District or the English coastline, but he also produced equally telling and arresting images of new cities such as Leeds, Newcastle and Dudley, where factories billow out their smoke into the dazzling sky and men lug cloth or mend walls or deliver milk. Turner seems genuinely filled with awe by the dynamic potential of the new manufacturing industries and the seemingly endless activity of Britain's workforce. In *Keelmen Heaving in Coals by Night*, an oil painting from 1835 now in the National Gallery of Art in Washington, vast ships sail through the night on the River Tyne, the silhouettes of tiny labourers visible out of the gloom, backlit by glowing torches and with the moonlight casting a silvery glow which breaks through the blanket of smog.

The previous year, Turner had emerged as a major chronicler of contemporary history thanks largely to the speed with which he could draw and paint. On the night of 16 October a tremendous fire consumed the Houses of Parliament. Turner rushed to the scene to see the inferno on the banks of the Thames and made numerous hurried sketches from a variety of different angles. In his studio, he later worked up nine watercolours and then began not one but two versions in oil, the first of which was shown at the British Institution in February and the second at the Royal Academy in May. The latter, which now hangs in the Cleveland Museum of Art, shows the view downstream on the south bank of the Thames near Waterloo Bridge, a furnace of orange soaring up and to the left and reflected in the water below to create what looks at first glance like an arrow of flames. The former, which now resides at the Philadelphia Museum of Art, is a view from just over Westminster Bridge near to where St Thomas's Hospital is now located, with a crowd of people gathered on the river bank in the foreground following the viewer's gaze into the wild flames which seem to have set the Thames itself on fire. Both are searing works of art in every respect, but the first version is perhaps more impressive when one realizes the way in which it was executed. When Turner arrived at the British Institute to hang the painting it was clearly unfinished. 'The picture sent in', a fellow painter recalled, 'was a mere dab of several colours and without form or void, like chaos before the creation.' It was common practice both at the Royal Academy and the British Institute to have three days before the exhibition for painters to make last-minute alterations to their works. This was called Varnishing Day, and famously Turner used this time not to touch up works but to paint entire canvases almost from scratch. His associate described the intense concentration of the artist:

> ... for three hours I was there – and I understood it had been the same since he began in the morning – he never ceased to work, or even once looked or turned from the wall on which his picture hung. All lookers-on were amused by the figure Turner exhibited in himself and the process he was pursuing with his picture.

After the work was completed Turner 'sidled off' without pausing to admire his work. Another onlooker commented: 'There, that's masterly, he does not stop to look at his work; he *knows* it is done, and he is off.' As he grew older, Turner developed a reputation as introverted, eccentric and rather misanthropic. He never married, had few friends and after his father's death in 1829 led an increasingly solitary and unsociable existence, remarkably so for one of his cultural stature. An associate remarked on his gruff manner and scruffy appearance:

> In the last twenty years of his life his short figure had become corpulent – his face, perhaps from continual exposure to the air, was unusually red, and a little inclined to blotches ... He generally wore what is called a black dress-coat, which would have been the better for brushing – the sleeves were mostly too long, coming down over his fat and not over-clean hands.

Despite his wealth, Turner's house and gallery on Queen Anne Street, which he had bought at the end of 1810, were reportedly filthy, with broken panes of glass that let in water. His paintings were allowed to grow mouldy, and one visitor sadly recalled the state of *Dido Building Carthage*: 'It was cracking – not in the ordinary way, but in long lines, like ice when it begins to break up. Other parts of the picture were peeling off – one piece ... just like a stiff ribbon turning over.'

Even though he lacked the social graces and etiquette that were expected in Regency and Victorian England, he was warmly accepted by his patrons, several of whom were equally eccentric. They played a vital role in his life, more than merely financial. He spent much of his time in their company, first with Walter Fawkes in his Yorkshire home at Farnley Hall – which he first visited in 1809 and subsequently almost every year up to 1824 – and then with George Wyndham, the third Earl of Egremont, at Petworth House in Sussex. Egremont was Turner's most important patron, buying his work from 1802 onwards. He spent long periods at both patrons' residences, painting within the grounds and using the homes as bases to explore the local countryside. Petworth became a favourite retreat in the 1820s and 1830s and provided a welcome refuge, particularly following his father's death. The house was enormous and filled with a great collection of contemporary British painting and sculpture. It was also home to other artists from time to time, although Turner was allocated his own private studio in the old North Library, with its near-perfect north-east light. His sense of pleasure and contentment at being in the house can be seen in the series of intimate sketches and paintings he produced, from his slightly furtive (even fly-on-the-wall) watercolour *of A Bedroom: A Lady Dressed in Black Standing with a Green-Curtained Bed – a Figure in the Doorway* from 1827 to the celebratory canvas depicting *Dinner in a Great Room with Figures in Costume* painted around 1835 (both Tate, London). When Lord Egremont died in 1837, Turner was deeply affected. Perhaps as a memorial, he painted *Interior at Petworth* soon after, an image which includes some of the Earl's vast art collection, both antique and contemporary, but where everything seems to be dissolving in a miasma of paint and light. After this pictorial lament was finished, Turner never returned to Petworth.

In addition to patronage, art criticism played an important, if often negative, role in his career. In Britain, the art critic was largely an invention of the eighteenth century, a profession which developed alongside the rise of the artists' academies where work was exhibited. The idea of a radical artist facing a barrage of mockery from cynical or uncomprehending critics is the stuff of avant-garde legend, and began in earnest in Paris in the 1860s and 1870s. In England, it began with the young Turner and flourished as he did. The Academy remained loyal and Turner found a young champion in his later years who turned out to be the most prolific and important critic who ever wrote on these shores – John Ruskin; but broadly speaking, the critical consensus was against Turner. Sir George Beaumont, a noted collector and amateur artist, airily dismissed Turner with the remark that 'he is perpetually aiming to be extraordinary, but rather produced works that are capricious and singular rather than great'. From his earliest seascapes, whose waves were compared to heavily veined slabs of marble, to his late work, his technique and use of paint were likened to custard, coal-dust, cream and, perhaps most infamously, to 'soapsuds and whitewash', a comment made about one of Turner's radical late oil paintings exhibited in 1842 and probably possessing the longest title in art history: *Snowstorm – Steamboat off a Harbour's Mouth Making Signals in Shallow Water, and Going by the Lead. The Author Was in this Storm on the Night the* Ariel *Left Harwich* (Tate, London).

According to Turner, he had asked some sailors to tie him to the mast of the boat for four hours so that he might experience the storm at first hand. It seems unlikely that at the age of sixty-seven he could have withstood such conditions for long. There is no evidence for a ship called *Ariel* at Harwich at this time, and Turner had not visited the east coast for a long time. The painting is more likely to be the product of strong memories and a visionary imagination. The subject is reminiscent of earlier paintings. It features a steamboat, a relatively modern invention, not as a glorification of man's technological achievement, but rather an indistinct vessel, a dark mass seemingly out of control and struggling on the high seas. The style is almost abstract, producing one of the most outlandish paintings of his entire career. Only close examination reveals the horizon and ship's mast amid the smoke, water and snow. Compositionally, he placed the horizon at an angle to capture the sensation of an uneven keel. Light is at the eye of the storm and the picture. Again, there is a strong vortical motion at work, but instead of just sucking the viewer into the image, it seems at one and the same time to spit one out, a dynamic push–pull force unlike anything previously painted.

With *Snowstorm* of 1842, Turner continued the theme he had begun to explore in his very first exhibited oil painting , the powerful domination of Man by nature. In *Rain, Steam and Speed – The Great Western Railway* (1844, National Gallery, London), Turner continued his expressive approach, but seemed to reverse the relationship between humanity and the surrounding world. It depicts a steam train surging out of the mist and rain on Brunel's new viaduct at Maidenhead. Like the steamboat in *Snowstorm* two years before, the train was a new but more startling invention. Turner was born in the age of the stagecoach; by the time of his death, the age of the railway was well under way. By 1841 the railway connected London and Bristol, and speed trials with specially modified trains reached the then incredible speed of 90 mph. This was a device the public both welcomed and feared. Turner was aware of the anxieties these loud, dirty engines generated in a hitherto tranquil countryside. He presents a forceful and uncompromising image. The dark shapes of the bridge and the train are powerful against the indistinct golden backdrop of the river and countryside. There are suggestions of the lazier, easygoing pace of the past – a boat and elegant bridge on the left, a plough far right. These contrast with the new and powerful future represented by the train, which detracts from the landscape by its size, speed and brutal force. Exhilaration and regret are mingled with alarm – not least for the poor hare that tears along the track, but which will be mown down any second by the monstrous machine.

Rain, Steam and Speed is a startling image produced by an even more radical technique, the culmination of years spent studying and rendering different qualities of light and atmospheric conditions. Many areas are thickly impastoed, whilst others are painted more thinly, a process that adds to the confusion and mystery of the scene in which the viewer seeks to make out shapes in the mist and rain. Turner blurs the

Rain, Steam and Speed – The Great Western Railway
1844, National Gallery, London

Ageing artists, with some notable exceptions, tend to reinforce what they know and believe; Turner, on the other hand, seemed to question one or two of the central assumptions in his art as he aged, most strikingly in this painting. It shows the landscape near Maidenhead along the Thames Valley. The sky is cloudy and it is pouring with rain but not threateningly so; the sun is thinly shining through, bathing the scene in a soft, hazy, wet light. Out of the mist, and adding to it with its billowing smoke, comes a steam train, hurtling down the track through the rain, moving from the centre of the painting to the right on a diagonal line that makes it seem to accelerate before our eyes.

On one small level, the scene is a piece of contemporary reportage, a topographical account of Isambard Kingdom Brunel's ambitious railway bridge – Maidenhead Viaduct – begun in 1837 and finished two years later. In addition, it shows the newly laid Great Western Railway line linking London with Bristol and Exeter. On another, more profound level, it is a study of speed, of an increasingly dynamic world in which the newly invented steam locomotive train gave the unprecedented sensation of travelling at close to a hundred miles an hour. According to John Ruskin, Turner stuck his head out of the window of a fast-moving train and wanted to convey something of the sensation he experienced. True or not, the picture combines both a detached viewpoint, observing the train's high-speed journey and the sense of a world fleetingly seen through the blurred vision of motion.

The application of paint reinforces the dynamism of the scene. Turner swirls and splashes it; sprays and scumbles. He used a variety of methods of applying paint – brushes, palette knives and fingers, even using a specially cultivated thumbnail to scratch out. Like much of his later work, the painting was clearly made very quickly, and the energy is apparent in the vigorous brushstrokes, some of which merge into the layers of paint beneath, the result of Turner's impatience in failing to allow the paint to dry before continuing his work.

For once, nature doesn't dominate; rather, it is threatened by technological progress. Ahead of the train, and disproportionately large, so that we can just about see it, is a hare racing down the track, terrified and on the verge of being mown down by what was described as the 'iron horse'.

Unlike previous paintings, not least *The Fighting Temeraire*, where Turner clearly resents the Industrial Revolution sweeping through Britain, his attitude is ambiguous. He was, after all, an artist who had benefited hugely from the expansion of rail travel. He was also clearly exhilarated by the sensation of speed. The work is therefore both a celebration and a lament for the passing of a more tranquil age, traces of which remain visible in the distance and in the water below. In many respects, Turner is acknowledging a new type of experience which could be called the industrial sublime.

distinction between painting as image-making and painting as physical process, which in itself anticipates the developments of abstract art in the early twentieth century. Perhaps only the greatest artists develop radical late styles: Michelangelo and Titian did and so did Rembrandt; Picasso and Matisse pushed their art to extremes in later life in the twentieth century; and so too did Turner in the nineteenth century. It is easy to overstate the case, to claim Turner as a proto-Modernist as if he intended to be so, which clearly he did not. Nonetheless, his late oil paintings begin to resemble watercolours or at least the two media seem to have converged in work which appears fluid, liquid almost – the most extreme example of which is *Norham Castle, Sunrise* (Tate, London), painted some time in the last five or six years of his life and left unfinished. It is a picture of translucent colour washes and almost indescribably delicate luminosity, a work which hovers on the edge of pure blinding vision. 'These are no longer pictures,' wrote the French neo-Impressionist Paul Signac of Turner's late paintings, 'but aggregations of colours, quarries of precious stone, painting in the most beautiful sense of the word.' Signac's immediate predecessors, the Impressionists

Norham Castle, Sunrise
c.1845–50, Tate, London
Norham Castle had long obsessed Turner as an artist and he had first begun to sketch the dramatic structure on the banks of the River Tweed on the borders of England and Scotland during his northern tour of 1797. He made various watercolour and ink drawings of the subject over the next three decades and visited again in 1831, when he made sketches on the spot. Some time towards the end of the following decade, he began his first and only painting of the subject, the culmination of years of study of both the scene itself and of light and atmosphere more generally.

It is a wonderfully tranquil image; the sun rises across a watery meadow in which a cow grazes contentedly, its reflection faintly visible below. The castle itself sits atop a rocky outcrop rendered in the most delicate washes of blue paint. That which is solid – the building, the rocks, even the cow – is rendered in translucent swaths of thin oil paint as if Turner is painting with watercolours; in turn, light is often rendered in thicker, impastoed areas of white paint applied with a palette knife. In this respect, our visual expectation is turned on its head and the effect is dazzling, a carefully orchestrated composition of soft colour and liquid light. The image is so fluid, it threatens to slide off the canvas.

It is a painting of intense visual perception, of close scrutiny, but it is also an image which proclaims the power of process, a celebration of light and vision and of painting itself. Numerous commentators have seen it as a forerunner of Modernist art, specifically of Impressionism and Abstract Expressionism, and there is no doubting the debt that painters like Claude Monet and Mark Rothko owed to Turner; indeed, they acknowledged it. This and other later paintings by Turner are radical works of art by any standards but there must be a note of caution. By Turner's definition, this was unfinished and therefore not for public display. It could be a sketch or the beginnings of an exhibition picture, a 'lay-in' to be completed perhaps on the walls of the Academy on Varnishing Day. In some respects, therefore, it could be our eyes – retrospectively armed with the knowledge of art history and coloured by the development of abstraction – that complete the work. But we know that Turner experimented increasingly in his later years and that in the face of widespread critical ridicule (or perhaps because of it) he continued to push at the boundaries of what painting was or might become. The most convincing view, perhaps, is that in this image of Norham Castle we get a privileged private view into the workings of a great painter who is still trying to resolve his art.

themselves, paid homage to Turner directly in a letter written in the mid-1880s and signed by Monet, Renoir, Degas and Pissarro, among others: 'A group of French painters united by the same aesthetic tendencies, struggling for ten years to bring art back to the scrupulously exact observation of nature, applying themselves with passion to the rendering of reality of forms in movement, as well as to the fugitive phenomenon of light, cannot forget that it has been preceded in this path by a great master of the English school, the illustrious Turner.'

In his early seventies, Turner moved to a house in Chelsea overlooking the Thames. He lived in anonymity and seclusion with his housekeeper Sophia Booth, disguising his identity as 'Admiral Puggy Booth'. He exhibited four oil paintings at the Royal Academy in the year before his death, some achievement for a man of seventy-five. His death came on 19 December 1851 at his Chelsea home. He was found by Dr Bartlett, who tended to his failing health during his last days. Bartlett noted, with a hint of Romantic vision or poetic licence, that before he passed away the room was darkened by the dull day. Moments later, as his spirit left him, 'the sun burst forth and shone directly on him with that brilliancy which he loved to gaze on and transfer the likeness to his paintings'. Turner was buried in St Paul's Cathedral according to his stipulated wishes, 'among my brothers in Art', as he put it.

Five years later, the nation received his vast personal collection of works – over 19,000 drawings and watercolours and around 300 oil paintings and sketches, following wranglings over Turner's frequently altered will. It was only when the Tate Gallery was opened in 1897 as an annexe to the National Gallery for the national collection of British art that Turner's work found a proper home and it took another ninety years for a new wing – the Clore Gallery – to be built to display all aspects of Turner's work permanently. This alone makes Turner unique in British art – the only artist to have established the conditions in which his work is viewed and assessed. But there was more – indeed, one specific request was carried out much earlier. On 19 March 1856, his *Dido Building Carthage* and *Sun Rising through the Vapour* were placed next to two paintings by the painter he held in great esteem, Claude Lorrain. They still remain side by side in the National Gallery nearly 150 years later, making Turner the only artist in London's great pantheon of painting to stipulate how his art should be placed specifically within the canon of Western art history.

Acknowledgements

The writing of this book has been a major project – and if we have cut a relatively straight path through the jungle of art history then we have a good number of people to thank. First and foremost, this book has been written in parallel with the TV series of the same name. These programmes have been made for Channel 5 in Britain – a channel that supports arts programming more actively than is ever publicly recognized. We must give great credit to the commissioning editors Michael Attwell and Kim Peat who represent TV executive control at its best. Equally, Channel 5 is unmatched in terms of its legal and financial support for independent companies like Seventh Art. Adam Tow, Katherine Lewis, and Alan Tott – thank you.

Also, a word for leading US video distributor Bill Ambrose, who has been a supporter with words and wallet for many years. To have someone who believes in public service media on your side is a great help.

Our gratitude goes to those consultants who gave generously of their time and knowledge: Dr Paul Joannides, Dr Charles Hope, Prof. Peter Cherry, Dr Joanna Woodall, Prof. William Vaughan, and Prof. Francis Ames-Lewis – they were an enormous aid to us, and to our two researchers Martina Cavicchioli and Dee Harding.

We must give thanks to the team at Seventh Art. All credit for the television series and this book must be shared with them. Their unceasing efforts, professionalism, good humour and, above all, their care to do their best for this project has, once again, been invaluable. The logistics of filming in over fifty museums and galleries should not be underestimated. We may take the credit for the words but none of this would have happened without Helena Berglund, Ben Harding, Helen Newnham, Angela Vermond, Jennifer Goodsell, Production Co-ordinator Julia Wilkie and Head of Production Amanda Wilkie without whom none of this gets off the starting block. They enabled us to film in numerous locations in Britain, Europe and America with one of the best crews around – sound recordist Chris Wright and cameraman Hugh Hood – and then get the material back to the two great editors Phil Reynolds and Duncan Weaver. Above all, credit must go to co-directors Ali Ray and Mehreen Saigo, whose dedication and craft pushed both the films and book towards the quality to which we aspire

In addition, thanks to the team at *Tate* magazine: Jessica Lack, Simon Grant, Chloe Kinsman, Matt Watkins, Chris Coombes, Phil Allison, Mary Keane-Dawson and Ian Massey for their encouragement and tolerance; to Stephen Coates for his vision and to Tanya Hudson for being so supportive and good natured throughout the entire project.

Finally, thanks and salutations to Walter Donohue at Faber for commissioning the book and never once wavering in his support or belief that it was worth writing, even if on the odd night out on the film shoot, we did.

This book is dedicated to Michael Attwell with respect and gratitude.

Phil Grabsky
Tim Marlow
Phillip Rance

Picture credits